Writing Research

A Guide to Curriculum Planning

ZB Zaner-Bloser

Acknowledgments

"Teach Writing as a Process Not Product (1972)." by Donald Murray. From *The Leaflet*, Fall 1972. Reprinted by permission of the New England Association of Teachers of English.

"Can Students Benefit from Process Writing?" by Arnold A. Goldstein and Peggy G. Carr. From National Assessment of Educational Progress: *NAEPfacts*, vol. I, no. 3 (April 1996).

"The Process Approach to Writing Instruction: Examining Its Effectiveness" by Pritchard, Ruie J., and Ronald L. Honeycutt. From *Handbook of Writing Research;* Charles A. Arthur, Steven Graham, and Jill Fitzgerald (eds). Copyright © 2006. Reprinted by permission of Guilford Press.

From "The Rewards of Writing" by Mark Overmeyer. Originally printed in *Understanding Our Gifted,* Spring 2008 (vol. 20, no. 3). www.our-gifted.com.

"Losing the Product in the Process" by Baines, Lawrence, Coleen Baines, Gregory Kent Stanley, and Anthony Kunkel. From *English Journal*, vol. 88, no. 5 (May 1999). Copyright © 1999 by the National Council of Teachers of English. Reprinted with permission.

"Training Writing Skills: A Cognitive Developmental Perspective." By Kellog, Ronald T. From *Journal of Writing Research*, vol. I, no. I (2008): I–26. Reprinted by permission.

With kind permission from Springer Science+Business Media: "Modeling the Development of Written Language." By Wagner, Richard K., Cynthia S. Puranik, Barbara Foorman, Elizabeth Foster, Laura Gehron Wilson, Erika Tschinkel, and Patricia Thatcher Kantor. From *Reading and Writing*, vol. 24 (2011): 203–220.

Reprinted with permission from *The Art of Teaching Writing* by Lucy McCormick Calkins. Copyright © 1986, 1994 by Lucy McCormick Calkins. Published by Heinemann, Portsmouth, NH. All rights reserved.

Reprinted with permission from *Breaking the Code: the New Science of Beginning Reading and Writing* by J. Richard Gentry. Copyright © 2006 by J. Richard Gentry. Published by Heinemann, Portsmouth, NH. All rights reserved.

Reprinted with permission from *What You Know by Heart* by Katie Wood Ray. Copyright © 2002 by Katie Wood Ray. Published by Heinemann, Portsmouth, NH. All rights reserved.

Strategy Instruction and the Teaching of Writing: A Meta-Analysis. By Steve Graham, From *Handbook of Writing Research;* MacArthur, Charles A., Steven Graham, and Jill Fitzgerald (eds). Copyright © 2008. Reprinted by permission of Guilford Press.

"The Effectiveness of a Highly Explicit, Teacher-Directed Strategy Instruction Routine." by Troia, Gary A., and Steve Graham. From *Journal of Learning Disabilities*, vol. 35., no 4, (2002): 290–305. Permission of SAGE Publications.

"Improving Fourth-Grade Students' Composition Skills: Effects of Strategy Instruction and Self-Regulation Procedures." By Glaser, Cornelia, and Joachim C. Brunstein. From *Journal of Educational Psychology,* vol. 99, no. 2 (2007): 297-310. Copyright © 2007 by the American Psychological Association. Reproduced with permission.

"Improving the Writing, Knowledge, and Motivation of Struggling Young Writers: The Effects of Self-Regulated Strategy Development With and Without Peer Support" by Harris, Karen R., Steve Graham, and Linda H. Mason. From *American Educational Research Journal*, vol. 42, no. 2 (2006): 295-340 Reprinted by Permission of SAGE Publications.

"Explicitly Teaching Strategies, Skills and Knowledge: Writing Instruction in Middle School Classrooms." By De La Paz, Susan, and Steven Graham. From *Journal of Educational Psychology*, vol. 94, no. 4 (2002): 687–698. Copyright © 2010 by the American Psychological Association. Reproduced with permission.

Reprinted with permission from *The Grammar Plan Book* by Constance Weaver. Copyright © 2007 by Constance Weaver. Published by Heinemann, Portsmouth, NH. All rights reserved.

"Investigating Narrative Writing by 9-11-year olds" by Beard, Rober, and Andrew Burrell. From *Journal of Research in Reading*, vol. 33, no. I (2010): 77-93. A journal of the United Kingdom Literacy Association.

"Teaching Argument Writing to 7- to 14-year-olds: An International Review of the Evidence of Successful Practice." by Andrews, Richard, Carole Togerson, Graham Low, and Nick McGuinn. From *Cambridge Journal of Education*, vol. 39, no.2 (2009): 291–310. Reprinted by permission of the publisher (Taylor & Francis Ltd, www.tandfonline.com)

With kind permission from Springer Science+Business Media: "Writing Development in Four Genres from Grades Three to Seven: Syntactic Complexity and Genre Differentiation." By Beers, Scott F., and William E. Nagy. From *Reading and Writing*, vol. 24 (2011): 183-202

"Children's Cognitive Effort and Fluency in Writing: Effects of Genre and of Handwriting Automatisation" by Thierry, Olive, Monik Favart, Caroline Beauvais, and Lucie Beauvais. From *Learning and Instruction,* vol. 19 (2009): 299-308. With permission from Elsevier.

Reprinted with permission from *Writing Essentials* by Regie Routman. Copyright © 2005 by Regie Routman. Published by Heinemann, Portsmouth, NH. All rights reserved.

"In Defense of Rubrics" by Spandel, Vicki. From *English Journal,* vol. 96, no. 1 (2006): 19-22. Copyright © 2006 by the National Council of Teachers of English. Reprinted with permission.

"Rubrics: Heuristics for Developing Writing Strategies." by De La Paz, Susan. From *Assessment for Effective Intervention,* vol. 34, no. 3 (2009): 134-146. Reprinted by Permission of SAGE Publications.

"Putting Rubrics to the Test: The Effect of a Model, Criteria Generation, and Rubric-Referenced Self-Assessment on Elementary School Students' Writing" by Andrade, Heidi L., Ying du, and Xiaolei Wang. From *Educational Measurement: Issues and Practice,* Summer 2008: 3–13. Reprinted by permission of John Wiley & Sons.

Reprinted from "Reliability and Validity of Rubrics for Assessment Through Writing" by Rezaei, Ali Reza, and Michael Lovorn. From *Assessing Writing,* vol. 15 (2010): 18-39. With permission from Elsevier.

"Writing in the 21st Century" by Yancey, Kathleen Blake. A Report From the National Council of Teachers of English, Copyright © February 2009. Reprinted with permission.

From "Summary of Findings" by Lenhart, Amanda, Sousan Arafeh, Aaron Smith and Alexandra Rankin Macgill from *Writing, Technology and Teens;* © 2008. Used by permission of the Pew Research Center's Internet & American Life Project.

"The Effect of Computers on Student Writing: A Meta-Analysis of Studies from 1992-2002" by Goldberg, Amie, Michael Russell, and Abigail Cook. From *The Journal of Technology, Learning and Assessment,* vol. 2, no. 1 (2003): 3–50. (Taylor & Francis Ltd, http://www.informaworld.com), reprinted by permission of the publisher.

"Laptops and Literacy: A Multi-Site Case Study." By Mark Warschauer. From Pedagogies, vol. 3 (2008): 52–67. Reprinted by permission of the publisher (Taylor & Francis Ltd, www.tandfonline.com).

"Laptops and Fourth-Grade Literacy: Assisting the Jump over the Fourth-Grade Slump" by Suhr, Kurt A., David A. Hernandez, Douglas Grimes, and Mark Warschauer From *The Journal of Technology, Learning and Assessment,* vol. 9, no. 51 (2010): 3–45. (Taylor & Francis Ltd, http://www.informaworld.com), reprinted by permission of the publisher.

"A Middle School One-to-One Laptop Program: The Maine Experience" by David Silvernail and the MLTI Research and Evaluation Team. From the University of Southern Maine, Maine Educational Policy Research Institute. Copyright © 2011 by the Center for Education Policy, Applied Research & Evaluation. www.usm.maine.edu/cepare/publications.htm.

ISBN   978-1-4531-0154-4

www.zaner-bloser.com

Printed in the United States of America

13 14 15 16 27475 5 4 3 2

SUSTAINABLE FORESTRY INITIATIVE

Certified Chain of Custody
Promoting Sustainable Forestry
www.sfiprogram.org
SFICOC-00993

Contents

Preface: Still Neglected? Writing in the 21st Century 8
  Steve Graham

Chapter 1   Teaching Writing as a Process 13

  Introduction. 14

  Teach Writing as a Process Not Product. .16
    Donald Murray

  Excerpts From
  Can Students Benefit from Process Writing? 20
    Arnold A. Goldstein and Peggy G. Carr, National Center

  Excerpts From
  The Process Approach to Writing Instruction: Examining Its Effectiveness . . 24
    Ruie J. Pritchard and Ronald L. Honeycutt

  The Rewards of Writing 28
    Mark Overmeyer

  Excerpts From
  Losing the Product in the Process. 32
    Lawrence Baines, Coleen Baines, Gregory Kent Stanley,
    and Anthony Kunkel

Chapter 2   Developing Writers 35

  Introduction. 36

  Excerpts From
  Training Writing Skills: A Cognitive Developmental Perspective 38
    Ronald T. Kellogg

  Excerpts From
  Modeling the Development of Written Language. 47
    Richard K. Wagner, Cynthia S. Puranik, Barbara Foorman, Elizabeth Foster,
    Laura Gehron Wilson, Erika Tschinkel, and Patricia Thatcher Kantor

  An Excerpt From
  Growing Up Writing: Grades K, 1, and 2. 60
    Lucy Calkins

Excerpts From
Five Phases of Intervention, Support, and Instruction—Up as Close as
You Can Get. 63
    J. Richard Gentry

Chapter 3   Teaching Writing Strategies 69

Introduction. 70

An Excerpt From
The Nature of Process Curriculum 72
    Katie Wood Ray

Excerpts From
Strategy Instruction and the Teaching of Writing 76
    Steve Graham

Excerpts From
The Effectiveness of a Highly Explicit, Teacher-Directed
Strategy Instruction Routine. 83
    Gary A. Troia and Steve Graham

Excerpts From
Improving Fourth-Grade Students' Composition Skills:
Effects of Strategy Instruction and Self-Regulation Procedures 96
    Cornelia Glaser and Joachim C. Brunstein

Excerpts From
Improving the Writing, Knowledge, and Motivation of Struggling Young
Writers: The Effects of Self-Regulated Strategy Development With and
Without Peer Support. 101
    Karen R. Harris, Steve Graham, and Linda H. Mason

Excerpts From
Explicitly Teaching Strategies, Skills, and Knowledge:
Writing Instruction in Middle School Classrooms. 113
    Susan De La Paz and Steve Graham

Chapter 4   Grammar, Genre, and Skills in
Teaching Writing 121

Introduction. 122

Contents

Excerpts From
Grammar to Enrich and Enhance Writing: A Smart Perspective 124
   Constance Weaver

Excerpts From
Investigating Narrative Writing by 9–11-Year-Olds 131
   Roger Beard and Andrew Burrell

Excerpts From
Teaching Argument Writing to 7- to 14-Year-Olds: An International Review
of the Evidence of Successful Practice 138
   Richard Andrews, Carole Torgerson, Graham Low, and Nick McGuinn

Excerpts From
Writing Development in Four Genres from Grades Three to Seven: Syntactic
Complexity and Genre Differentiation 145
   Scott F. Beers and William E. Nagy

Excerpts From
Children's Cognitive Effort and Fluency in Writing: Effects of Genre
and of Handwriting Automatisation 154
   Thierry Olive, Monik Favart, Caroline Beauvais, and Lucie Beauvais

Chapter 5   **Writing Traits: Rubrics and Assessment** 167

Introduction. 168

Excerpts From
An Investigation of the Impact of the 6+1 Trait Writing Model on
Grade 5 Student Writing Achievement. 170
   Michael Coe, Makoto Hanita, Vicki Nishioka, Richard Smiley

An Excerpt From
Make Assessment Count. 180
   Regie Routman

In Defense of Rubrics 184
   Vicki Spandel

Excerpts From
Rubrics: Heuristics for Developing Writing Strategies 190
   Susan De La Paz

Excerpts From
Putting Rubrics to the Test: The Effect of a Model, Criteria Generation,
and Rubric-Referenced Self-Assessment on Elementary School
Students' Writing 199
   Heidi L. Andrade, Ying Du, and Xiaolei Wang

Excerpts From
Reliability and Validity of Rubrics for Assessment Through Writing 205
   Ali Reza Rezaei and Michael Lovorn

Chapter 6   New Technology, New Writing? 215

Introduction 216

Excerpts From
Writing in the 21st Century: A Report from the
National Council of Teachers of English 218
   Kathleen Blake Yancey

Executive Summary From
Writing, Technology and Teens 224
   Amanda Lenhart, Sousan Arafeh, Aaron Smith, and
   Alexandra Rankin Macgill

Excerpts From
The Effect of Computers on Student Writing: A Meta-Analysis of Studies
from 1992 to 2002 232
   Amie Goldberg, Michael Russell, and Abigail Cook

Excerpts From
Laptops and Literacy: A Multi-Site Case Study 239
   Mark Warschauer

Excerpts From
Laptops and Fourth-Grade Literacy: Assisting the Jump over the
Fourth-Grade Slump 245
   Kurt A. Suhr, David A. Hernandez, Douglas Grimes, and Mark
   Warschauer

Excerpts From
A Middle School One-to-One Laptop Program: The Maine Experience . . . 251
   David L. Silvernail, Caroline A. Pinkham, Sarah E. Wintle, Leanne C.
   Walker, Courtney L. Bartlett

Still Neglected?
Writing in the 21st Century

Steve Graham, Ed.D.

Professor and Currey Ingram Chair in Special Education and Literacy
Vanderbilt University

First, the bad news. Although writing scores on national tests have increased slightly over the last two decades, the most recently reported National Assessment of Educational Progress (NAEP) findings show that among a representative sample of eighth grade students, 31% achieved a "proficient" (29%) or "advanced" (2%) level on the writing assessment (Salahu-Din, Persky, & Miller, 2008). According to the NAEP, a *proficient* achievement level "represents solid academic performance. Students reaching this level have demonstrated competency over challenging subject matter" whereas *basic* "shows only partial mastery of prerequisite knowledge and skills that are fundamental for proficient work at a given grade" (Salahu-Din et al., 2008, p. 6). In short, more than two-thirds of U.S. students do not have grade-level writing skills at Grade 8. The numbers at Grade 12 are even more troubling: only 24% of students taking the writing assessment scored as proficient or advanced, leaving more than three-quarters of students at or below basic achievement of the writing level we should expect for a student getting ready to graduate from high school (Salahu-Din et al., 2008, p. 37).

> **Students are still not getting the instruction and practice they need to become skilled writers.**

In an era of blogs, tweets, and wikis—a flowering of public writing—it may be surprising that writing instruction in the schools is not similarly blooming. But many educators agree that students are still not getting the instruction and practice they need to become skilled writers.

In 2003, the National Commission on Writing issued *The Neglected "R": The Need for a Writing Revolution* (NCOW, 2003), which called for schools to double the amount of time students spent writing (p. 3) because at that time, most elementary students spent fewer than three hours per week writing (p. 20; also see Cutler & Graham, 2008). But seven years later, a national survey found that elementary students still wrote for only an average of two hours per week (Gilbert & Graham,

2010, p. 503)—about 25 minutes per day—and received slightly more than an hour's writing instruction each week. Students wrote paragraphs and short pieces, not longer texts. Despite the data that show writing is a crucial skill for both higher education and career, students do not receive enough instruction and practice in the classroom, and teachers do not get the training they need to teach writing (Cutler & Graham, 2008; Gilbert & Graham, 2010).

Next Steps for Teaching Writing

Now, the good news: We *do* know what can work to help students in the writing classroom and beyond. Decades of increasingly more rigorous research have given us solid leads on instruction that can make a difference. In the reports *Writing Next* (Graham & Perin, 2007) and *Informing Writing* (Graham, Harris, & Hebert, 2011), published for the Carnegie Corporation by the Alliance for Excellent Education, as well as a more recent report conducted solely with elementary grade students (Graham, Kiuhara, McKeown, & Harris, 2012), the effects of specific types of writing instruction were reviewed and summarized. These reports recommend multiple research-proven strategies to help student writing proficiency; they include the following:

- A focus on the process of writing, with special emphasis on the stage of prewriting, in a writing workshop-based environment
- An emphasis on strategies to approach the writing situation and specific steps for carrying out the different processes of writing
- The teaching of genre; sentence construction; and handwriting, typing, and spelling skills
- The inclusion of models and self-assessment with context-specific rubrics
- The use of technology tools such as word processing

This book intends to highlight the important research taking place that will help us develop writing classroom practices that work for our students.

Developing Process Approaches

Chapter 1 highlights the history of and research in process writing. Since the 1970s, the process approach to writing has been used increasingly as the base instructional model in language arts (Pritchard & Honeycutt, 2006). With this approach, teachers identify and model the stages of writing (prewriting, drafting, editing, revising, proofreading, and publishing) to help students understand and work through their own writing process. The process approach is also embedded in the Common Core State Standards (CCSS) for English Language Arts (Common Core State Standards Initiative, 2010; see especially standards under "Production and Distribution of Writing"). Student writing is the center of inquiry in a way that, prior to the 1970s, it had not been. Now we know, thanks to research on the process approach, that the planning and revising stages are especially crucial to students' writing achievement.

One consequence of the process approach's focus on student writing is the idea that we as teachers try to meet students where they are and listen to what they try to tell us. That perception sets the stage for the research in Chapter 2 that asks "How do writing skills develop?" and "What instruction might be appropriate for different levels of development in our students?" Without the process approach and the work of early adopters to simply watch what students *do* as they write, teachers and researchers like Lucy Calkins may not have come up with insights that propelled our instruction forward about encouraging children to "write" wherever they can start and helping them build from there.

The Use of Strategies

Critics of a process approach to writing claim that sometimes teachers have difficulty with helping students build the skills they need. But process-based approaches easily accommodate strategy instruction, as the research in Chapter 3 describes. *Writing Next* identifies strategy instruction as having the greatest effect on the quality of adolescents' writing in numerous studies. Asking students to consciously adopt a strategy, trying it on to see if it "fits," like a shirt, and evaluate its usefulness is an important part of the research that suggests this self-awareness is a crucial component of strategy instruction.

Incorporating Skills

As educators, we have been discussing our options for embedding skills in the writing curriculum for at least three decades. In the era of high-stakes testing, grammar is an easy assessment target—but research has demonstrated time and again that teaching grammar in isolation does not promote student learning or the application of grammar concepts in student writing. In Chapter 4, much of the research demonstrates that what works is teaching writing skills, along with genre study, for example, within a student's writing process. Part of writing instruction, many authors point out, includes the development of "mini lessons" in these subjects that put instruction at the point of use—when students need those skills to get on with the discovery of what they want to say.

Rubrics and Traits

Large-scale research on the 6+1 Traits® of writing has just been published, and we are happy to excerpt that important report here. This research shows the success of the 6+1 Traits model in scientifically validated ways—confirming what teachers who have adopted the tool have discovered in their classroom practice. Traits and rubrics complement both process and strategy instruction because they give students the opportunity to reflect on their *process* as well as assess their *progress*. The research analyzed in *Informing Writing* also supports trait-based tools: trait-based rubrics help students set goals for their writing.

Technology Tools

In the mid 1980s, language arts teachers started to wonder whether the personal computer and word processing could be used in the classroom, not just to type up a final copy but to assist in the writing process. Since that time, the opportunities for technology use in the writing process have increased exponentially. *Writing Next* identified the use of word processing tools as composing and revising tools—we have not begun to tap the potential of Web 2.0 communication tools in helping our students find authentic outlets for their writing. In the final chapter of *Writing Research: A Guide to Curriculum Planning*, we have pulled together solid research and analysis that will guide us as we plan for technologies we cannot yet imagine that our future students will use.

Conclusion

The breadth and depth of research in writing development and instruction make one thing clear: in the 21st century, even with new tools and technologies making breakthroughs in our understanding, there is still a lot to understand about how different approaches and methods can impact students' specific writing skills and their general achievement in language and literacy. But as a result of decades of inquiry, we do know that there are some approaches to writing instruction that are solidly supported by ongoing research: process writing, a strategies approach that includes genre-based instruction, the incorporation of writing skills instruction within the context of students' composing, the use of rubrics and models for guidance and self-assessment of the six traits of effective writing, and a thoughtful approach to incorporating technology in the writing process.

References

Common Core State Standards Initiative (2010). *Common core state standards for English language arts & literacy in history/social studies, science, and technical subjects.* Available from http://www.corestandards.org/the-standards/english-language-arts-standards

Cutler, L., & Graham, S. (2008). Primary grade writing instruction: A national survey. *Journal of Educational Psychology, 100*(4), 907–919.

Gilbert, J., & Graham, S. (2010). Teaching writing to elementary students in grades 4–6: A national survey. *The Elementary School Journal, 110*(4), 494–518.

Graham, S., Harris, K.R., & Hebert, M. (2011). *Informing writing: The benefits of formative assessment.* Washington, DC: Alliance for Excellent Education (commissioned by the Carnegie Corporation of New York).

Graham, S., Kiuhara, S., McKeown, D., & Harris, K.R. (2012). A meta-analysis of writing instruction for students in the elementary grades. Forthcoming.

Graham, S., & Perin, D. (2007). *Writing next: Effective strategies to improve writing of adolescent middle and high school.* Washington, DC: Alliance for Excellent Education (commissioned by the Carnegie Corporation of New York).

National Commission on Writing. (2003). *The neglected "R": The need for a writing revolution.* New York: College Entrance Examination Board.

Pritchard, R. J., & Honeycutt, R. L. (2007). Best practices in implementing a process approach to teaching writing. In S. Graham, C. A. MacArthur, & J. Fitzgerald (Eds.), *Best practices in writing instruction* (pp. 28–49). New York: Guilford.

Salahu-Din, D., Persky, H., & Miller, J. (2008). *The nation's report card: Writing 2007.* Washington, DC: National Center for Education Statistics, Institute of Education Sciences, U.S. Department of Education.

Chapter 1

Teaching Writing as a Process

"I channeled John Dewey. He says if you want to be a good teacher, don't teach reading and writing. Teach students."

A.BACALL

Introduction

As many of the articles in Chapter 1 point out, by the 21st century, *the writing process* has become a ubiquitous part of language arts instruction. But it is worthwhile to remember how innovative pioneers like **Donald Murray** in the 1970s upended writing instruction, outlining the radical notion that what was interesting and important about writing was not the final product, but the process of getting to it.

In the manifesto "Teach Writing as a Process Not Product," Murray identifies the three general stages of the process—prewriting, writing, and rewriting—that make up "unfinished writing," which is the real subject of inquiry in the writing classroom. Putting students' writing at the core of instruction frees the student to make choices and "discover his own meaning"; teachers become, in Murray's words, "coaches, encouragers, developers, creators of environments." He encourages teachers to be patient and not rush to "help" students by doing their thinking for them, especially in the prewriting stage. Giving over classroom time for winding through the writing process, allowing students generous time to discover their own truths, results in a product that "may be worth your reading," according to Murray.

Since Murray and his compatriots introduced "process" as the focus of instruction, many teachers and researchers have augmented or realigned these stages, and both the process and its instruction have become subjects of academic research. The investigation reported in the second article by **Arnold Goldstein** and **Peggy Carr** finds that prewriting activities generally helped students achieve higher scores on the National Assessment of Educational Progress (NAEP) in Writing. During 1992, approximately 22,500 students took the writing assessment and in addition were asked about their teachers' approach to writing instruction. Students in grades 8 and 12 who reported that their teachers always asked them to purposefully perform some elements of a structured approach to writing had higher scores than students whose teachers did not. In addition, as the authors point out, "Students who reported they were asked both to plan their writing and write multiple drafts all the time had higher average proficiency scores than students who always did one or the other but not both of these activities." The authors caution that their findings support certain techniques associated with the process approach to writing but that individual student writers may or may not find all techniques equally useful; they conclude, however, that generally "the use of techniques such as planning and preparation of more than one draft is related to higher performance."

Other, more recent studies support aspects of the process approach to writing instruction. In the chapter's third article excerpt, **Ruie Pritchard** and **Ronald Honeycutt** provide an overview of research on the process approach and the changes in instruction that have come about as a result. They point out that one change since what they term as the "anything-goes" model of the process approach is that some aspects of writing can be directly taught, including self-regulation strategies and genre constraints. Instruction in the writing process has evolved to encompass more teacher direction and has resulted in student achievement. However, research findings are often mixed or contradictory, and very large-scale experimental studies have not been undertaken because the "process model evolved in practice more quickly than did supporting research and theories." Recently some academics question whether the process approach deemphasizes the product too much in an era where high-stakes tests determine student and school achievement, creating another debate about the writing curriculum.

Teacher-researcher **Mark Overmeyer,** in the fourth article in this chapter, asks, "Should we be more concerned with process or product?" but weighs in thoughtfully on the side of process *in the service of* production: "[I]n the writing classroom we should consider paying more attention to the rituals of practicing than the rituals of publishing." By watching his high-achieving students, Overmeyer concludes that focusing on products diminishes a student's ability to become a better writer because it increases the pressure of literary perfection. Instead, teachers should focus on the practice of writing in the classroom and publish writing only rarely. In a sense, Overmeyer argues that the best instruction does not focus on the finished writing needed by a state assessment: the way to help students become better writers for those assessments is to discover what writing strategies work best for them. And that means making their composing process the focus of the writing classroom.

On a different side of the debate, in the final article, **Lawrence Baines, Coleen Baines, Gregory Stanley,** and **Anthony Kunkel** wonder, "If teaching writing as a process has had such a tremendous effect on the attitudes and achievement of students, why isn't the evidence on its behalf more convincing?" They contend that in pure process classrooms they observed, teachers never corrected "errors" in language use or grammar for fear of damaging a student's self-esteem. They ask which is more important, "self-esteem or achievement," and suggest that the rejection of grammatical convention does not help students who will at some point need to use standard English.

Teach Writing as a Process Not Product

Donald Murray

The Essential Don Murray: Lessons from America's Greatest Writing Teacher,
Pages 1–5, ©2009 Heinemann.

Most of us are trained as English teachers by studying a product: writing. Our critical skills are honed by examining literature, which is finished writing; language as it has been used by authors. And then, fully trained in the autopsy, we go out and are assigned to teach our students to write, to make language live.

Naturally we try to use our training. It's an investment and so we teach writing as a product, focusing our critical attentions on what our students have done, as if they had passed literature in to us. It isn't literature, of course, and we use our skills, with which we can dissect and sometimes almost destroy Shakespeare or Robert Lowell, to prove it.

Our students knew it wasn't literature when they passed it in, and our attack usually does little more than confirm their lack of self-respect for their work and for themselves; we are as frustrated as our students, for conscientious, doggedly responsible, repetitive autopsying doesn't give birth to live writing. The product doesn't improve, and so, blaming the student—who else?—we pass him along to the next teacher, who is trained, too often, the same way we were. Year after year the student shudders under a barrage of criticism, much of it brilliant, some of it stupid, and all of it irrelevant. No matter how careful our criticisms, they do not help the student since when we teach composition we are not teaching a product, we are teaching a process.

> To be a teacher of a process such as this takes qualities too few of us have, but which most of us can develop. We have to be quiet, to listen, to respond. We are not the initiator or the motivator; we are the reader, the recipient.

And once you can look at your composition program with the realization you are teaching a process, you may be able to design a curriculum which works. Not overnight, for writing is a demanding, intellectual process; but sooner than you think, for the process can be put to work to produce a product which may be worth your reading.

What is the process we should teach? It is the process of discovery through language. It is the process of exploration of what we should know and what we feel about what we know through language. It is the process of using language to learn about our world, to evaluate what we learn about our world, to communicate what we learn about our world.

Instead of teaching finished writing, we should teach unfinished writing, and glory in its unfinishedness. We work with language in action. We share with our students the continual excitement of choosing one word instead of another, of searching for the one true word.

This is not a question of correct or incorrect, of etiquette or custom. This is a matter of far higher importance. The writer, as he writes, is making ethical decisions. He doesn't test his words by a rule book, but by life. He uses language to reveal the truth to himself so that he can tell it to others. It is an exciting, eventful, evolving process.

This process of discovery through language we call writing can be introduced to your classroom as soon as you have a very simple understanding of that process, and as soon as you accept the full implications of teaching process, not product.

The writing process itself can be divided into three stages: *prewriting, writing,* and *rewriting.* The amount of time a writer spends in each stage depends on his personality, his work habits, his maturity as a craftsman, and the challenge of what he is trying to say. It is not a rigid lock-step process, but most writers most of the time pass through these three stages.

Prewriting is everything that takes place before the first draft. Prewriting usually takes about 85 percent of the writer's time. It includes the awareness of his world from which his subject is born. In prewriting, the writer focuses on that subject, spots an audience, chooses a form which may carry his subject to his audience. Prewriting may include research and daydreaming, note-making and outlining, title-writing and lead-writing.

Writing is the act of producing a first draft. It is the fastest part of the process, and the most frightening, for it is a commitment. When you complete a draft you know how much, and how little, you know. And the writing of this first draft—rough, searching, unfinished—may take as little as one percent of the writer's time.

Rewriting is reconsideration of subject, form, and audience. It is researching, rethinking, redesigning, rewriting—and finally, line-by-line editing, the demanding, satisfying process of making each word right. It may take many times the hours required for a first draft, perhaps the remaining 14 percent of the time the writer spends on the project.

How do you motivate your students to pass through this process, perhaps even pass through it again and again on the same piece of writing?

First by shutting up. When you are talking he isn't writing. And you don't learn a process by talking about it, but by doing it. Next by placing the opportunity for discovery in your student's hands. When you give him an assignment you tell him what to say and how to say it, and thereby cheat your student of the opportunity to learn the process of discovery we call writing.

To be a teacher of a process such as this takes qualities too few of us have, but which most of us can develop. We have to be quiet, to listen, to respond. We are not the initiator or the motivator; we are the reader, the recipient.

We have to be patient and wait, and wait, and wait. The suspense in the beginning of a writing course is agonizing for the teacher, but if we break first, if we do the prewriting for our students they will not learn the largest part of the writing process.

We have to respect the student, not for his product, not for the paper we call literature by giving it a grade, but for the search for truth in which he is engaged. We must listen carefully for those words that may reveal a truth, that may reveal a voice. We must respect our student for his potential truth and for his potential voice. We are coaches, encouragers, developers, creators of environments in which our students can experience the writing process for themselves.

Let us see what some of the implications of teaching process, not product are for the composition curriculum.

Implication No. I. The text of the writing course is the student's own writing. Students examine their own evolving writing and that of their classmates, so that they study writing while it is still a matter of choice, word by word.

Implication No. 2. The student finds his own subject. It is not the job of the teacher to legislate the student's truth. It is the responsibility of the student to explore his own world with his own language, to discover his own meaning. The teacher supports but does not direct this expedition to the student's own truth.

Implication No. 3. The student uses his own language. Too often, as writer and teacher Thomas Williams points out, we teach English to our students as if it were a foreign language. Actually, most of our students have learned a great deal of language before they come to us, and they are quite willing to exploit that language if they are allowed to embark on a serious search for their own truth.

Implication No. 4. The student should have the opportunity to write all the drafts necessary for him to discover what he has to say on this particular subject. Each new draft, of course, is counted as equal to a new paper. You are not teaching a product, you are teaching a process.

Implication No. 5. The student is encouraged to attempt any form of writing which may help him discover and communicate what he has to say. The process which produces "creative" and "functional" writing is the same. You are not teaching products such as business letters and poetry, narrative and exposition. You are teaching a process your students can use—now and in the future—to produce whatever product his subject and his audience demand.

Implication No. 6. Mechanics come last. It is important to the writer, once he has discovered what he has to say, that nothing get between him and his reader. He must break only those traditions of written communication which would obscure his meaning.

Implication No. 7. There must be time for the writing process to take place and time for it to end. The writer must work within the stimulating tension of unpressured time to think and dream and stare out windows, and pressured time—the deadline—to which the writer must deliver.

Implication No. 8. Papers are examined to see what other choices the writer might make. The primary responsibility for seeing the choices is the student's. He is learning a process. His papers are always unfinished, evolving, until the end of the marking period. A grade finishes a paper, the way publication usually does. The student writer is not graded on drafts any more than a concert pianist is judged on his practice sessions rather than on his performance. The student writer is graded on what he has produced at the end of the writing process.

Implication No. 9. The students are individuals who must explore the writing process in their own way, some fast, some slow, whatever it takes for them, within the limits of the course deadlines, to find their own way to their own truth.

Implication No. 10. There are no rules, no absolutes, just alternatives. What works one time may not another. All writing is experimental.

None of these implications require a special schedule, exotic training, extensive new materials or gadgetry, new classrooms, or an increase in federal, state, or local funds. They do not even require a reduced teaching load. What they do require is a teacher who will respect and respond to his students, not for what they have done, but for what they may do; not for not for what they have produced, but for what they may produce, if they are given an opportunity to see writing as a process, not a product.

Excerpts From

Can Students Benefit From Process Writing?

Arnold A. Goldstein and Peggy G. Carr,
National Center for Education Statistics

NAEPfacts, Vol. I, April 1996, Pages I–5.

Data from the 1992 National Assessment of Educational Progress (NAEP) in Writing indicate that "teachers' encouragement of...process-related activities was strongly related to average writing proficiency."(1) Students whose teachers encouraged certain aspects of process writing averaged higher performance on the NAEP writing assessment.

> **Students whose teachers encouraged certain aspects of process writing averaged higher performance on the NAEP writing assessment.**

The 1992 writing assessment was administered to a representative national sample of approximately 7,000 4th-grade students, 11,000 8th-grade students, and 11,500 12th-grade students from about 1,500 public and private schools across the country. NAEP assessed students' ability to accomplish three purposes for writing: informative, persuasive, and narrative. Students in grade 4 were asked to respond to two 25-minute writing tasks; students in grades 8 and 12 were asked to respond to either two 25-minute tasks or one 50-minute task. Preceding each task, students were given a blank page with instructions to encourage pre-writing. Students, teachers, and administrators in all three grades were also asked about instructional content; instructional practices; school and teacher characteristics; school conditions; and student background, student activities, and home environment.

Teachers' Encouragement of Process Writing

Students in grades 8 and 12 (but not grade 4) were asked the extent to which their teachers asked them to do the following activities:

- Plan their writing;
- Make a formal outline before they write;
- Define their purpose and audience;
- Use sources or resources other than their textbook;
- Write more than one draft of a paper.

About half or more of 8th- and 12th-grade students reported their teachers always asked them both to plan their writing and to write more than one draft. High percentages of students (about 70 percent of 8th-graders and 76 percent of 12th-graders) also reported their teachers always asked them either to plan their writing or to write more than one draft, or to do both. On the other hand, about one-fourth of students (29 percent of 8th-graders and 24 percent of 12th-graders) were never asked to do either of those activities.

TABLE I. Students' reported frequency and average proficiency, by teachers' encouragement of process writing: Grades 8 and 12

Teachers' encouragement	Percent of students			Average proficiency scores		
	Always	Sometimes	Never	Always	Sometimes	Never
How often does your English teacher ask you to do the following:						
Plan your writing:						
Grade 8	55	38	8	270	253	248
Grade 12	63	30	7	292	278	269
Make a formal outline before you write:						
Grade 8	32	46	22	264	262	258
Grade 12	33	49	19	285	288	285
Define your purpose and audience:						
Grade 8	27	45	28	268	261	257
Grade 12	43	39	19	293	284	278
Use sources or resources other than your textbook:						
Grade 8	37	51	12	265	262	254
Grade 12	45	46	9	288	288	272
Write more than one draft:						
Grade 8	49	40	12	269	257	248
Grade 12	52	37	11	293	281	272
Always plan and draft:						
Grade 8	32	38	29	274	262	248
Grade 12	39	37	24	296	286	272

NOTE: The standard errors of the estimated percentages range from 0.4 to 1.1; standard errors of the proficiencies range from 0.9 to 2.7. It can be said with 95 percent confidence for each population of interest, the value for the whole population is within plus or minus two standard errors of the estimate for the sample. In comparing two estimates, one must use the standard error of the difference. Percentages may not total 100 percent due to rounding error.

SOURCE: National Assessment of Educational Progress (NAEP), 1992 Writing Assessment.

Average NAEP proficiency scores associated with the various techniques are also shown in Table 1. The highest possible score on the NAEP scale is 500. The data indicate that students who reported being always asked to do certain elements of a structured approach to writing had higher average NAEP scores than those who reported never being asked to do them. For example, 8th-graders who reported always being asked to plan their writing had an average score of 270, compared with only 248 for those never asked to plan their writing. Large differences in average writing scores were also evident between 8th-graders who reported always being asked to define the purpose and audience, to use sources or resources other than the textbook, or to write more than one draft, and those never asked to do these activities. Similar differences appeared for 12th-graders for these activities. In the case of making a formal outline before writing, however, the difference was much smaller (as for 8th-graders) or nonexistent (12th-graders).

> Students who reported they were asked both to plan their writing and write multiple drafts all the time had higher average proficiency scores than students who always did one or the other but not both of these activities.

Students who reported they were asked both to plan their writing and write multiple drafts all the time had higher average proficiency scores than students who always did one or the other but not both of these activities. Eighth-grade students who reported always being asked both to plan their writing and write more than one draft averaged 274, compared with 262 for those asked to always do one or another of these activities. For 12th-graders the corresponding scores were 296 and 286. Students asked to do neither of these activities always had the lowest average scores, 248 for 8th-graders and 272 for 12th-graders.

Discussion

Are process writing techniques helpful for effective writing? Evidence from the 1992 NAEP assessment in writing supports research in the field that several process writing techniques are associated with higher writing proficiency skills. In addition, NAEP provides evidence about which techniques have the greatest potential for positive outcomes.

Students of teachers who always encourage particular elements of process writing, such as planning and defining purpose and audience, were found to be generally better writers than students of teachers who

Teaching Writing as a Process

reportedly never encourage these activities. Similarly, average writing ability is higher among students whose teachers emphasize more than one process writing strategy. The 1992 NAEP assessment offered direct evidence that use of pre-writing activities is associated with the highest average proficiency scores. There is some conflicting evidence, however. The writing proficiency of students who reported their teachers always encourage various pre-writing activities (Table 1) attained higher scores than other students. Yet on the 1992 NAEP assessment, students who actually used unrelated notes or drawings, wrote different versions, or wrote first drafts performed about the same as those who did no pre-writing. Only those who used lists or outlines, or diagrams, outperformed those who showed no evidence of pre-writing. Perhaps students' actual practice in a test situation does not always conform to what is taught, especially in response to time pressure or low motivation (the NAEP has no individual consequences for the student).

The focus of process-oriented writing instruction is to stimulate students to think about their writing and reflect on their ideas. Writing is an individual activity, and students will often benefit by using some strategies and not others. While process-oriented instruction may not lead to better writing in all students, the use of techniques such as planning and preparation of more than one draft is related to higher performance.

Notes

All differences reported are statistically significant at the .05 level with adjustments for multiple comparisons. Associations between instructional variables and performance do not imply direct causation. The effectiveness of educational approaches could result from students' prior learning, their receptivity, teacher preparedness, having access to the necessary resources, and other factors.

(1) Arthur N. Applebee, Judith Langer, Ina V. S. Mullis, Andrew S. Latham, Claudia A. Gentile, *NAEP 1992 Writing Report Card,* National Center for Education Statistics, Report No. 23-W01 (Washington, D.C.: U.S. Government Printing Office, June 1994), p. 178.

(2) Linda Flower and John R. Hayes, "The Cognitive Process Theory of Writing," *College Composition and Communication,* 32, 365-387 (1981).

(3) George Hillocks, Jr., *Research on Written Composition* (Urbana, IL: National Conference on Research in English, 1986), Chapter 1.

Excerpts From

The Process Approach to Writing Instruction: Examining Its Effectiveness

Ruie J. Pritchard and Ronald L. Honeycutt

Handbook of Writing Research, Pages 275–290, ©2006 Guilford.

The understanding of what constitutes the writing process instructional model has evolved since the 1970's, when it emerged as a pedagogical approach. In the early years, it was regarded as a nondirectional model of instruction with very little teacher intervention. In his review of research on composition from 1963 to 1982, Hillocks (1984) concluded that the teacher's role in the process model is to facilitate the writing process rather than to provide direct instruction; teachers were found "*not* to make specific assignments, *not* to help students learn criteria for judging writing, *not* to structure activities based on specific objectives,…*not* to provide exercises in manipulating syntax, *not* to design activities that engage students in identifiable processes of examining data" (p. 162; emphasis in original). It is not surprising that the research Hillocks summarizes showed minimal impact on the quality of writing products as a result of this "natural process mode."

In the formative years, the process approach model was regarded as applying mainly to stories, was linear and prescriptive, merged proofreading and editing as the same thing, and usually did not involve direct instruction—a sort of anything-goes model whereby the process was valued over the product. In this early model, a simplistic pedagogy resulted: After their teacher describes the four stages, students recall and rehearse the steps, use the process to produce a story, and get

> **As a result of new theories, new research, and the changing status of writing in the curriculum, the process model has evolved.**

into groups to share their stories and gain feedback. In the literature in special education, such instruction to help students plan, organize, and carry out a writing task is called teaching "plans of action" (Gersten & Baker, 2001). Such plans comprise only some of the procedural tasks of the current process model.

Today, most researchers of the process model recognize that it involves both procedural knowledge and many other kinds of strategies that can be nurtured and directly taught, including activating schemata to access prior knowledge; teaching self-regulation strategies; helping students understand genre constraints; guiding students in re-visioning and in editing surface errors; providing structured feedback from teachers and peers; teaching the differences between reader- and writer-based prose; developing audience awareness and effects of audience on style, content, and tone; and dealing with emotional barriers, to name a few. In general, those studies that view the process model as encompassing more teacher direction in the process show positive effects on the quality of students' writing, on their view of themselves as writers, and on their understanding of the writing process. For example, a meta-analysis of 13 studies with learning disabled students (Gersten & Baker, 2001) concluded that an effective comprehensive writing program in special education should entail explicit teaching of "(a) the steps of the writing process and (b) the critical dimensions of different writing genres…as well as (c) structures for giving extensive feedback to students on the quality of their writing from either teachers or peers" (p. 251). Our review of the literature reveals that these elements also characterize effective writing instruction within regular education classroom settings.

> Critics of the process approach argue that attention to the processes of creating texts has made writing products into by-products.

Furthermore, current researchers recognize that as a writer matures and internalizes the overall procedures and strategies for producing texts in various genres, these become automatized. They occur more efficiently throughout the writing process, and not in sequential steps, as noted in the change in the professional literature in referring to the writing process as "recursive." Furthermore, the emphasis today on state academic standards is influencing how the process model is implemented and tested. In his argument that assessment creates artificial conditions for applying the writing process, Schuster (2004) sarcastically says that state writing tests should really be labeled "state drafting tests" (p. 378). As a result of new theories, new research, and the changing status of writing in the curriculum, the process model has evolved. Teaching the process model now demands careful scaffolding and creating lessons that traverse the entire process; researching the process model in all its inclusiveness is a multilayered process demanding a variety of research methodologies. As we learn more about what is entailed in teaching and learning the writing process, the definition and the pedagogy of the process model are likely to change.

Where Do We Go from Here?

Critics of the process approach argue that attention to the processes of creating texts has made writing products into by-products. "The process has become so ubiquitous as to mean anything, or perhaps more precisely, it has come to mean almost nothing. Tragically, the art and soul of writing have been lost in the 'process'" (Baines, Baines, Stanley, & Kunkel, 1999, p. 72). Proponents of the process approach say it is only through valuing the process that we help our students find the art and soul of writing.

Our reading of the current literature reveals that most researchers assert that writing and the writing process are best understood as complex phenomena that include not only procedural strategies for going through the writing process to generate text but also a multitude of other strategies to develop specific schemata. These include strategies to help writers understand the context for writing, to tap general background knowledge and reading ability, to sharpen cognitive processes for problem solving, to create emotional dispositions and attitudes about writing, to develop micro-level skills such as spelling, transcription, and sentence construction, as well [as] a macro-level understanding about organization, conventions, cohesion, audience, genre, and topic, to name a few. To complicate matters, findings from reports on the various subprocesses of the writing process contradict one another (van den Bergh & Rijlaarsdam, 2001). These strategies and subprocesses need to be explored in conjunction with the process model; since writing proficiency is recognized as a developmental process, longitudinal studies are especially needed.

As a result of the complexity of studying writing processes that are so inclusive, multi-layered, and overlapping, few purely experimental studies have been conducted, and fewer yet on a large scale or with the same population over time. Even when variables are highly controlled, researchers in writing concede that their studies cannot account for all the factors that influence the final product. For example, some studies suggest, but have not proven, that the process approach is most applicable to creating narratives. Theorists have surmised that as the writing process approach evolved, it became fused with personal writing, and this flawed understanding of the process model has persisted with practitioners and researchers (Stotsky, 1995). Needed, and in some cases under way, are studies about the comparative impact of the process approach to teaching various genres of writing. Another persisting misconception is that the process model does not entail direct instruction. In the beginning, the holistic emphasis on developing a writer's ownership of his or her writing, of creating authentic audiences, and of providing multiple sources of feedback somehow dominated educators' interest. Studies of the subprocesses of writing were not prominent in the research and still need to be studied as variables influencing writing products.

Since the process approach provided an instructional alternative at a time when traditional methods grounded in rhetorical theory were being challenged, the process model evolved in practice more quickly than did supporting research and theories. Many theories have been used to study writing, such as the cognitive process theory of Flower and Hayes (1981), the natural process model of Peter Elbow (1973) and Donald Murray (1985), and the mental growth model of James Moffett (1981, 1992). Not all derived from or were tested by research. Practitioners still need theories of teaching writing that are firmly grounded in research. This, in turn, should provide a foundation for what professionals consider best practices for enhancing student writing performance.

References

Baines, L., Baines, C., Stanley, G. K., & Kunkel, A. (1999). Losing the product in the process. *English Journal, 88*(5), 67–72.

Elbow, P. (1973). *Writing without teachers.* New York: Oxford University Press.

Flower, L., & Hayes, J. R. (1981). A cognitive process theory of writing. *College Communication and Composition, 32*(4), 365–387.

Gersten, R., & Baker, S. (2001). Teaching expressive writing to students with learning disabilities: A meta-analysis. *Elementary School Journal, 101*(3), 251–272.

Hillocks, G. (1984). What works in teaching composition: A meta-analysis of experimental treatment studies. *American Journal of Education, 93*(1), 133–170.

Moffett, J. (1981). *Active voice.* Montclair, NJ: Boynton/Cook.

Moffett, J. (1992). *Detecting growth in language.* Portsmouth, NH: Heinemann.

Murray, D. (1985). *A writer teaches writing* (2nd ed.). Boston: Houghton Mifflin.

Schuster, E. H. (2004). National and state writing tests: The writing process betrayed. *Phi Delta Kappan, 85*(5), 375–378.

Stotsky, S. (1995). The uses and limitations of personal or personalized writing in writing theory, research, and instruction. *Reading Research Quarterly, 30*(4), 758–776.

van den Bergh, H., & Rijlaarsdam, G. (2001). Changes in cognitive activities during the writing process and relationships with text quality. *Educational Psychology, 21*(4), 373–385.

The Rewards of Writing

Mark Overmeyer

Understanding Our Gifted, Spring 2008, Pages 6–8.

In *Bird by Bird*, Annie Lamott compares writing to a tea ceremony: "That thing you had to force yourself to do—the actual act of writing, turns out to the best part. It's like discovering that while you thought you needed the tea ceremony for the caffeine, what you really needed was the tea ceremony. The act of writing turns out to be its own reward" (Lamott, 1994, p. xxvi).

Lamott's ideas resonate with me as both a writer and as a teacher of writing. When I think of the many students I have worked with over the years, I remember their writing in particular....I often call my friends to share examples, amazed at how writing from elementary and middle school students can elicit the same reaction as the writing of a beloved novelist or poet. Lamott is right: The act of writing is full of rewards, and I think this is true about the teaching of writing as well.

But I worry a bit in these days of high stakes testing that we are more concerned about product than process in the writing classroom, and this can have a negative impact on all our students. I have worked with hundreds of advanced learners and gifted students over the years, and the subject they tend to struggle with most is writing. One message that is clear in every book I have read by novelists and poets is that writing,

---

Should we be more concerned with process or product?

---

even for professionals, does not come easily. Or to state it more clearly: It does not always come easily. Some days, the words and ideas flow, and other days they do not. Writing is different from other subjects because it can be like starting over again every day. One year, my advanced 6th graders read the novel *Watership Down* by Richard Adams, and each day we had rich discussions. Although sometimes we had to work harder to understand the text, my students were never unable to read the book. But some days, these same literate, eager students could not find the right words to express themselves in an essay or a story. It almost seemed as if they had "forgotten" how to write. I understand now that this is not because students aren't trying—it is because we may be too product oriented.

Writing as a Process

If we forget Lamott's idea of ceremony—the rituals and routines—of a successful writing classroom, we may send the wrong message to our students about the very nature of writing as a process. If we focus our attention only on the product, we will forget the rich processes that lead us to a product we will want to share. And since there is not one process for all writers, we need to build in rituals that enable students to discover what works best for them.

After having dozens of conversations with students about their processes, I am convinced that one of the best ways to uncover methods that may help students become better writers is to talk with them. Some possible questions that can jumpstart a discussion follow:

- How do you come up with ideas for writing?
- What can you do to effectively get ready to write? Do you like to create a plan, or do you just like to write?
- In what environments do you write most effectively? Do you like music, or do you need it to be quiet? Do you like to be alone, or are you okay with others being around?
- Do you like to talk about your ideas before you write, or would you prefer to get started first?
- What do you do when you are assigned a piece of writing to which you must respond, and you do not like the prompt?
- What do you do when you get stuck while you are writing?

It is important to keep in mind that when discussions about these topics happen, the teacher must act as a researcher and then respond to the thoughts students bring to the table. For example, when I discussed these very topics with a group of 6th graders, the class was split on the idea of music. Some thought music helped them to think, while

> One of the worst enemies some of our gifted students bring to writing is perfectionism.

others were distracted by it. We decided together that the most logical compromise at school was to have no music during sustained writing times because the music might distract others. Since some liked to talk prior to writing, and others liked to just think, we timed the talking block so that those who liked to talk could do so, and those who needed quiet knew that their time to think and process would come soon. But since writing is done at home as well as school, all the discussions helped students to think about what might help them in multiple environments.

So what do we do about products? How can we help our students become more effective at producing writing once they become comfortable with a process?

Writing as Product

One of the worst enemies some of our gifted students bring to writing is perfectionism. I think one reason many gifted students are more prone to this difficulty may lie, paradoxically, in books. Many of my most gifted students seem to inhale books. They read two or three books a week. These same students have not necessarily been my best writers, and I wonder if this is because they don't allow themselves time to practice. They are too product oriented and set out to write the next great Harry Potter fantasy. Because their vision is so overwhelming, they give up before they get much of a start.

One of the foundations of good lesson planning is to ask students to activate schema or background knowledge. Some students struggle because they have too little background knowledge, but some of our advanced students may struggle because they have too much schema about books and writing. In other words, when a teacher asks them to write a narrative, they immediately associate fiction with the books they are reading, and this seems like a nearly impossible task. I am not suggesting that our students cannot write books. Christopher Paolini famously began his dragon trilogy with the book *Eragon* when he was a teenager and has since become a very successful writer. However, the reality is that most of our students, no matter how gifted, will probably not write novels in our classes, and we are probably not equipped to help them write large amounts of text.

> **The bulk of writing our students do should be seen as practice.**

So how can we balance this mismatch between what our students read and what we ask them to do in school?

I turn to writer and teacher Natalie Goldberg for advice. She recommends that we be kind to ourselves. When we put too much pressure on ourselves, we often shut down. I do not believe our advanced writers *mean* to create a negative environment for their own writing, but they often have such high expectations for themselves that they shut down. The bulk of writing our students do should be seen as practice. Much like a soccer coach works with a team for weeks before the first game, we need to allow our students time to engage in meaningful, short exercises that will help them to become stronger writers. They should talk about their writing with others often, write and revise frequently, share regularly, and publish to perfection only rarely. I am suggesting here that in the writing classroom we should consider paying more attention to the rituals of practicing than the rituals of publishing.

Writing as a Surprise

Above all, we owe our students the truth. We need to let them know that writing is different from other subjects. Math and science can help us wrap our minds around the patterns in the universe, and reading can help us understand the human condition.

But writing is unique because it always involves the creation of something new. And because writing is always an act of creation, we may often find ourselves surprised.

> We can actually learn what we really think, or what we really want to say, by writing it down.

These surprises become the norm when students are asked to practice writing regularly. During one visit to a 1st grade classroom last spring, the teacher and I took the children outside and spent time drawing what we noticed. When we returned, we talked about the many ways we might write down our thoughts. During sharing time, many students focused on the concrete nature of their observations with sentences like these:

I see a tree.
The car is noisy.
I see clouds.

Our surprise that day came from a student who has not lived in America for very long. She wrote and shared the following sentence: *The flrs r lking for lit* (The flowers are looking for light.).

When I asked this child to share how she came up with this idea, she was unable to tell me, partially because she had limited English but also because she wasn't truly sure. This student exemplifies one of my strongest beliefs about writing: Sometimes we not only surprise the reader by what we write, but we surprise ourselves. We can actually learn what we really think, or what we really want to say, by writing it down. We aren't always sure how the words will fall, and we may even feel lost, but like the flowers in the 1st grade piece above, if we know our own process—and if we believe in writing as ceremony—we can always find our way.

Reference

Lamott, A. (1994). *Bird by bird*. New York: Random House.

Excerpts From

Losing the Product in the Process

Lawrence Baines, Coleen Baines, Gregory Kent Stanley,
and Anthony Kunkel

The English Journal, Vol. 88, May 1999, Pages 67–72.

Few researchers would dare dispute that the process movement has done wonders to improve the teaching of writing. Emig's *The Composing Processes of Twelfth Graders* [1971] and other publications of the late 1960s and early 1970s made the point that a strictly grammatical approach to writing did not reflect the way that students actually wrote. In 1973 the National Writing Project was established to help promulgate the concept that writing might not necessarily follow the circumscribed steps suggested in the lessons available in textbooks, many of which focused upon intricacies of outlining, grammar, and spelling. Later, Flower and Hayes [1981, 1984] contributed some handy flowcharts that seemed to map out rather neatly the cognitive processes associated with the writing process. At the end of the millennium, "the writing process" has become so accepted as the paradigm for composition that even Warriner's [1988] now devotes huge sections of its erstwhile grammatical textbook to "the process."

> Regrettably, one consequence of the widespread emergence of "the process" is that the word *error* has been banished from teachers' vocabularies.

Still, the extent to which teaching writing as a process affects student achievement and attitudes is somewhat uncertain. Despite over two million teacher graduates from the National Writing Project alone..., the latest National Assessment of Educational Progress (NAEP) writing results reveal that the overall writing performance of students has stagnated since the inception of the NAEP assessment of writing some fourteen years ago. Moreover, the data also indicate that students' perceptions of writing haven't changed much either. If teaching writing as a process has had such a tremendous effect on the attitudes and achievement of students, why isn't the evidence on its behalf more convincing?

"The Process" and Student Error

Regrettably, one consequence of the widespread emergence of "the process" is that the word *error* has been banished from teachers' vocabularies. Amid our observations of three hundred classrooms, no teacher ever said, "That is wrong," or "This is an error." When we asked teachers what they looked for when they evaluated student writing, we were more likely to get a sermon on the damaging psychological effects of "bleeding red ink all over the page" than a statement regarding attributes of good writing.

Overwhelmingly in our observations, the quality of writing was presented more as a personal choice than a desired goal. That is to say, in conversations with teachers, many claimed that good writing could not be suitably quantified and that bad writing was really not so bad once you understood the plethora of factors behind it—the student's home environment, ethnicity, social life, popularity, absentee record, former teachers.

Perhaps many who teach "the process" have begun to confuse the act of grading with the gentle art of correcting. While teachers of "the process" often graded papers without correcting them, they seldom corrected papers without grading them. Predictably, the excommunication of error has caused repercussions in many postsecondary institutions. Many adolescents first learn as college freshmen that they aren't flawless masters of the language, when their English professors, usually more concerned with the quality of a piece of writing than the fragile psyche of its author, return the first batch of papers.

A Paradigm That Needs Breaking

In the classrooms we observed, the obsession with process, at times, crowded out the hard, dirty work of learning how to write well. Grammar, spelling, vocabulary, or sentence structure were rarely, if ever, mentioned. Although we are not nostalgic about the painfully dull and irrelevant practice of teaching writing through decontextualized drill, we feel that many teachers of "the process" have too flippantly rejected the prospect that a student somewhere might eventually need to know the rule of grammar regarding subject and verb agreement. There is nothing heinous about informing individual students where their writing falters from standard English. Once informed, these students can at least have the option of learning standard English so that they can use it appropriately, should they find themselves in a position where such knowledge may be required—in a job, for example.

> Perhaps many who teach "the process" have begun to confuse the act of grading with the gentle art of correcting.

So, what can teachers do to improve how writing is taught and learned? For one thing, they can consider allowing the idea of *error* back into the classroom. Although a student may experience some unpleasant disequilibrium when an error is identified, the experience is not something from which most students will be unable to recover. While it is commendable to be concerned with students' sensitivities, the self-esteem of most adolescents is a little beyond being manipulated by gold stars or push-button pleasantries, anyway. Rather than post a "No Hunting Allowed!" sign on the door, as Kirby, Liner, and Vinz [1988] suggest, to dissuade students from making rude remarks about each other's writing, perhaps a teacher could post a "Constructive Comments Welcome!" sign and help students track and analyze their progress towards overcoming their most common mistakes.

Teachers of writing might also loosen up with regard to "the process" that students use to get to the endpoint of a piece of writing. Most worthwhile writing begins in the gut or the heart and has little to do with the lockstep allegiance to the simplistic mantra of "brainstorm/draft/revise." Even most advocates of "the process" acknowledge that students who care about their subject will write more convincingly than students who don't.

Finally, teachers of writing might reconsider their goals for student writing. Which is more important—self-esteem or achievement, standard English or dialect, process or product? In the current educational climate, a teacher acknowledging that one piece of writing might be more lucid, more moving, more eloquent—or dare we say it?—better than another would be tantamount to treason. In the never-ending struggle to preserve self-esteem, nothing can be said that might offend or hurt another's feelings. As a result, "the process" has become so ubiquitous as to mean anything, or perhaps more precisely, it has come to mean almost nothing. Tragically, the art and soul of writing have been lost in the process.

References

Emig, Janet. *The Composing Processes of Twelfth Graders*. Urbana, IL: NCTE, 1971.

Flower, Linda, and John Hayes. "Images, Plans and Prose." *Written Communication* (Jan. 1984): 120–60.

———. "A Cognitive Process Theory of Writing." *College Composition and Communication* 32 (1981): 365–87.

Kirby, Dan, Tom Liner, and Ruth Vinz. *Inside Out*. Portsmouth, NH: Heinemann-Boynton/Cook, 1988.

Warriner, John. *English Composition and Grammar: An Introductory Course*. Orlando, FL: Harcourt Brace, 1988.

Developing Writers

Introduction

As Don Murray wrote in an earlier chapter, "writing is a demanding, intellectual process." Recent research in cognitive development has helped teachers and others understand the real complexity of producing writing and has illuminated why many children struggle to put their thoughts into words. In the first article of this chapter, **Ronald Kellogg** announces that people need at least two decades of writing practice to advance from the beginning stages of composing skills to something close to the skill of professional writers—from knowledge-telling, simply "telling what one knows" without regard to audience, to knowledge-crafting, in which a skilled writer not only carefully imagines the audience but attempts to anticipate a reader's interpretation of the text. Students' difficulty with revising, Kellogg surmises, is a result of the difficulty of keeping the author, the text, and the reader in mind all at once, which is primarily a question of cognitive development. Younger writers are simply unable to keep all of the complexities in their limited working memory. Kellogg's stages of writing development align with cognitive development trajectories to illustrate what students can be expected to accomplish in early and later grades.

Using theories of cognitive development, researchers recently began attempting to model children's writing development and to identify what are developmental versus individual differences in students' skills. In the second article in this chapter, **Richard Wagner and his colleagues** describe an experiment that attempts to determine the developmental differences between writers in Grade 1 and Grade 4. They found a wide variety of developmental differences in the written compositions of students at different grades. Interestingly, they also discovered a strong relationship between handwriting fluency and writing at both grades, which suggests that handwriting fluency may free up "attentional resources that can be devoted to planning and composing when writing." The researchers also conclude there may be a more complicated relationship in which "the perceptual and motor aspects of handwriting become associated and even integrated with language networks." They speculate that the relationship between spelling and composing may similarly be cognitively complex—as the authors of the fourth article also conclude. (See Zaner-Bloser's *Handwriting Research: A Guide to Curriculum Planning* and *Spelling Research: A Guide to Curriculum Planning* guides for more studies on the relationship between handwriting/spelling and composing.)

From a teacher-researcher perspective, **Lucy Calkins** examines the developmental relationship between drawing and writing for very young students. In the third article of this chapter, she describes how children approach drawing as a rehearsal for writing. She surmises that "[i]n their drawings, children take one bit of the world and hold it still for a moment; then, with the picture lying in front of them, they begin work on the accompanying words." To make a drawing helps them select what to write about. It also helps them create narrative, which is based on action: when children's drawings start to show characters acting, their writing begins to tell a chronological story. But, Calkins cautions, at some point children do not need to keep weaving drawing and writing together, and teachers should identify at what point students should be directed into writing more and drawing less to communicate their ideas. They can also, perhaps as early as the second grade, encourage students to rely more on oral language as rehearsal for composing: Whereas in early years, children's drawing skill exceeds their written language development, "by second grade," Calkins explains, "the goal is often to have writing catch up to talking." Attending to children's natural language development, teachers can plan writing instruction that meets their students' needs and takes advantage of their changing, individual skills.

Exploring those critical moments of a child's transition from drawing to writing words and sentences, **J. Richard Gentry** examines in the final article the development of writing and spelling skills in early childhood. Using examples of student writing from kindergarten through Grade 2, Gentry identifies five specific and identifiable stages of early literacy. In Stage 0, children are scribbling and drawing but are not yet forming letters. In the next stage, children form letters, perhaps in support of their drawings, but these letters do not match the sounds of the words they are trying to write. In Stage 2, students write letters that mostly correspond to the beginning and ending sounds of words they are trying to spell. Stage 3 is characterized by more complete invented spelling, where the letters represent each sound (whether correctly or not). In Stage 4, students spell in "chunks" that follow familiar phonics patterns—a point Gentry identifies as "breaking the code" of written English and the crucial step toward skilled reading and writing. Gentry emphasizes using the right teaching tools for each unique stage by providing short examples of the kinds of things teachers might say and do to support a student's writing development.

Excerpts From

Training Writing Skills: A Cognitive Developmental Perspective

Ronald T. Kellogg

Journal of Writing Research, Vol. I, 2008, Pages I–26.

Development of writing skills

The development of written composition skills are conceived here as progressing through three stages, as illustrated in Figure 1. It takes at least two decades of maturation, instruction, and training to advance from (1) the beginner's stage of using writing to tell what one knows, to (2) the intermediate stage of transforming what one knows for the author's benefit, and to (3) the final stage of crafting what one knows for the reader's benefit. The first two stages are well-established by developmental research and typically mastered by advanced high school and college students (Bereiter & Scardamalia, 1987). The third is seldom discussed, perhaps because it characterizes only mature adults who aim to become skilled professional writers (Kellogg, 2006).

FIGURE I. Macro-stages in the cognitive development of writing skill

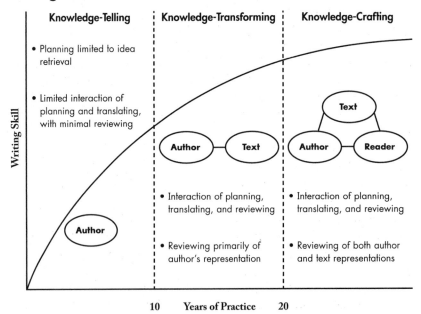

The three stages shown in Figure 1 are intended to demarcate three macro-stages of writing development. Writing skill is shown as continuously improving as a function of practice, as is typical for perceptual-motor and cognitive skills in general. The micro-changes underlying the gradual improvement that drive the transition to the next macro-stage fall beyond the scope of the present article. But, in general, it is assumed that both the basic writing processes of planning, language generation, and reviewing, plus the mental representations that must be generated and held in working memory, undergo continuous developmental changes through maturation and learning within specific writing tasks. As a consequence of the task specificity, a child might be operating at a more advanced stage in writing, say, narrative texts, assuming these are most practiced, compared with persuasive texts.

Author, text, and reader representations

In the most advanced stage of knowledge-crafting, the writer is able to hold in mind the author's ideas, the words of the text itself, and the imagined reader's interpretation of the text. The representations of the author, the text, and the reader must be held in the storage components of working memory and kept active by allocating attention to them (Traxler & Gernsbacher, 1993). Thus, for expert writers, not only are the basic processes of planning, sentence generation, and reviewing juggled successfully, but so are three alternative representations of content. The author's ideas, comprehension of what the text currently says, and the interpretations of an imagined reader may be quite different mental representations.

> In the most advanced stage of knowledge-crafting, the writer is able to hold in mind the author's ideas, the words of the text itself, and the imagined reader's interpretation of the text.

By contrast, during earlier stages of a writer's development, the text and reader representations may be either relatively impoverished or sufficiently detailed but not adequately maintained in working memory during text composition. A young child of, say, 6 years of age might have only a partial representation of how the text actually reads in comparison to a much richer representation of his or her own ideas. Gradual gains in writing skill within the stage of knowledge-telling across several years of writing experience would stem from growth in the child's ability to represent the text's literal meaning. Similarly, a 12 year old might be aware of the prospective reader, but this reader representation may be too unstable to hold in working memory. Although such a developing writer's audience awareness might well guide, say, word choices in language generation at the moment of transcription, the reader representation would not be available for reviewing the text, if it cannot be maintained adequately in working memory.

As shown in Figure 1, then, the stage of knowledge-telling is dominated by the author's representation. By the stage of knowledge-transforming, the text representation is both sufficiently detailed and stable enough to maintain in working memory to permit an interaction between the author and text representations. Yet the reader representation is not yet routinely entered into the interaction in working memory until the stage of knowledge-crafting. It must first become sufficiently elaborate and stable to maintain *and* working memory resources must be available to coordinate all three representations. The key point made here is the heavy demands made on working memory by planning, sentence generation, and reviewing processes limit not only the coordination of these basic cognitive processes, but also the maintenance and use of the three distinct representations underlying the composition of expert writers.

Knowledge-telling

The initial stage of knowledge-telling consists of creating or retrieving what the author wants to say and then generating a text to say it. The author is not entirely egocentric in knowledge-telling and can begin to take into account the reader's needs. Specifically, by the time children are beginning to write they realize that another person's thoughts about the world may differ from their own. By about the age of 4, children have acquired a theory of mind that allows them to take another's perspective (Wellman, 1990; Wellman, Cross, & Watson, 2001). This helps them to plan what they need to say or write to communicate their ideas.

> Knowledge-telling consists of creating or retrieving what the author wants to say and then generating a text to say it.

However, it would appear that the writer's representation of what the text actually says to him or her and, to an even greater degree, how the prospective reader would interpret the text as written are impoverished early on in writing acquisition. As the child develops during middle childhood and adolescence, first the text representation, and then the reader representation, gradually become richer and more useful to the composer. The assumption made here is that the author must first be able to comprehend what the text actually says at a given point in the composition (i.e., possesses a stable text representation) before he or she can imagine how the text would read to another person (i.e., acquire a reader representation). It is further assumed that these representations must be constructed by the writer in a stable form before he or she can hold these representations in working memory and make use of them in planning and reviewing. Extending McCutchen's (1996) analysis of how working memory limitations constrain planning, language generation, and reviewing, it is proposed here that the three representations of the author, text, and reader are not fully accessible in working memory until the most advanced stage of knowledge-crafting is achieved.

What is known empirically is that writers operating at the initial knowledge-telling stage of development clearly struggle with understanding what the text actually says. As Beal (1996) observed, young writers who compose by telling their knowledge have trouble seeing the literal meaning of their texts, as those texts would appear to prospective readers. The young author focuses on his or her thoughts not on how the text itself reads. The verbal protocols collected by Bereiter and Scardamalia (1987) of children clearly document the essential focus on the author's representation rather than the text and reader representations. The text produced is essentially a restatement of their thoughts.

Knowledge-transforming

The second stage of knowledge-transforming involves changing what the author wants to say as a result of generating the text. It implies an interaction between the author's representation of ideas and the text representation itself. What the author says feeds back on what the author knows in a way not observed in knowledge-telling. Reviewing the text or even ideas still in the writer's mind can trigger additional planning and additional language generation. In reading the text, the author builds a representation of what it actually says. At times such reviewing may lead to a state of dissonance between what the text says and what the author actually meant, but it can also become an occasion for rethinking afresh the author's ideas (Hayes, 2004). During knowledge-transforming, the act of writing becomes a way of actively constituting knowledge representations in long-term memory (Galbraith, 1999) rather than simply retrieving them as in knowledge-telling. Verbal

> During knowledge-transforming, the act of writing becomes a way of actively constituting knowledge representations in long-term memory.

protocols of writers at the stage of knowledge-transforming reveal extensive interactions among planning, language generation, and reviewing in this stage of development (Bereiter & Scardamalia, 1987). The text actually produced is a greatly condensed version of the author's thought processes. When the transition to knowledge-transforming is completed, it is clear that the writer can maintain and use both the author and text representations.

Knowledge-crafting

The third stage characterizes the progression to professional expertise in writing. The writer must maintain and manipulate in working memory a representation of the text that might be constructed by an imagined reader as well as the author and text representations. Notice that this stage now involves modeling not just the reader's view of the writer's message but also the reader's interpretation of the text itself. In knowledge-crafting, the writer shapes what to say and how to say it with the potential reader fully in mind. The writer tries to anticipate different ways that the reader might interpret the text and takes these into account in revising it. As Sommers (1980; p. 385) observed in journalists, editors, and academics, "experienced adult writers imagine a reader (reading their product) whose existence and whose expectations influence their revision process."

Holliway and McCutchen (2004) stressed that the coordination of the author, text, and reader representations "builds on multiple sources of interpersonal, cognitive, and textual competencies" and may well account for most of the difficulties that children experience with revision. In an early study of expert versus novice differences in writers, Sommers (1980) documented that professional writers routinely and spontaneously revise their texts extensively and globally, making deep structural changes. They express concern for the "form or shape of their argument" as well as "a concern for their readership" (p. 384). By contrast, college freshmen made changes primarily in the vocabulary used to express their thoughts. Lexical substitutions predominated rather than semantic changes. The students seemed to view their assignment primarily as an exercise in knowledge-telling and did not "see revision as an activity in which they modify and develop perspectives and ideas..." (p. 382). There seemed to be little interaction between the text and author representation in her sample of college freshmen, let alone a focus on a reader representation.

> In knowledge-crafting, the writer shapes what to say and how to say it with the potential reader fully in mind.

It is too strong a statement to suggest that adolescents and young adults always fail to make changes in meaning or take into account the needs of the reader as they review. For example, Myhill and Jones (2007) reported that students aged 14 to 16 can verbalize such concerns when prompted to comment on their writing processes after a writing session. As many as half of their sample of 34 students commented on revisions made to improve coherence and add text in addition to avoiding repetition and making it sound better in general. It is suggested, though, that working memory limitations in holding and manipulating representations of how the reader interprets the text, while simultaneously managing the author and text representations, is a fundamental brake on the writing skill of developing writers throughout childhood, adolescence, and young adulthood. It helps to explain, for example, why adolescent writers do not routinely and spontaneously make the kinds of deep structural revisions found in experienced adult writers.

> Working memory limitations in holding and manipulating representations of how the reader interprets the text, while simultaneously managing the author and text representations, is a fundamental brake on the writing skill of developing writers throughout childhood, adolescence, and young adulthood.

Finally, interventions that prompt the writer to "read-as-the-reader" explicitly focus working memory resources on the reader representation. These are effective in improving the revising activities of 5th and 9th graders (Holliway & McCutchen, 2004) as well as of college students (Traxler & Gernsbacher, 1993). However, it is unclear from these studies what costs are incurred when limited attention and storage capabilities are focused on the reader representation rather than on the author and text representations. In all of these studies, the task involved writing a text that described a geometric figure to the reader and thus possibly limited the importance of interactions between author and text representations and knowledge-transforming. That is to say, the act of composing a draft and revising it did not demand an intensive discovery of what the author thinks about the topic, as would be necessary in an open-ended persuasive task as opposed to a descriptive task using a limited set of perceptually available stimuli.

To summarize the studies reviewed here and the argument made, even young children understand that they must take into account the reader's thoughts as they compose a message in oral and written communication during the first stage of knowledge-telling. Yet, being aware of a fictional reader in generating text is different from being able to read the text as it is currently written from another person's perspective. Audience awareness should be regarded as a necessary, but not sufficient, condition for eventually developing the capacity to read and interpret the author's own text from the standpoint of an imagined or fictional reader. An additional necessary condition is having a sufficiently developed working memory system to coordinate the author, text, and reader representations concurrently with relative ease. Executive attention, in particular, must be fully mature and effectively deployed to maintain and manipulate all three of these representations as the writer recursively plans, generates, and reviews the emerging text. In knowledge-crafting, the reader's interpretation of the text must feed back to the way the text reads to the author and to the message the author wishes to convey in the first place. Knowledge-crafting, then, is characterized by a three-way interaction among representations held in working memory. The author can spontaneously engage in deep conceptual revisions as well as surface revisions to a text to try to make certain that readers see matters the way the author does. By anticipating in detail the responses of readers to an existing text, the writer operating at the level of knowledge-crafting engages in extensive revisions at all levels of the text.

> Audience awareness should be regarded as a necessary, but not sufficient, condition for eventually developing the capacity to read and interpret the author's own text from the standpoint of an imagined or fictional reader.

The concept of knowledge-crafting proposed here draws from the work of Walter Ong. About 30 years ago, Ong (1978) argued that a skilled author creates a fictional audience for the text to understand its meaning from the prospective readers' point of view. In contrast to oral communication, the audience for written communication is not actual, but fictional, a product of the writer's imagination that can play an active role in composition. As Ong explained, "the writer must anticipate all the different senses in which any statement can be interpreted and correspondingly clarify meaning and to cover it suitably." To effectively interpret the text from the reader's point of view, the author is forced to think about and decide what knowledge the reader already knows that need not be made explicit in the text.

It is important to remember that the process of reviewing ideas and text is not limited to the revision phase of composition. It is usually embedded in the composition of a first draft, along with planning and language generation. The reviewing of ideas alone—perhaps held solely as mental representations or perhaps recorded as visual-spatial symbols or brief, cryptic verbal notations—can even occur during prewriting before a first draft is undertaken. Highly extensive reviewing during prewriting and drafting characterize the strategy of attempting to produce a perfect rather than a rough first draft (Kellogg, 1994). Thus, the capacity to see the text from the perspective of the reviewer can be put to use during the composition of a first draft rather than delayed until revising an initial effort, depending on the strategy adopted by the author. For example, experienced scientists show a wide range of individual composing strategies (Rymer, 1988). Whereas some use a linear strategy of extensive planning during prewriting before starting a draft, others jump right in with a very rough draft and revise endlessly. Both the specific task and the medium or tool used for writing influence the choice of composing strategies (Van Waes & Schellens, 2003). Regardless of the particular composition strategy employed, what characterizes the knowledge-crafting of expert writers is the capacity to keep in mind how a reader would interpret the text as well as representing the author's ideas and what the text, in its present form, communicates to the author and to the reader.

References

Beal, C. R. (1996). The role of comprehension monitoring in children's revision. *Educational Psychology Review, 8,* 219–238.

Bereiter, C., & Scardamalia, M. (1987). *The psychology of written composition.* Hillsdale, NJ: Lawrence Erlbaum Associates.

Galbraith, D. (1999). Writing as a knowledge-constituting process. In M. Torrance, & D. Galbraith (Eds.), *Studies in writing: Vol. 4. Knowing what to write: Conceptual processes in text production* (pp. 139–160). Amsterdam: Amsterdam University Press.

Hayes, J. R. (2004). What triggers revision? In L. Allal, L. Chanquoy, & P. Largy (Eds.), *Revision of written language: Cognitive and instructional processes* (pp. 9–20). Boston/Dordrecht, Netherlands/New York: Kluwer.

Holliway, D. R., & McCutchen, D. (2004). Audience perspective in young writers' composing and revising. In L. Allal, L. Chanquoy, & P. Largy (Eds.), *Revision of written language: Cognitive and instructional processes* (pp. 87–101). Boston/Dordrecht, Netherlands/New York: Kluwer.

Kellogg, R. T. (1994). *The psychology of writing.* New York: Oxford University Press.

Kellogg, R. T. (2006). Professional writing expertise. In K. A. Ericsson, N. Charness, P. J. Feltovich, & R. R. Hoffman (Eds.), *The Cambridge handbook of expertise and expert performance* (pp. 389–402). New York: Cambridge University Press.

McCutchen, D. (1996). A capacity theory of writing: Working memory in composition. *Educational Psychology Review, 8,* 299–325.

Myhill, D. & Jones, S. (2007) More than just error correction. *Written Communication, 24,* 323–343.

Ong, W. (1978). Literacy and orality in our times. In T. J. Farrell and P. A. Soukup (2002) (Eds.) *An Ong reader: Challenges for further inquiry/Walter J. Ong* (pp. 405–428). Cresskill, NJ: Hampton Press.

Rymer, J. (1988). Scientific composing processes: How eminent scientists write journal articles. In D. A. Jollife (Ed.) *Advances in writing research, volume two: Writing in academic disciplines.* Norwood, NJ: Ablex.

Sommers, N. (1980). Revision strategies of student writers and experienced writers. *College Composition and Communication, 31,* 378–387.

Traxler, M. J., & Gernsbacher, M. A. (1993). Improving written communication through perspective-taking. *Language and Cognitive Processes, 8,* 311–334.

Van Waes, L., & Schellens, P. J. (2003). Writing profiles: The effect of the writing mode on pausing and revision patterns of experienced writers. *Journal of Pragmatics, 35,* 829–853.

Wellman, H. M. (1990). *The child's theory of mind.* Cambridge, MA: MIT Press.

Wellman, H. M., Cross, D., & Watson, J. (2001). Meta-analysis of theory-of-mind development: The truth about false belief. *Child Development, 72,* 655–684.

Excerpts From

Modeling the Development of Written Language

Richard K. Wagner, Cynthia S. Puranik, Barbara Foorman, Elizabeth Foster, Laura Gehron Wilson, Erika Tschinkel, and Patricia Thatcher Kantor

Reading and Writing, Vol. 24, 2011, Pages 203–220.

Although models of reading have been proposed since the turn of the last century, the first model of writing to gain traction was that proposed by Hayes and Flower (1980), Hayes (1996). According to the Hayes and Flower model, writing consists of three parts: planning, translating, and reviewing. Hayes (1996) revised the original model by incorporating aspects beyond the cognitive processes used in writing such as motivation for writing, the writing context, and working memory. He also reconceptualized the original cognitive processes into the broader categories of reflection, text production, and text interpretation.

Subsequently, a simple view of writing was proposed as an analogy to the simple view of reading, in which writing can be explained in terms of ideas and spelling (Juel, Griffith, & Gough, 1986). Another simple view of writing was proposed by Berninger et al. (2002) to capture the instructional components that research on effective writing instruction had found to be effective in facilitating writing development—explicit instruc-

> Compared to older expert writers, young novice writers show only rudimentary preparation in the form of reflection and planning before beginning writing.

tion in transcription (handwriting and spelling) coupled with the executive functions in the original Hayes and Flower model (planning, translating, and reviewing/revising) all taught with strategies (Graham & Harris, 2005; Harris, Graham, Mason, & Friedlander, 2008) to generate written text at different levels of language (words, sentences, and text). More recently, writing models have been expanded to reflect the fact that writing is an extraordinarily complex strategic activity that operates under constraints that affect other kinds of cognitive and language processing (Berninger & Winn, 2006; Torrance & Galbraith, 2006). It also is important to acknowledge that writing is done for a purpose in a sociocultural context (Nystrand, 2006). Models of writing have been proposed for adult skilled writers (e.g., the original 1980 Hayes and Flower model and the revised 1996 Hayes model) and for developing child writers (e.g., Berninger & Swanson, 1994). Finally, it is important to distinguish aspects of writing that are relatively unique to writing and aspects that are shared with reading and oral language (Mehta, Foorman, Branun-Martin, & Taylor, 2005; Shanahan, 1984, 1988, 2006; Shanahan & Lomax, 1986).

The nature of writing changes with development (Berninger & Chanquoy, in press). Compared to older expert writers, young novice writers show only rudimentary preparation in the form of reflection and planning before beginning writing. The writing task is viewed as writing what they know about a topic. Substantial differences are also found in text generation (i.e., the mental production of the to-be-written message) and transcription (i.e., transcribing the message into written text).

> Writing in the early grades consists primarily of learning to write letters, to spell, and compose short texts, but transitions by fourth grade into more extended writing as a way of learning about a topic.

Younger novice writers revise minimally relative to older more experienced writers (see McCutchen, 2006, for a review of developmental changes in writing). Finally, writing in the early grades consists primarily of learning to write letters, to spell, and compose short texts, but transitions by fourth grade into more extended writing as a way of learning about a topic (Berninger, Abbott, Whitaker, Sylvester, & Nolen, 1995). This of course is analogous to the idea of a developmental change in reading from learning to read to reading to learn.

In the area of reading, techniques such as confirmatory factor analysis (CFA) and structural equation modeling (SEM) have proven valuable for testing alternative models of individual and developmental differences (see e.g., Wagner, Torgesen, Laughon, Simmons, & Rashotte, 1993; Wagner, Torgesen, & Rashotte, 1994). These techniques have been applied in studies of written language, albeit with less frequency. For example, Abbott and Berninger (1993) and Graham, Berninger, Abbott, Abbott, and Whitaker (1997) reported structural equation modeling studies of handwriting, spelling, and composition. These studies provided evidence of strong roles for handwriting and spelling in composition, even for intermediate writers.

In previous studies that have addressed the factors of writing, a wide variety of variables have been studied, including quantitative measures of amount of writing done (e.g., numbers of words or sentences), qualitative ratings of overall writing quality, and quantitative variables at the discourse-level, sentence-level, and word-level (Sanders & Schilperood, 2006; Nelson & Van Meter, 2007).

Recent research by Puranik, Lombardino, and Altmann (2008) represents an integration of these lines of inquiry by exploring the underlying structure of writing using analyses of more fine grained variables. Writing samples were obtained using a retelling paradigm in which a story was read to students and they were asked to write what they remembered from the story. Results from an exploratory factor analysis were interpreted as support for three factors: productivity (i.e., how much writing was done), complexity (i.e., the density of writing and length of sentences), and accuracy (i.e., whether the writing was free from spelling and punctuation errors).

> The present study was designed to evaluate alternative models of the structure of individual and developmental differences in writing.

The present study was designed to evaluate alternative models of the structure of individual and developmental differences in writing. A better understanding of these differences could inform our understanding of writing development. Models of the structure of individual and developmental differences in writing also would have implications for scoring writing samples....Our study also represents a replication of the Puranik et al. (2008) study and an extension of it in four ways. First, writing samples were obtained by requiring students to generate a story from a prompt as opposed to asking them to retell a story that was read to them. Second, confirmatory factor analysis was used in an attempt to confirm the framework that was proposed on the basis of the initial exploratory factor analysis. Third, the framework was expanded by including variables that represented the macro-organizational level of text structure (using a topic sentence, number and logical ordering of ideas). Fourth, given the strength of relations between handwriting fluency and various measures of written language found in previous studies (Graham et al., 1997), the construct of handwriting fluency was added to the analyses.

Method

Participants

Writing samples were collected from 208 1st- and 4th-grade students who were sampled from two public schools in a small southeastern city. Writing samples were obtained from all first-and fourth-grade students whose parents provided consent.

Of the 208 writing samples collected, 186 were coded and the remaining 22 samples were not coded because the students did not complete the task or because the writing was considered illegible by at least two coders. The coded writing samples included 98 from 1st-grade students and 88 from 4th-grade students.

Measures

The measures consisted of a compositional writing sample and two handwriting fluency measures.

Compositional writing sample

To obtain the writing sample, the task was introduced by saying:

> We are going to write about choosing a pet for the classroom. When you are writing today, I want you to stay focused and keep writing the whole time. Don't stop until I tell you to. Also, if you get to a word that you don't know how to spell, sound it out and do your best. I'm not going to help you with spelling today. If you make a mistake, cross out the word you don't want and keep writing. Don't erase your mistake because it will take too long. Keep writing until I say stop.

A demonstration of crossing out a word on the board was given. Participants then were instructed:

> Remember, today we are writing about choosing a pet for your classroom. Imagine that you could have any animal in the world for a classroom pet. What would that animal be? Explain why you would like to have that animal for a classroom pet.

> Remember to write the whole time, cross out any mistakes and do not erase them, and sound out any words you can't spell.

Students were given 10 min to write. Students who stopped writing before the time was up were prompted:

> What more could you write about choosing this pet?

Handwriting fluency

Handwriting fluency was assessed by an alphabet handwriting fluency task and a sentence copying fluency task. These tasks were introduced by saying:

> We're going to play a game that will show me how well and quickly you can write. First, you are going to write the lowercase or small letters of the alphabet as fast and as carefully as you can. Then I'm going to ask you to copy a sentence as fast and carefully as you can. Don't try and erase any of your mistakes, just cross them out and go on.

The alphabet handwriting fluency task was administered by saying:

> When I say "ready, begin," you are going to write the small letters of
> the alphabet as fast and as carefully as you can. Keep writing until I say
> stop. If you make a mistake, draw a line through the letter and keep
> going. Ready, begin.

Students were given 60 s to complete the task. The score was the
number of letters correctly printed regardless of order. For the sentence
copying fluency task, the sentence to be copied was printed on the board.
The students were then instructed:

> We are going to do some more writing. This time, I want you to copy
> this sentence, (point to the sentence on the paper) 'The quick brown fox
> jumps over the lazy dog,' as many times as you can while writing as fast
> and carefully as you can. I'm going to time you again, and it's important
> that you write the whole time until I say stop. If you get to the end of the
> sentence, start over again. If you make a mistake, draw a line through it
> and keep going. When I say stop, please stop writing and put down
> your pencil. Ready, begin.

Students were given 60 s to complete the task. The score was the
number of words correctly copied in order.

Writing variables coded

Written samples were transcribed into a computer database according to Systematic Analysis of Language Transcript conventions (SALT,
Miller & Chapman, 2001) by two trained coders. T-units were used as
the unit of segmentation (Scott & Stokes, 1995; Scott & Windsor, 2000)
and written samples were analyzed using a modification of Nelson, Bahr,
and Van Meter's (2004) protocol for analyzing written language. A
T-unit is defined as the shortest grammatically allowable sentence into
which language can be divided, or minimally terminable unit. It refers to
a dominant clause and its dependent clauses. Ten variables were coded.

Macro-organization

Three variables were coded that represented the higher level organization of the writing sample:

1. *Topic.* Whether a topic sentence was present or not.

2. *Logical ordering of ideas.* Logical ordering of ideas was rated on a
   1-to 4-point rating scale.

3. *Number of key elements.* One point was given each for the presence
   of a main idea, body, and conclusion, yielding a maximum possible
   score of three.

Complexity

Two variables were used to represent the complexity with which the writing sample conveyed information:

4. *Mean length of T-unit.* A commonly used measure of syntactic complexity obtained by dividing total number of words by the number of T-units.

5. *Clause density....* Clause density is the ratio of the total number of clauses (main and subordinate) divided by the number of T-units.

Productivity

Two variables represented how much writing was accomplished:

6. *Total number of words.* Total number of words was the number of words produced in writing by the child. Words or phrases that did not relate to the prompt such as "The end" or "That's all I remember" were deleted when calculating total number of words. Incomplete sentences or phrases, usually found at the end of the written sample, were also omitted when calculating total number of words.

7. *Number of different words.* This measure of lexical diversity was automatically generated by SALT.

Spelling and punctuation

Three variables represented spelling and punctuation:

8. *Number of spelling errors....* Number of spelling errors was the sum of spelling errors in a child's written sample.

9. *Number of capitalization errors.*

10. *Number of errors involving a period.* Errors included missing and unnecessary use of end periods.

Procedure

The three tasks were group administered in the students' classrooms by their teachers with members of the research team in the classroom to monitor task administration and answer any questions.

Results

We were interested in the magnitude of developmental differences between first and fourth grade samples for each of the 10 composition variables and the 2 handwriting fluency variables (Table 1).

TABLE I. Descriptive statistics for the composition and handwriting fluency variables and effect sizes and significance tests associated with developmental differences between the first- and fourth-grade samples

		1st Grade M (SD)		4th Grade M (SD)		Cohen's D	t
Macro-organization							
1.	Topic	0.78	(0.41)	0.97	(0.18)	0.56	3.78***
2.	Logical ordering of ideas	2.81	(0.94)	3.44	(0.62)	0.80	5.42***
3.	Number of key elements	2.00	(0.61)	2.37	(0.55)	0.67	4.46***
Complexity							
4.	Mean length of T-units	7.07	(2.03)	9.84	(2.10)	0.94	6.36***
5.	Clause density	1.25	(0.27)	1.51	(0.29)	0.91	6.24***
Productivity							
6.	Total number of words	43.77	(18.00)	112.32	(41.09)	2.17	15.04***
7.	Number of different words	28.06	(9.71)	62.76	(17.30)	2.48	17.14***
Spelling and punctuation							
8.	Number of spelling errors	5.99	(5.10)	5.14	(5.08)	0.16	1.09
9.	Number of capitalization errors	2.23	(2.23)	1.57	(2.10)	0.28	1.96
10.	Number of period errors	1.32	(1.80)	1.05	(1.50)	0.16	1.07
Handwriting fluency							
11.	Alphabet printing fluency	8.39	(5.02)	22.19	(11.47)	1.65	11.12***
12.	Sentence copying fluency	6.98	(3.25)	20.64	(5.73)	2.69	17.08***

*** $p < .001$

An interesting pattern of differences emerged. Large differences between first-and fourth-grade means were noted for variables associated with the productivity and handwriting fluency constructs. These effect sizes ranged from 1.7 to 2.7 in magnitude. Moderate differences were noted for variables associated with macrostructure organization and complexity, with effect sizes ranging from 0.6 to 0.9. Finally, minimal differences were noted for variables associated with spelling and punctuation, with effect sizes ranging from .16 to .28.

In first grade, handwriting fluency was significantly and moderately related to three of the four factors of written composition, with the strongest relation found for productivity. This seems reasonable in that young children who are more fluent in handwriting are able to generate longer writing samples. What is more remarkable is the magnitude of the relations between handwriting fluency and the factors of writing in fourth grade. The magnitude of the relation between handwriting fluency and productivity is nearly double that found in first grade. Even more surprising was the magnitude of the relation between handwriting fluency and macro-organization.

Discussion

The results of our study replicate and extend the results of Puranik et al. (2008)....The magnitude of developmental differences between first- and fourth-grade students was remarkably variable, with effect sizes ranging from near 0 to 2.7.

The most striking result was the strength of relations between handwriting fluency and both macro-organization and productivity for the fourth-grade sample. We imagined that handwriting fluency might place a strong constraint on all aspects of writing for first-grade students, but did not expect it to be as strongly related to written composition for fourth-grade students. However, Graham et al. (1997) reported standardized path coefficients in the range of .5–.7 from handwriting fluency to composition quality as well as composition fluency for large samples of students from first through sixth grade.

> The most striking result was the strength of relations between handwriting fluency and both macro-organization and productivity for the fourth-grade sample.

What might explain the striking relations between handwriting fluency and written composition, including macro aspects of organization of writing for fourth-grade students? One possibility is that an individual who is fluent at handwriting fluency has more attentional resources that can be devoted to planning and composing when writing compared to an individual who is not fluent at handwriting and must devote attentional resources to this aspect of writing. Flower and Hayes (1980) provided an apt description of the processing demands of writing:

> As a dynamic process, writing is an act of dealing with an excessive number of simultaneous demands or constraints. Viewed this way, a writer in the act is a thinker on full-time cognitive overload (p. 33, cited by Torrance & Galbraith, 2006).

A large literature that includes both correlational and experimental methods supports this explanation of relations between handwriting fluency and higher-level aspects of writing (Alves, Castro, Sousa, & Stromqvist, 2007; Chanquoy & Alamargot, 2002; Christensen, 2005; Connelly, Campbell, MacLean, & Barnes, 2006; Connelly, Dockrell, & Barnett, 2005; Dockrell, Lindsay, & Connelly, 2009; Graham et al.,

1997; McCutchen, 2006; Olive, Alves, & Castro, in press; Olive & Kellogg, 2002; Peverly, 2006; Torrance & Galbraith, 2006). The argument that handwriting fluency affects higher level aspects of writing because of capacity limitations is analogous to that made to explain the relation between fluent decoding and comprehension.

> **It is also possible that measures of handwriting fluency actually tap deeper and richer language centers than might be assumed.**

In addition to direct or mediating effects of handwriting fluency on higher level aspects of writing, it is also possible that measures of handwriting fluency actually tap deeper and richer language centers than might be assumed. The idea here is that as a result of considerable writing experience over years, the perceptual and motor aspects of handwriting become associated and even integrated with language networks, much as graphemes and letter strings become attached to corresponding phonemes and morphemes. As a result, relations between handwriting fluency and higher level aspects of writing and language more generally might actually be bidirectional: handwriting fluency influences higher level writing directly or as a mediator, but also is a by-product of the development of higher levels aspects of writing and language.

Interpretation of the spelling and punctuation (i.e., accuracy in Puranik et al., 2008) construct may not be as straightforward as it first appears to be. Fayol (1997) argues that punctuation is an integral part of transforming thought into the linear dimension that writing requires. As such, it may be more related not only to thought but also to

> **Findings from this study highlight the need to assess individual students' strengths and weaknesses at the word, sentence, and discourse level such that intervention can be tailored to meet those needs.**

simple grammar. Relatedly, a recent fMRI study by Richards, Berninger, and Fayol (2009) reported that spelling activated areas of the brain associated with thought.

Finally, we note a close correspondence between three of the factors described in the present study and a level of language framework that has been applied to writing (Whitaker, Berninger, Johnston, & Swanson, 1994): Our macro-organization factor corresponds to the text level; our complexity factor corresponds to the sentence level; and our productivity factor corresponds to the word level. Our findings substantiate potential intraindividual differences in the three levels of language (Whitaker et al., 1994; Puranik et al., 2008). Findings from this study highlight the need to assess individual students' strengths and weaknesses at the word, sentence, and discourse level such that intervention can be tailored to meet those needs. The findings from this study also extend previous research by showing that more than handwriting fluency is involved in transcription. Similar to analyzing writing at different levels of language, analyses of transcription errors should include spelling, and punctuation.

References

Abbott, R. D., & Berninger, V. W. (1993). Structural equation modeling of relationships among developmental skills and writing skills in primary- and intermediate-grade writers. *Journal of Educational Psychology, 85,* 478–508.

Alves, R. A, Castro, S. L., Sousa, L., & Stromqvist, S. (2007). Influence of typing skill on pause-execution cycles in written composition. In M. Torrance, L. van Waes, & D. Galbraith (Eds.), *Writing and cognition: Research and applications* (pp. 55–65).

Berninger, V. W., Abbott, R. D., Whitaker, D., Sylvester, L., & Nolen, S. B. (1995). Integrating low- and high-level skills in instructional protocols for writing disabilities. *Learning Disabilities Quarterly, 18,* 293–309.

Berninger, V. W., & Chanquoy, L. (in press). Writing development: What writing is and how it changes over early and middle childhood. In E. Grigorenko, E. Mambrino, & D. Priess (Eds.), *Handbook of writing: A mosaic of perspectives and views.* New York: Psychology Press.

Berninger, V., & Swanson, H. L. (1994). Modifying Hayes and Flower's model of skilled writing to explain beginning and developing writing. In E. Butterfield (Ed.), *Children's writing: Toward a process theory of development of skilled writing* (pp. 57–81). Greenwich, CT: JAI Press.

Berninger, V. W., Vaughan, K., Abbott, R., Begay, K., Byrd, K., & Curtin, G. (2002). Teaching spelling and composition alone and together: Implications for the simple view of writing. *Journal of Educational Psychology, 94,* 291–304.

Berninger, V. W., & Winn, W. (2006). Implications of advancements in brain research and technology for writing development, writing instruction, and education evolution. In C. MacArthur, S. Graham, & J. Fitzgerald (Eds.), *Handbook of writing research* (pp. 96–114). New York: Guilford.

Chanquoy, L., & Alamargot, D. (2002). Working memory and writing: Evolution of models and assessment of research. *Annee Psychologique, 102,* 363–398.

Christensen, C. A. (2005). The role of orthographic-motor integration in the production of creative and well-structured written text for students in secondary school. *Educational Psychology, 25,* 441–453.

Connelly, V., Campbell, S., MacLean, M., & Barnes, J. (2006). Contribution of lower-order letter and work fluency skills to written composition of college students with and without dyslexia. *Developmental Neuropsychology, 29,* 175–198.

Connelly, V., Dockrell, J., & Barnett, J. (2005). The slow handwriting of undergraduate students constrains overall performance in exam essays. *Educational Psychology, 25,* 99–107.

Dockrell, J., Lindsay, G., & Connelly, V. (2009). The impact of specific language impairment on adolescents' written text. *Exceptional Children, 75,* 427–436.

Fayol, M. (1997). On acquiring and using punctuation: A study of written French. In J. Costermans & M. Fayol (Eds.), *Processing interclausal relationships: Studies in the production and comprehension of text* (pp. 157–178). Mahwah, NJ: Lawrence Erlbaum.

Flower, L. S., Hayes, J. R. (1980). The dynamics of composing: Making plans and juggling constraints. In L. W. Gregg & E. K. Steinberg (Eds.), *Cognitive processes in writing* (pp. 31–50). Hillsdale, NJ: Erlbaum.

Graham, S., Berninger, V. W., Abbott, R. D., Abbott, S. P., & Whitaker, D. (1997). Role of mechanics in composing of elementary school students: A new methodological approach. *Journal of Educational Psychology, 89,* 170–182.

Graham, S., & Harris, K. R. (2005). *Writing better: Effective strategies for teaching students with learning difficulties.* Baltimore, MD: Paul H. Brookes.

Harris, K. R., Graham, S., Mason, L., & Friedlander, B. (2008). *Powerful writing strategies for all students.* Baltimore, MD: Paul H. Brookes.

Hayes, J. R. (1996). A new framework for understanding cognition and affect in writing. In C. M. Levy & S. Ransdell (Eds.), *The science of writing: Theories, methods, individual differences, and applications* (pp. 1–27). Mahwah, NJ: Lawrence Erlbaum.

Hayes, J. R., & Flower, L. (1980). Identifying the organization of writing processes. In L. Gregg & E. Steinberg (Eds.), *Cognitive processes in writing: An interdisciplinary approach* (pp. 3–30). Mahwah, NJ: Lawrence Erlbaum.

Juel, C., Griffith, P., & Gough, P. (1986). Acquisition of literacy: A longitudinal study of children in first and second grade. *Journal of Educational Psychology, 78,* 243–255.

McCutchen, D. (2006). Cognitive factors in the development of children's writing. In C. MacArthur, S. Graham, & J. Fitzgerald (Eds.), *Handbook of writing research* (pp. 115–130). New York: Guilford.

Mehta, P. D., Foorman, B. R., Branum-Martin, L., & Taylor, W. P. (2005). Literacy as a unidimensional multilevel construct: Validation, sources of influence, and implications in a longitudinal study in grades 1 to 4. *Scientific Studies of Reading, 9,* 85–116.

Miller, J., & Chapman, R. (2001). Systematic analysis of language transcripts (Version 7.0) [computer software]. Madison, WI: Waisman Center, University of Wisconsin-Madison.

Nelson, N. W., Bahr, C., & Van Meter, A. (2004). *The writing lab approach to language instruction and intervention.* Baltimore, MD: Paul H. Brookes Publishing Co., Inc.

Nelson, N. W., & Van Meter, A. M. (2007). Measuring written language ability in narrative samples. *Reading & Writing Quarterly, 23,* 287–309.

Nystrand, M. (2006). The social and historical context for writing research. In C. MacArthur, S. Graham, & J. Fitzgerald (Eds.), *Handbook of writing research* (pp. 11–27). New York: Guilford.

Olive, T., Alves, R. A., & Castro, S. L. (in press). Cognitive processes in writing during pauses and execution periods. *European Journal of Cognitive Psychology.*

Olive, T., & Kellogg, R. T. (2002). Concurrent activation of high- and low-level production processes in written composition. *Memory & Cognition, 30,* 594–600.

Peverly, S. T. (2006). The importance of handwriting speed in adult writing. *Developmental Neuropsychology, 29,* 197–216.

Puranik, C., Lombardino, L., & Altmann, L. (2008). Assessing the micro-structure of written language using a retelling paradigm. *American Journal of Speech-Language Pathology, 17,* 107–120.

Richards, T. L., Berninger, V. W., & Fayol, M. (2009). fMRI activation differences between 11-year-old good and poor spellers' access in working memory to temporary and long-term orthographic representations. *Journal of Neurolinguistics, 22,* 327–353.

Sanders, T. J. M., & Schilperood, J. (2006). Text structure as a window on the cognition of writing: How text analysis provides insights in writing products and writing processes. In C. MacArthur, S. Graham, & J. Fitzgerald (Eds.), *Handbook of writing research* (pp. 386–402). New York: Guilford.

Scott, C., & Stokes, S. (1995). Measures of syntax in school-age children and adolescents. *Language, Speech, and Hearing Services in Schools, 26,* 309–317.

Scott, C., & Windsor, J. (2000). General language performance measures in spoken and written discourse produced by school-age children with and without language learning disabilities. *Journal of Speech, Language, and Hearing Research, 43,* 324–339.

Shanahan, T. (1984). Nature of the reading-writing relation: An exploratory multivariate analysis. *Journal of Educational Psychology, 76,* 466–477.

Shanahan, T. (1988). The reading-writing relationship: Seven instructional principles. *Reading Teacher, 41,* 636–647.

Shanahan, T. (2006). Relations among oral language, reading, and writing development. In C. MacArthur, S. Graham, & J. Fitzgerald (Eds.), *Handbook of writing research* (pp. 171–183). New York: Guilford.

Shanahan, T., & Lomax, R. G. (1986). An analysis and comparison of theoretical models of the reading-writing relationship. *Journal of Educational Psychology, 78,* 116–123.

Torrance, M., & Galbraith, D. (2006). The processing demands of writing. In C. MacArthur, S. Graham, & J. Fitzgerald (Eds.), *Handbook of writing research* (pp. 67–80). New York: Guilford.

Wagner, R. K., Torgesen, J. K., Laughon, P., Simmons, K., & Rashotte, C. A. (1993). Development of young readers' phonological processing abilities. *Journal of Educational Psychology, 85,* 1–20.

Wagner, R. K., Torgesen, J. K., & Rashotte, C. A. (1994). The development of reading-related phonological processing abilities: New evidence of bi-directional causality from a latent variable longitudinal study. *Developmental Psychology, 30,* 73–87.

Whitaker, D., Berninger, V., Johnston, J., & Swanson, L. (1994). Intraindividual differences in levels of language in intermediate grade writers: Implications for the translating process. *Learning and Individual Differences, 6,* 107–130.

Growing Up Writing:
Grades K, 1, and 2

Lucy Calkins

The Art of Teaching Writing, Pages 83–89, ©1994 Heinemann.

Children can write sooner than we ever dreamed was possible. Most children come to school knowing a handful of letters, and with these they can write labels and calendars, letters and stories, poems and songs. They will learn to write by writing and by living with a sense of "I am one who writes." This self-perception will give children the eyes to see, and they will notice the conventions of written language everywhere.

> Not just the act of drawing but the picture itself provides a supportive framework for young writers.

They will learn about punctuation, spelling, purposes for writing, and the many rhythms of written language from billboards and environmental labels and books. They will ask about the monogram letters on their bath towels and the words on their sweatshirts. They will imitate their big sister's cursive writing, they will gather knowledge from all the writing and all the writers in their world. Their growth as writers is spectacular. All over the world, there are six- and seven-year-olds who write with voice, skill, and confidence. Sometimes it helps us as teachers and as parents if we can anticipate some of the continuums along which growth in writing may happen.

Changes That Occur as Children's Writing Is Supported by, and Eventually Separated from, Their Drawings

Five-year-old Chris opens his book to a blank page and takes hold of his pencil. Cheerfully I ask, "What are you going to write?" The boy stares at me as if astounded by the stupidity of my question. "How should I know?" he says. "I haven't drawed it yet."

Like many four-, five-, and six-year-olds, Chris rehearses for writing by drawing. This does not mean that his drawings are important only as preludes to writing. In fact, the drawings are far more important to Chris than the writing; the drawings take up most of his time and most of his paper, and they convey most of his story. When I say that Chris's drawings are rehearsals for writing, I also do not mean that his drawings accomplish the purposes we, as adults, normally connect with rehearsal. As he draws, Chris does not weigh one topic against another, nor does he anticipate an audience's response to his story or plan the direction his writing will take. In the block area, Chris does not begin with armchair speculation over what he will build. Instead he piles one block on top of another until he announces, "I'm makin' a tower." So, too, in the writing area he does not begin by thinking about his final product but by drawing the conventional person; then, in the middle of drawing, he announces, "This is gonna be my brother."

For older children, rehearsal for writing will involve living one's life as a writer, noticing all that it contains. Rehearsal will also involve rereading one's notebook to consider various topics, planning a story, thinking about making something for someone, worrying over the audiences' responses, and gathering notebook entries with an eye toward future writing. In order to do this, the writer must have a wide-lens sense of time. The writer must be able to anticipate that the work begun today will exist tomorrow. Chris, like many kindergarten, first-, and second-grade children, tends to operate more in the present tense, in the here and now. He doesn't spend a lot of time anticipating his tomorrows. He doesn't fret about whether his writing topic is "good enough" any more than he frets about whether his block tower will be acceptable. He writes the way he plays with blocks—for the sake of the

> When action enters children's drawing, their texts tend to change from "all-about" books into narratives or chronologically ordered books.

activity more than for the creation of a final product.

Drawings must also help youngsters with the problem of selection. The world involves such a rapid flux of activities and ideas, and writing is so slow, so limited, that selection is a problem even for skilled writers. How much more true this must be for beginning writers! In their drawings, children take one bit of the world and hold it still for a moment; then, with the picture lying in front of them, they begin work on the accompanying words.

About fifteen years ago, Don Graves, Susan Sowers, and I spent several years conducting a major study of children and their writing. As part of this study, Sowers found that when action enters children's drawing, their texts tend to change from "all-about" books into narratives or chronologically ordered books. Action entered into children's drawings especially after they began drawing their figures in profile. Now horses could be led on a rope, people could kiss and dance together, dogs could drink out of their bowls. Characters could interact with each other and with their settings...and different written texts resulted.

Because of the many ways in which drawing contributes to early writing, I encourage kindergarten and first-grade teachers to provide their children with thin marker pens and with an assortment of unlined and experience-chart paper, with some stapled into small, informal books, and some left as individual sheets.

Having spoken so extensively about the ways in which drawing can support children's early writing, let me also say that in some first- and most second-grade classrooms I discourage teachers and children from regarding drawing as an integral part of the writing process. In some primary classrooms, I ask teachers, "Why not steer them away from drawings?"

Let me be clear that when I suggest, at some point, that children move away from writing only captions under drawings, I'm not advocating moving away from artwork. Although it is not always necessary for writing to weave in and out of drawing, it is certainly necessary for our classrooms to support all kinds of artistic exploration. I selected my sons' nursery school largely because of the centrality of the "cut and color" table at that school, and because, instead of having teacher-directed art projects, the school encourages free exploration with pens, paints, and clay. I think it's very important that the painting easel always be available as an option in primary classrooms. There is no question in my mind that the habits of mind one develops in composing a diorama or a clay sculpture are very similar to the habits of mind one develops in writing. In both instances, the composer needs to ask, "How shall I go about making something lovely? What medium might work best?" The artist, like the writer, explores one possibility and then another, drafting and revising. With paint, clay, and fabric, the artist, like the writer, creates imaginary worlds and invites others to live inside them.

> We can introduce drawing as a form of rehearsal, but then we must watch for signs indicating that a child no longer needs to weave drawing and writing together.

Teachers are sometimes baffled to find that first I recommend drawing as a way of rehearsing for writing and then later, I discourage it. The point is that no solution works for every child and no solution works forever. We can introduce drawing as a form of rehearsal, but then we must watch for signs indicating that a child no longer needs to weave drawing and writing together.

Excerpts From

Five Phases of Intervention, Support, and Instruction— Up as Close as You Can Get

J. Richard Gentry

Breaking the Code: the New Science of Beginning Reading and Writing,
pages 46, 74–88 ©2006 Heinemann.

Observing, writing, reading, and listening to children talk about what they are thinking are all wonderful ways to get up close to what's happening inside a child's brain with literacy.... In this chapter I want to show you what some teachers and I see when we look closely at a child's writing and talk with them about it.

Seeing a Writer's Phase of Development

Question 1: Is this child using letters? If only scribbles, wavy writing, or looping writing is used and no letters are present, it's Phase 0.

Question 2: Is this child using letters but not matching any of the letters to sounds? If letters are used but no sounds are represented, it's Phase 1.

Question 3: Is this child using letters and getting mostly beginning and ending sounds? If mostly beginning and ending sounds are represented but some sounds are missing, it's Phase 2.

Question 4: Is this child supplying a letter for each sound? If you can finger spell the invented words and get results similar to what you see in the child's invented spelling, it's Level 3.

Question 5: Does this child usually spell in chunks of phonics patterns? If you can see that the child is spelling in chunks of familiar phonics patterns, it's Level 4.

Intervening, Supporting, and Teaching a Level 0 Writer

The sample in Figure 7.3 shows Horacio's production in August near the beginning of kindergarten. He came to school unable to write his name. His teacher might start by praising his picture and his writing approximations, which she refers to as "wavy writing," in their conversation. "You are ready to write your name!" she explains as she models and

FIG. 7.3 Horacio's Level 0 Writing

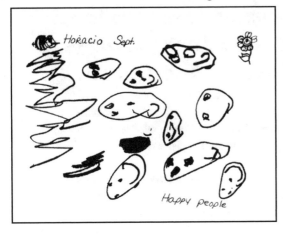

pronounces his letters. She might show him where to start and watch him trace it.

But then she sees other opportunities. Perhaps she will clap out the syllables in his name: *Ho-ra-ci-o, Ho-ra-ci-o* for sound work with phonological analysis. Perhaps she will place the adult underwriting at the bottom of the page after Horacio tells that his wavy writing says "happy people," and together they will practice reading words and phrases…. Perhaps she will ask how many of the letters in *Horacio* he can name. Perhaps they will explore the concept of what a word is. …These little conversations are exercises in metalinguistic awareness as Horacio begins to build a register for words and concepts about language such as *word, letter, sound, syllable, beginning sound, whole word, spell, write, read,* and the like. There are wonderful opportunities to teach, support, and nudge Level 0 writers forward each and every time that they write, and as you can see, a plethora of teaching and learning opportunities grow out of Horacio's first attempts at writing.

Intervening, Supporting, and Teaching a Level I Writer

Leslie's teacher listens as Leslie gives an elaborate verbal account of her trip to her grandmother's house in the country, where she took a

FIG. 7.4 Leslie's Level I Writing

walk in the pasture and was suddenly surrounded by a "flock of butterflies." "Let's write about that!" Her teacher exclaims, "A flock of butterflies. You can write it on these lines." Then picking up a yellow highlighter the teacher draws four consecutive lines for each word separating them appropriately for word spaces, making the "butterflies" line the longest since it is a long word with many letters, and

64

finger pointing as she "reads" the highlighted lines saying the word that Leslie will be writing on each line for "a flock of butterflies." The lines show that individual words are separated by spaces in print. Now Leslie is ready to write on her own—" a flock of butterflies"—making decisions about what letters to use and how to take it from this point. Her Level 1 writing is shown in Figure 7.4.

As with Level 0, Level 1 writing presents a plethora of possibilities for teaching into the writing. One of the greatest possibilities for significant literacy growth to come out of a piece such as this is to return to the piece after the Level 1 writing is completed and make a reading-writing connection through adult underwriting.

Intervening, Supporting, and Teaching a Level 2 Writer

Figure 7.5 shows a piece of Level 2 writing that is all ready for adult underwriting. Moments later, the piece looks like the version in Figure 7.6 and there is lots of reading and rereading of it. The adult underwriting properly provides the conventional form, which is much better for reading.

FIG. 7.5 Level 2 Writing Ready for Adult Underwriting

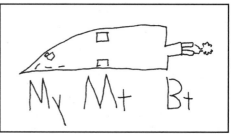

In a conference or whole-class mini-lesson, many opportunities for teaching, extending, and supporting this Level 2 writer present themselves. For example, the teacher might decide it's a good time to nudge Michael to create more volume.... The piece in Figure 7.6 might also present opportunities for instructional support for decoding.... Michael will read both the kid writing and the adult writing and eventually he will depend more on the memorization of the adult underwriting for reading (because it has more cues). Perhaps he'll learn to read the word *boat* on sight, and he may even learn to spell it. It's perfectly normal for kindergarteners to read many more words than they can spell, because spelling the word is harder.

FIG. 7.6 Level 2 Writing After Adult Underwriting is Added

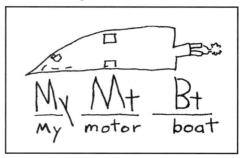

FIG. 7.8 Sarah's Stories with Level 3 Spelling

Intervening, Supporting, and Teaching a Level 3 Writer

Sarah was exactly on grade level when I met with her in September. She had volunteered to be interviewed in front of about fifty teachers and administrators and I showed them the writing samples pictured in Figure 7.8, all short, three- or four-line stories.

FIG. 7.9 Sarah's Longer Story

Sarah read a selection from her basal [reader] fluently for me in front of our audience of teachers and from all signals appeared to be functioning exactly as expected on beginning first-grade level. As bright as she appeared, I thought it might be nice to model an instructional intervention for the group—not intended to remediate, but simply to challenge her and take her one notch higher. Having bonded with

Sarah and having discovered that she was enthralled with her little dog, Chiquita, we chatted at length in front of our audience about Chiquita—what Chiquita ate, where she slept; and when I asked Sarah to tell us a very funny story about Chiquita, she told the story of Chiquita's Bath. I guided Sarah through a first-then-next-last framework, and in a few minutes she completed the wonderful fourteen-line story shown in Figure 7.9. This production gave her brain a workout with fifty-one words for writing and reading as compared to her usual fifteen-word average.

Intervening, Supporting, and Teaching a Level 4 Writer

Children's writing often shows the teacher exactly what patterns need practice or verifies which of the patterns that have been taught.... Figure 7.14 shows the writing of a beginning second grader, Tameka, whom we can celebrate because Tameka has definitely broken the code.

FIG. 7.14 Tameka's Level 4 Writing

Good THING to Eat

I like STRALBARES and i like ORRANGE.

I like tomato SUPE and I like PECHIS.

I like apples and I like BROCLE.

I like COLEFLAWORE TO, you know.

I like corn and I like green BENES.

I like FRIDE CEKEN and I like BARBO Q CEKEN TO.

But most of all I like HO MAED SPOGATE.

THOSS things are good for you.

That's why I put them down.

While the piece is not particularly elaborate writing and shows dialect diversity and a few vocabulary constraints (i.e., *thing* instead of *things; orange* instead of *oranges; ho maded* instead of *homemade*) those would provide opportunities for learning in the writing revision. The sample demonstrated Tameka's high level of word knowledge and her use of a chunking strategy for invented spelling. ...She had reached the point where good explicit spelling instruction would dramatically increase her word knowledge and writing (and reading) precision.

Tameka had broken the code and with explicit instruction, her word knowledge and use of the English language would soar. She would be on her own and on her way as a writer and reader. With more years of word study in elementary school, Tameka would master English print with potential to use language gracefully, powerfully, and eloquently as a life-long reader, for her own benefit and perhaps for yours and for mine.

Chapter 3

Teaching Writing Strategies

"Here's my 'What I did over the weekend' report. However, there were a few seconds I couldn't account for."

Reprinted with permission. www.CartoonStock.com

Introduction

As **Katie Wood Ray** writes in *What You Know by Heart,* a nuanced approach to writing instruction should offer students both *understandings* and *strategies.* In the first excerpt of this chapter, she advocates sharing with students what writers think about as they write and what they know from experience about the process of writing. She identifies this "understanding" as academic content that is different from factual information but that is nevertheless rigorous and important. The second facet of the writing process is "strategy," which emphasizes what writers *do* to start and keep writing: "We try things as writers as we engage in the journey of this process, and these things we do can become things we might suggest another writer try." Emphasizing that teachers of writing must be writers themselves, and based on her experience in the classroom, Ray suggests that understandings and strategies form a writing curriculum that benefits student writers.

Ray's experience is borne out by a growing body of research, which suggests that explicitly teaching strategies can have a great impact on student writing. **Steve Graham,** in the next article, analyzes 39 experimental and quasi-experimental studies to reach conclusions about the impact of explicit instruction in writing strategies on student performance. He concludes that all studies found significant effects on student writing achievement and that many studies also suggest these positive effects are maintained over time. In assessing the studies' findings, Graham also notes that positive changes were achieved regardless of the type of student, the grade level, the strategy explicitly taught, or the writing genre studied. By gathering these disparate studies in one meta-analysis, Graham demonstrates the substantial weight of research evidence on the benefits of strategy instruction.

Students with learning disabilities especially seem to benefit from explicit instruction in planning. As **Gary Troia** and **Steve Graham** find in their experimental study of children with learning disabilities (LD), explicit instruction in planning strategies is more effective for this group than is a purely process-based approach. Children in the treatment group were taught planning strategies—"setting appropriate goals, brainstorming ideas, and effectively organizing those ideas"—accompanied by highly teacher directed instruction. Children in the control group received modified process instruction. Troia and Graham discovered significant differences in both aspects of the children's narrative writing: measures of "product" (i.e., essay length and overall quality) and measures of "process" (i.e., planning time and complete thoughts jotted down). Children with LD who received explicit strategy instruction wrote higher quality stories and showed a greater increase in the time they spent planning their stories, compared to the students who received only process writing instruction.

Some versions of strategy-based writing instruction include "self-regulation activities," which, according to researchers **Cornelia Glaser** and **Joachim Brunstein,** emphasize self-reflection in three general areas—planning the writing, monitoring the implementation of a strategy, and assessing performance of the strategy. Glaser and Brunstein set up a quasi-experimental study to compare students taught strategies for writing with and without the addition of self-regulation activities such as using a checklist, or rubric, against which to assess their own writing. One finding was that students taught self-regulation procedures with strategy instruction tended to maintain a higher performance in writing five weeks after instruction ended, whereas students taught only strategies tended to regress to the same achievement levels as prior to the strategy instruction five weeks later. The authors also tentatively speculate that self-regulation activities help generalize writing strategies to other kinds of writing tasks.

Struggling writers especially benefit from strategy instruction with self-regulation, as **Karen Harris, Steve Graham,** and **Linda Mason** discuss in the next article; in their study, they add peer support to self-regulated strategy instruction given to the experimental group of second grade students (two control groups received either strategy-only or writing workshop instruction). Rather than relying solely on teachers, the students helped each other to apply the strategies, identify where they could be used, and assess whether they were used successfully. Peer support appeared to result in longer and qualitatively better stories when coupled with self-regulated strategy instruction for struggling second-grade writers.

As the last article in the chapter confirms, strategy instruction helps older student writers as well. In this study, students were taught strategies for planning, drafting, and revising their essays as well as writing skills such as transition words and vocabulary. Researchers **Susan De La Paz** and **Steve Graham** show that students provided with strategy instruction that also incorporated these skills "produced essays that were longer, contained more mature vocabulary, and were qualitatively better than" essays developed by the group of students who did not receive strategy instruction. Additionally, this type of instruction may help students achieve higher scores on high-stakes tests such as statewide writing assessments.

An Excerpt From

The Nature of Process Curriculum

Katie Wood Ray

What You Know by Heart, Pages 10–14, ©2002 Heinemann.

As teachers, we know that every encounter we have with writing is essentially an act of curriculum development. Our experiences with writing are essentially experiences with the *process of writing,* the process that leads us on a journey that begins with having an idea and ends with that idea going out to an audience in some finished, written form. As teachers of writing, we ask our students to go on this journey of process again and again and we support them with teaching as they travel.

Thinking It Through

Before reading on, you might try thinking about what you already know about these questions of process. You might choose a part of the process—say revision—and jot down a list of some things you know writers think about and do as they revise. As you make the list, ask yourself, "How do I know this? Where am I getting this curriculum knowledge?"

The curriculum we offer students in this teaching comes from everything we know about how someone goes on the journey of process. We are searching, basically, for the answers to two questions:

What kinds of things do writers think about, and why do they think about these things? (understandings)

What kinds of things do writers do, and how and why do they do them? (strategies)

Let's open those two ideas up just a little now and think about what kinds of things we are trying to learn (so we can teach) as we write like teachers of writing.

Understandings

Recently, in a conference with a second grader, I listened as a young writer explained to me that he had been working for several days on the draft of a story I could see laid out in front of him. "Let me ask you a question," I said. "Do you think about this story when you're away from school? Away from writing workshop? Do you think about it when you're at home or out playing or doing chores with your mom or dad?"

"No," he said. "Not really."

"Hmm..." I replied. I had my teaching direction. I opened my notebook and showed this young writer pages in it that were marked with different codes and I explained that these were pages where I put ideas for the writing project I was working on at the time. "I think about it all the time," I told him. "Even when I'm not actually writing it, I'm still thinking about it and talking about it to other people and having ideas for it." I helped him think about how he might live like this for awhile, live like a writer consumed by a project. We imagined him thinking of his story while he was on the playground, talking through ideas with friends and family, dreaming about it at night. Together we envisioned what it might look like if he tried this: *think like a writer when you're away from your writing desk.* We parted with an agreement to talk again in a day or two about how this had gone for him.

The curriculum I offered this young writer during our conference, the *what* of what I taught him (the specific content) is something I know about writing because I have experienced it firsthand. I know that when writers are working on a piece of writing over time, they don't just think about it at the writing desk, they think about it off and on all the time. This is an essential *understanding* I have about writing. Much of the curriculum around the process of writing is a lot like this, and a lot of times it looks and feels so different from more traditional, empirical kinds of curriculum—the steps of mitosis, for instance, or states and capitals.

> We have to get comfortable with the fact that students need help understanding how it is a person does this writing work, that they need these understandings just as much as they need to know where apostrophes go or different options for structuring a text or how to write compelling leads.

Sometimes when we teach children *understandings* about writing, the teaching feels not quite solid enough at first. But later, when we see what a difference these understandings can make in students' writing, later when this little second-grade boy comes to school and announces he has some great new ideas for his story because he thought about it all last evening, then we realize the rigor behind the teaching. We have to get comfortable with the fact that students need help understanding how it is a person does this writing work, that they need these understandings just as much as they need to know where apostrophes go or different options for structuring a text or how to write compelling leads.

Because we have been on journeys through the writing process, there are lots of things we understand about how that journey goes. We know what kinds of things a person thinks about when on this journey, and all of these things are important curriculum. Offering students this curriculum helps them develop important understandings about their work as writers and ultimately helps them do things better.

> Students need to know what kinds of things writers do, throughout the process, to get their writing done. They need to know strategies for getting ideas; growing ideas; and drafting, revising, and editing those ideas for publication.

We will develop lots of these understandings because we write ourselves, but we can also listen to other writers and be watchful for what we can learn from their understanding about the process. For example, in an interview with Karen Hesse I found on Scholastic's website, this author says of writing, "There are times that the writing goes so well that I feel I have been given a gift. Then there are times it goes so slowly, it feels like torture. But I know that if I stay at the computer—if I keep at it with every word and every image—it will be okay."

When we read this quote like teachers of writing, we find a very important understanding in it: *sometimes you just have to keep at it, even when it feels like torture.* This becomes something we can teach students about the process of writing. When we see writers struggling with how hard writing can be at times, we tell them about Karen Hesse, and we help them come to understand that this is a normal part of the process. This important understanding will help them steer through the waters of "things being hard" and come to the other side.

Strategies

In addition to having a lot of understandings about how someone goes through the process of writing, when we write ourselves we also know what kinds of things a person does to get through this journey, and these too become important curriculum in the form of strategies we can suggest. *You might try listing all the parts you want to include; or, you could take an entry and try asking questions about it just to get your thinking going, or, get someone else to read it, tell it back to you, and then listen to see if it made sense.* We try things as writers as we engage in the journey of this process, and these things we do can become things we might suggest another writer try. The nature of this kind of curriculum is strategic.

Students need to know what kinds of things writers do, throughout the process, to get their writing done. They need to know strategies for getting ideas; growing ideas; and drafting, revising, and editing those ideas for publication. As teachers of writing, we pay very close attention to exactly what it is we are doing as we write, how we are doing it, and why we are doing it. We have to pay attention so that we can teach students—in a strategic way—how to do these same things.

We also pay attention when our co-teachers of writing talk about going through this process. We listen for the action verbs in what they say. We need to know what they do because, whatever it is, it becomes something our students might do as well. For example, in that same interview with Karen Hesse on Scholastic's website, we learn that Karen often looks at a photograph of someone as she is writing, that this helps her develop realistic characters. This becomes something we might suggest that students try when writing fiction: *try finding a photograph of someone to represent your character and keep that photo with you as you write your character's story* (just like Karen Hesse does). This becomes a piece of strategic curriculum.

Layers and layers of understandings and strategies make up the curriculum of process. As teachers of writing, we have to know how to turn our experiences with writing into this kind of writing curriculum. We have to live with a very real sense of the future, knowing that students wait for us at the end of our writing process.

Thinking It Through

What do your students already know about you as a writer? Do they see you as being like them (someone who writes) in that way?

They will want to know, "How was it? Did it go okay? What can you tell me about the ride?" We represent, in living, breathing form, a person who has "been there and done that" when it comes to writing. When we get together in summer writing institutes and courses on writing, I think we need tee shirts that say, "My teacher went to writing camp and all I got was this great curriculum."

References

Hesse, Karen. "Authors and Books-Author Studies-Karen Hesse-Interview Transcript." Retrieved from www.scholastic.com.

Excerpts From

Strategy Instruction and the Teaching of Writing

Steve Graham

In this chapter, I examine the effectiveness of one of these approaches, namely, strategy instruction.... I employed meta-analysis to examine the overall impact of strategy instruction on students' writing performance immediately following instruction and at maintenance. Generalization to different genres and across persons-settings was also examined. I attempted to (1) typify strategy instruction effects on post-test, maintenance, and generalization measures of writing performance, and (2) investigate the relationship between study features and study outcomes. This included examining whether study outcomes were related to student type (learning disability, poor writer, average writer, or good writer), grade (elementary or secondary), genre (narrative or expository), cognitive process (planning, revising/editing, or both), instructor (graduate assistant/researcher or teacher), and type of instruction (the Self-Regulated Strategy Development [SRSD] or other approaches).

Methods for the Review
Location and Selection of Studies

For the purpose of this review, strategy instruction studies in writing were defined as empirical investigations in which school-age students (grades 1–12) were taught one or more strategies for planning (including translating plans into text), revising, or editing text. This included the three cognitive processes—planning, translating, and reviewing—included in the model developed by Hayes and Flower (1980). Because the primary goal of strategy instruction is thoughtful and independent use of the target strategies, studies included in this review also had to meet the following criteria: (1) Students had to be shown how to use the strategy (i.e., modeling); (2) there were at least 3 or more days of instruction; and (3) instruction progressed toward students' independent use of the strategy. Included in the review were experimental studies involving group comparisons (strategy instruction vs. control), as well as single-subject design investigations. The group studies included both true experiments (i.e., random assignment to treatments) and quasi-experiments (random assignment to treatments was not employed) that contained a control condition. Single-subject design studies were limited to multiple-baseline design investigations (see Kratochwill & Levin, 1992). With this type of design, treatment is systematically and sequentially introduced to each set of students at a time (a set can be one or more students). Prior to the introduction of the treatment, each student's writing is assessed over time to establish a baseline of typical performance. A functional relationship between the treatment (i.e., strategy instruction) and students' progress on the dependent measure is established if performance improves only after the introduction of treatment, and if the noninstructed students' performance stays at or near preintervention levels across baseline. I did not include single-subject studies involving reversal designs, because the effects of strategy instruction cannot be removed by terminating treatment (a basic assumption underlying such designs). Effect sizes were analyzed separately for group and single-subject design studies.

Thirty-nine studies were located that were suitable for inclusion in this review.... Twenty of these investigations involved group comparisons, and the other 19 were single-subject design studies.... The

> **Strategy instruction is effective in improving students' writing performance.**

most common type of planning strategy taught in these studies involved planning a composition in advance of writing by brainstorming and organizing ideas for the basic parts of the composition (e.g., for persuasive writing, this usually involved generating possible ideas for reasons, counter-reasons, examples, and elaborations) using the resulting plan to write the paper, and modifying and upgrading the plan while writing (see, e.g., De La Paz, 2001; Sawyer, Graham, & Harris, 1992). The most common revising strategy involved the use of specific criteria to evaluate the composition (see, e.g., Englert et al., 1991; Graham & MacArthur, 1988).

Conclusions

The primary finding from this meta-analysis was that strategy instruction is effective in improving students' writing performance. When all measures are added together, the mean [effect size, or ES] immediately following strategy instruction in 20 group comparison studies was 1.15. When key measures, such as writing quality, elements, length, and revisions, were considered separately, the impact was still large, because ESs at posttest for these indices were 1.21, 1.89, 0.95, and 0.90, respectively. The impact of strategy instruction on writing mechanics was relatively weak (mean ES at posttest = 0.30), however, even though this was typically measured in studies where revising-editing strategies were taught. To place these ESs in context, the most successful intervention, the environmental mode, in Hillocks's (1984) seminal meta-analysis of different methods for teaching writing had an average effect size of 0.44.

The findings from the 19 single-subject design studies support those from the group comparison studies. Immediately following instruction, the mean [percentage of overlapping data, or PND] when all variables are included in the tabulation, was 89% (90% or greater indicates that a treatment is very effective). For the most frequently graphed measure, elements, the posttest PND was 95%, and it was 89% for both writing quality and revisions.

> Strategy instruction not only had a strong impact on students' writing immediately following instruction but these effects were also maintained over time and generalized.

A major issue in strategy instructional research is whether effects are maintained over time and are generalized to new tasks and situations (Graham, Harris, MacArthur, & Schwartz, 1991). Although the findings from this analysis must be viewed as tentative, since maintenance was only assessed in 54% of the studies reviewed and generalization (to genre or persons/settings) in just 38%, average ESs generally rivaled or exceeded those from baseline. For example, overall effects for the group comparison studies for maintenance, generalization to genre, and generalization to setting-person were 1.32, 1.13, and 0.93, respectively. For the single-subject design studies, mean PND at maintenance and for generalization to persons-settings was in the very effective range (above 90%). Thus, strategy instruction not only had a strong impact on students' writing immediately following instruction but these effects were also maintained over time and generalized.

The impact of strategy instruction appears to be extremely robust, because the effects on students' writing were not related to the type of student who received instruction, their grade-level placement, the type of cognitive process or strategy taught, or the genre that served as the focal point for instruction. There was a relationship, however, between magnitude of ES and how the writing strategies were taught in the group comparison studies. Investigations using the SRSD model (Harris & Graham, 1996, 1999) of instruction yielded a mean ES at posttest that was almost double the average ES obtained by researchers who did not use this approach. Such a relationship was not replicated in the analysis of single-subject design studies, however. Nevertheless, it is important to note that mean ES were large for both SRSD and non-SRSD groups and single-subject design studies.

There was also a relationship between ES and who delivered instruction (teachers vs. graduate assistants/researchers) in the single-subject design studies. When teachers delivered instruction, PND was larger at posttest and maintenance. This finding must be interpreted cautiously, however, because the variables included in calculating PND were limited only to those that were graphed by researchers, and PND does not measure magnitude of improvement (it only measures what percentage of posttreatment observations exceed the largest score during baseline). Furthermore, even though there was no statistically significant difference for type of instructor in the group comparison studies ($p = .06$), the mean ES for graduate assistants/researchers was one-half of a standard deviation larger at posttest than it was for teachers (a similar difference was evident at maintenance, but the number of ESs for teachers was too small to allow for a statistical comparison). Again, it is important to note that writing strategy instruction was effective no matter who delivered it.

References

References marked with an asterisk indicate studies included in the meta-analysis.

Albertson, L. R., & Billingsley, E. E. (2001). Using strategy instruction and self-regulation to improve gifted students' creative writing. *Journal of Secondary Gifted Education, 12,* 90–101.*

Beal, C., Garrod, A., & Bonitatibus, G. (1993). Fostering children's revision skills through training in comprehension monitoring. *Journal of Educational Psychology, 82,* 275–280.*

Bryson, M., & Scardamalia, M. (1996). Fostering reflectivity in the argumentative thinking of students with different learning histories. *Reading and Writing Quarterly: Overcoming Learning Difficulties, 12,* 351–384.*

Cole, K. (1992). Efficacy and generalization of instruction in sequential expository writing for students with learning disabilities. Unpublished doctoral dissertation, Northern Illinois University, DeKalb, IL.*

Danoff, B., Harris, K. R., & Graham, S. (1993). Incorporating strategy instruction within the writing process in the regular classroom: Effects on the writing of students with and without learning disabilities. *Journal of Reading Behavior, 25,* 295–319.*

De La Paz, S. (1999). Self-regulated strategy instruction in regular education settings: Improving outcomes for students with and without learning disabilities. *Learning Disabilities Research & Practice, 14,* 92–106.*

De La Paz, S. (2001). Teaching writing to students with attention deficit disorders and specific language impairments. *Journal of Educational Research, 95,* 37–47.*

De La Paz, S. (2005). Teaching historical reasoning and argumentative writing in culturally and academically diverse middle school classrooms. *Journal of Educational Psychology, 97,* 139–158.*

De La Paz, S., & Graham, S. (1997a). Effects of dictation and advanced planning instruction on the composing of students with writing and learning problems. *Journal of Educational Psychology, 89,* 203–222.*

De La Paz, S., & Graham, S. (1997b). Strategy instruction in planning: Effects on the writing performance and behavior of students with learning disabilities. *Exceptional Children, 63,* 167–181.*

De La Paz, S., & Graham, S. (2002). Explicitly teaching strategies, skills, and knowledge: Writing instruction in middle school classrooms. *Journal of Educational Psychology, 94,* 291–304.*

Englert, C., Raphael, T., Anderson, L., Anthony, H., Steven, D., & Fear, K. (1991). Making writing and self-talk visible: Cognitive strategy instruction writing in regular and special education classrooms. *American Educational Research Journal, 28,* 337–373.*

Fitzgerald, J., & Markham, L. (1987). Teaching children about revision in writing. *Cognition and Instruction, 4,* 3–24.*

Gambrell, L., & Chasen, S. (1991). Explicit story structure instruction and the narrative writing of fourth- and fifth-grade below-average readers. *Reading Research and Instruction, 31,* 54–62.*

Glaser, C. (2004). Improving the fourth-grade students' composition skills: Effects of strategy instruction and self-regulatory procedures. Unpublished doctoral dissertation, University of Pottsburg, Germany.*

Graham, S., & Harris, K. R. (1989b). Improving learning disabled students' skills at composing essays: Self-instructional strategy training. *Exceptional Children, 56,* 201–214.*

Graham, S., Harris, K. R., MacArthur, C., & Schwartz, S. (1991). Writing and writing instruction with students with learning disabilities: A review of a program of research. *Learning Disability Quarterly, 14,* 89–114.

Graham, S., Harris, K. R., Mason, L. (2005). Improving the writing performance, knowledge, and motivation of struggling young writers: The effects of Self-Regulated Strategy Development. *Contemporary Educational Psychology, 30,* 207–241.*

Graham, S., & MacArthur, C. (1988). Improving learning disabled students' skills at revising essays produced on a word processor: Self-instructional training. *Journal of Special Education, 22,* 133–152.*

Graham, S., MacArthur, C., Schwartz, S., & Page-Voth, V. (1992). Improving the compositions of students with learning disabilities using a strategy involving product and process goal setting. *Exceptional Children, 58,* 322–334.*

Harris, K. R., & Graham, S. (1985). Improving learning disabled students' composition skills: Self-control strategy training. *Learning Disabilities Quarterly, 8,* 27–36.*

Harris, K. R., & Graham, S. (1996). *Making the writing process work: Strategies for composition and self-regulation.* Cambridge, MA: Brookline.

Harris, K. R., & Graham, S. (1999). Programmatic intervention research: Illustrations from the evolution of self-regulated strategy development. *Learning Disability Quarterly, 22,* 251–262.

Hayes, J., & Flower, L. (1980). Identifying the organization of writing processes. In L. Gregg & E. Steinberg (Eds.), *Cognitive processes in writing* (pp. 3–30). Hillsdale, NJ: Erlbaum.

Hillocks, G. (1984). *Research on written composition: New directions for teaching.* Urbana, IL: ERIC Clearinghouse on Reading and Communications Skills.

Kratochwill, T., & Levin, J. (1992). *Single-case research design and analysis: New directions for psychology and education.* Hillsdale, NJ: Erlbaum.

MacArthur, C., Schwartz, S., & Graham, S. (1991). Effects of a reciprocal peer revision strategy in special education classrooms. *Learning Disability Research and Practice, 6,* 201–210.*

Moran, M., Schumaker, J., & Vetter, A. (1981). *Teaching a paragraph organization strategy to learning disabled adolescents* (Research Report No. 54). Lawrence: University of Kansas Institute for Research in Learning Disabilities.*

Reynolds, C., Hill, D., Swassing, R., & Ward, M. (1988). The effects of revision strategy instruction on the writing performance of students with learning disabilities. *Journal of Learning Disabilities, 21,* 540–545.*

Saddler, B., Moran, S., Graham, S., & Harris, K. R. (2004). Preventing writing difficulties: The effects of planning strategy instruction on the writing performance of struggling writers. *Exceptionality, 12,* 3–18.*

Sawyer, R., Graham, S., & Harris, K. R. (1992). Direct teaching, strategy instruction, and strategy instruction with explicit self-regulation: Effects on the composition skills and self-efficacy of students with learning disabilities. *Journal of Educational Psychology, 84,* 340–352.*

Schumaker, J., Deshler, D., Alley, G., Warner, M., Clark, E, & Nolan, S. (1982). Error monitoring: A learning strategy for improving adolescent performance. In W. Cruickshank & J. Lerner (Eds.), *Best of ACLD* (Vol. 3, pp. 170–183). Syracuse, NY: Syracuse University Press.*

Sexton, R. J., Harris, K. R., & Graham, S. (1998). The effects of self-regulated strategy development on essay writing and attributions of students with learning disabilities in a process writing setting. *Exceptional Children, 64*, 295–311.*

Simmons, D., Kame'enui, E., Dickson, S., Chard, D., Gunn, B., & Baker, S. (1994). Integrating narrative reading comprehension and writing instruction for all learners. In C. Kinzer & D. Len (Eds.), *Multidimensional aspects of literacy research, theory, and practice.* Chicago, IL: National Reading Conference.*

Stoddard, B., & MacArthur, C. (1993). A peer editor strategy: Guiding learning disabled students in response and revision. *Research in the Teaching of English, 27,* 76–103.*

Tanhouser, S. (1994). Function over form: The relative efficacy of self-instructional strategy training alone and with procedural facilitation for adolescents with learning disabilities. Unpublished doctoral dissertation, Johns Hopkins University, Baltimore, MD.*

Troia, G., & Graham, S. (2002). The effectiveness of a highly explicit, teacher-directed strategy instruction routine: Changing the writing performance of students with learning disabilities. *Journal of Learning Disabilities, 35,* 290–305.*

Troia, G. A., Graham, S., & Harris, K. R. (1999). Teaching students with learning disabilities to mindfully plan when writing. *Exceptional Children, 65,* 215–252.*

Vallecorsa, A., & deBettencourt, L. (1997). Using a mapping procedure to teach reading and writing skills to middle grade students with learning disabilities. *Education and Treatment of Children, 20,* 173–188.*

Wallace, G., & Bott, D. (1989). Statement-pie: A strategy to improve the paragraph writing skills of adolescents with learning disabilities. *Journal of Learning Disabilities, 22,* 541–553.*

Welch, M. (1992). The PLEASE strategy: A metacognitive learning strategy for improving the paragraph writing of students with mild disabilities. *Learning Disability Quarterly, 15,* 119–128.*

Welch, M., & Jensen, J. (1990). Write, P.L.E.A.S.E.: A video-assisted strategic intervention to improve written expression of inefficient learners. *Remedial and Special Education, 12,* 37–47.*

Wong, B. Y. L., Butler, D. L., Ficzere, S. A., & Kuperis, S. (1996). Teaching low achievers and students with learning disabilities to plan, write, and revise opinion essays. *Journal of Learning Disabilities, 29,* 133–145.*

Yeh, S. (1998). Empowering education: Teaching argumentative writing to cultural minority middle-school students. *Research in the Teaching of English, 33,* 49–83.*

Excerpts From

The Effectiveness of a Highly Explicit, Teacher-Directed Strategy Instruction Routine: Changing the Writing Performance of Students with Learning Disabilities

Gary A. Troia and Steve Graham

Journal of Learning Disabilities, Vol. 35, July/August 2002, Pages 290–305.

An important component of effective writing is planning. This is especially evident in the behavior of skilled writers. Flower and Hayes (1980), for instance, found that adults usually develop goals to guide the composing process, generating and organizing writing content to meet their objectives. Gould (1980) reported that business executives spend about two thirds of their composition time planning, whereas Kellogg (1987) indicated that college students devote about one fourth of their writing time to planning. High levels of planning are especially apparent in the composing behavior of professional writers. For example, Joyce Carol Oates, the author of almost 70 books, has noted that she often produces 1,000 pages of notes for every 250 printed pages (Arana-Ward, 1997). Similarly, Kathy Reichs, author of *Deja Dead*, constructs an outline for each chapter and develops character files and timelines (Minzesheimer, 1997).

> An important goal in writing instruction for students with LD, therefore, is to help them become more planful, integrating into their writing the same types of planning strategies that are employed by more skilled or sophisticated writers.

In contrast, children with learning disabilities (LD) tend to employ an approach to writing that minimizes the role of planning, especially planning in advance (Graham & Harris, 1996; Thomas, Englert, & Gregg, 1987). These students typically convert writing tasks into telling what they know about the topic (McCutchen, 1988). They plan as they write, summoning from memory any information that is somewhat relevant, writing it down, and using each preceding idea to stimulate the generation of the next one. A Peanuts® cartoon featuring a disheveled

Peppermint Patty captures this approach to writing. Sharing her paper with the class, she reads that wind blows your hair around as you walk to school, that once you get there you don't have a comb, and that wind gives you something to write about when you are out of ideas and can't see what you are writing. With this retrieve-and-write approach, little attention is directed to the development of rhetorical goals, the constraints imposed by the topic, the organization of the text, or the needs of the reader (Graham & Harris, 2000).

An important goal in writing instruction for students with LD, therefore, is to help them become more planful, integrating into their writing the same types of planning strategies that are employed by more skilled or sophisticated writers. One way of accomplishing this objective is to directly teach these students planning strategies that can be used during or in advance of writing, such as brainstorming or semantic webbing (Graham & Harris,

> **We examined if basic planning strategies could be taught effectively to students with LD using an explicit and highly teacher-directed procedure.**

1997a). This approach has been quite successful, as explicit instruction in planning strategies has resulted in improved writing performance for students with LD in almost 20 studies.

The present study extends previous research on teaching planning strategies to students with LD in three important ways. First, we examined if basic planning strategies could be taught effectively to students with LD using an explicit and highly teacher-directed procedure. Fourth- and fifth-grade students with LD were taught how to incorporate three common planning strategies into their current approach to writing: setting rhetorical goals, brainstorming ideas, and effectively organizing those ideas. The teaching routine used in this study employed a variety of components that are considered essential to effective strategy instruction (Graham, Harris, & Troia, 1998), including teacher description and modeling of the target strategies; individually tailored support (scaffolding) that was faded as students moved toward independent use of the strategies; explanations about how the strategies work and what potential impact they have on performance; clarifications of when, where, and how the strategies could be used in the future; homework assignments designed to extend the use of the strategies to different settings and tasks; and feedback on the effects of using the strategies. Although the bulk of this instruction (i.e., modeling the strategies and providing scaffolded assistance in applying them) involved collaboration and dialogue between instructor and students, the participating children played a less active role in other aspects, as instructors provided students with information on how the strategies work, what their potential effects are, when and where to use them, and how to make possible modifications in their use. The instructor also took responsibility for providing students with specific feedback on how the strategies affected their writing performance. When such information was provided in the writing strategy studies reviewed earlier, it typically was gained through interactive dialogue between students and the instructor.

Second, the present study extends prior research on teaching planning strategies to students with LD by comparing the effects of such instruction to the process approach to writing instruction.... Although [the process approach] is the most common approach to writing instruction in the elementary grades and has been advocated for use with students with LD by some authors (e.g., Wansart, 1988; Zaragoza & Vaughn, 1992), critics have maintained that it is not powerful enough for some students, particularly those with special needs (see Graham & Harris, 1994, 1997b). They argued that this approach relies too heavily on informal or incidental methods of learning and that many students with learning difficulties do not acquire a variety of cognitive and metacognitive strategies and skills unless frequent and comprehensive explicit instruction is provided (Brown & Campione, 1990).

> We anticipated that teacher-directed strategy instruction would have a more positive impact on the story writing performance of students with LD than process writing instruction.

In the present study, students were randomly assigned either to a strategy instruction or to a process approach to writing condition. The process writing condition mirrored the approach used in the participating students' schools, where children spent most of their writing time drafting, editing, revising, and publishing their compositions but no special attention was placed on advance planning; it was neither emphasized nor discouraged. Thus, some of the key features of exemplary writing process instruction were not part of the process writing condition in this study, primarily because they were not prominent features in the participants' classroom writing programs.

The third and final extension of previous research involves the effectiveness of brainstorming when it is more open-ended and not specifically tied to the structural features of the genre under consideration. In most previous strategy instruction studies in which students with LD applied this strategy, brainstorming was more constrained, as students with LD generated ideas for specific elements or parts of a story or essay in advance of writing (e.g., De La Paz & Graham, 1997; Englert et al., 1991; Graham & Harris, 1989; Sawyer, Graham, & Harris, 1992). In the present study, students were taught to generate a list of possible ideas to use in their stories. Although students in both the strategy and the process writing conditions were familiarized with the basic parts of a story and persuasive essay prior to the collection of baseline data, they were not shown how to brainstorm ideas for specific elements.

We anticipated that teacher-directed strategy instruction would have a more positive impact on the story writing performance of students with LD than process writing instruction. Specifically, it was expected that the stories written by students assigned to the strategy instruction condition would be longer and qualitatively better than the stories produced by their peers in the process writing condition. However, no specific predictions were made concerning transfer of strategy instruction to an uninstructed genre, persuasive essay writing.

Method

Participants

Twenty fourth- and fifth-grade students with LD from two suburban elementary schools in a mid-Atlantic school district participated in the present study.

Assignment to Conditions

The participants were randomly assigned to either an experimental treatment group receiving advance planning strategy instruction or a comparative treatment group receiving a modified version of process writing instruction. The comparative treatment approach was compatible with the process writing instruction that students regularly received in their classrooms (see Calkins, 1981, 1986; Graves, 1983).

Treatment

For the experimental treatment group, instruction was criterion based. Students in the process writing condition participated in the same number of instructional sessions as students in the strategy training condition and wrote on the same topics....The advance planning strategies taught to the participants in the strategy instruction group included the following: identifying the purposes of the activity and setting appropriate goals, brainstorming ideas, and organizing those ideas. The acronym STOP & LIST (Stop, Think Of Purposes, and List Ideas, Sequence Them), printed on a small chart, was used to facilitate the teaching of these components. The process writing instruction delivered to the students in the process writing group was segmented into four steps: writing a rough draft, revising the rough draft, proofreading and editing, and publishing the final version. These steps were printed on a chart to facilitate instruction. In both conditions, the SPACE [setting, problems, actions, consequences, emotions] chart listing the five elements of a narrative was used to facilitate story writing.

Measures

Prior to scoring, all written plans and compositions collected during pretest, posttest, and maintenance probe sessions were typed, and spelling, punctuation, and capitalization errors were corrected. This eliminated any potential bias that mechanical factors such as handwriting or spelling might exert during the scoring process. All identifying information was removed from the papers as well.

Product Measures. Two product measures were used to evaluate students' stories and opinion essays: length and overall quality. For composition length, the word count function of a word processing software package was used to score all stories and essays. Stories and essays were scored for overall quality using an analytic rating scale developed for each writing genre.

Process Measures. Two process measures were used for both stories and essays: advance planning time and propositions in written plans. The instructor recorded the advance planning time (i.e., elapsed time between the instructor's prompt to begin and the initiation of writing) in seconds for each probe using a stopwatch. Propositions were defined as written utterances that correspond to a complete thought and include a predicate (Stein & Glenn, 1979).

Results

Product Measures

Stories. Significant treatment group differences were evident in posttest difference scores for story quality, $t(18) = 2.11$, $p = .05$, favoring the strategy instruction group (ES = 1.00). However, posttest gains in story length were not significantly different between groups, $t(18) = -0.23$, $p = .82$.

Essays. There were no significant differences between groups in posttest difference scores for essay quality, $t(18) = -1.40$, $p = .18$, or essay length, $t(18) = 0.58$, $p = .57$.

TABLE 2. Pretest, Posttest, Maintenance, and Difference Scores on Writing Measures for Stories

Dependent product measure	Strategy instruction		Process writing instruction		t	df
	M	SD	M	SD		
Quality						
Pretest	4.58	1.74	5.45	.88		
Posttest	5.00	1.55	4.83	.71		
Maintenance	5.20	1.93	3.65	.98		
Pre/post difference	0.43	1.40	−0.63	.71	2.11*	18
Pre/maintenance difference	0.60	1.97	−2.30	.86	3.03*	18
Length						
Pretest	92.50	57.26	86.90	31.67		
Posttest	93.50	50.91	91.90	36.56		
Maintenance	121.00	90.45	50.20	14.70		
Pre/post difference	1.00	44.75	5.00	30.38	−0.23	18
Pre/maintenance difference	49.20	41.25	−36.40	18.39	4.24*	8
Advance planning time						
Pretest	0.15	.24	0.15	.24		
Posttest	6.10	7.67	0.25	.42		
Maintenance	1.80	.84	1.00	1.00		
Pre/post difference	5.95	7.69	0.10	.32	2.40*	18
Pre/maintenance difference	1.70	.67	0.90	.89	1.60	8
Propositions in plans						
Pretest	0.00	.00	0.00	.00		
Posttest	4.95	7.29	0.00	.00		
Maintenance	0.00	.00	0.00	.00		
Pre/post difference	4.95	7.29	0.00	.00	2.15*	18
Pre/maintenance difference	0.00	.00	0.00	.00	n/a	

NOTE: Pre/post differences were calculated for all 10 students in each group, whereas pre/maintenance differences were calculated for only those 5 children in each group who were able to complete maintenance probes. *$p \leq .05$.

Process Measures

Stories. There was a significant group difference in posttest difference scores for advance planning time, $t(18) = 2.40$, $p = .03$, favoring the strategy instruction group (ES = 1.46), and for written planning propositions, $t(18) = 2.15$, $p = .05$, again favoring the strategy instruction group (ES = 1.36). Examination of the scores reported in Table 2 shows that children in the strategy instruction group spent more time (approximately 6 minutes, compared with less than 1 minute at pretest) planning their stories in advance after treatment, but the amount of time devoted to advance planning by students in the process writing group remained virtually unchanged from pretest to posttest (less than 1 minute). It should be recalled that advance planning time refers to the elapsed time before composing is begun, so that it includes written planning time, mental planning time, or both.

Essays. No significant group differences were observed in posttest difference scores for essay planning time, $t(18) = -0.27, p = .79$.

Discussion

In the present study, students with LD learned to set rhetorical goals, brainstorm ideas, and organize their ideas prior to writing stories. The procedures used to teach these strategies were explicit and relied heavily on teacher direction. Instructors modeled how to use the strategies and provided students with scaffolding as they learned to apply them. Such collaborative support is common in current approaches to strategy instruction (e.g., Deshler & Schumaker, 1986; Englert et al., 1991; Graham et al., 1998). Moreover, instructors provided students with information on the rationale, value, impact, and general applicability of the three planning strategies. According to several observers (Poplin, 1988; Wong, 1994), teachers often use this same approach to deliver this critical information. However, many researchers have recommended and employed a more interactive approach to promote the development of this knowledge, using dialogue, observation, and student reflection (Englert et al., 1991; Harris & Graham, 1996; Wong, 1994, 1997).

Consistent with our predictions, teaching students with LD three basic planning strategies via an explicit and highly teacher-directed approach had a positive, albeit modest, impact on their writing performance. Immediately following the instruction that focused on story writing, students who were taught to use these strategies wrote stories that were qualitatively better than those produced by their peers assigned to the process writing condition. Some caution must be exercised in interpreting performance on the maintenance story writing probe administered 4 weeks later, as only half the students were available for testing at this point, but the findings were again consistent with predictions. Students who were taught the planning strategies produced not only qualitatively better stories than their process writing group peers, but longer stories as well.

It should further be noted that students with LD in the present study were taught the same three planning strategies as students with LD in a previous study by Troia et al. (1999). Although learning these strategies had a positive effect on the length and schematic structure of students' stories in this previous investigation, the impact on overall story quality was minimal. Troia et al. (1999) indicated that improvements in quality were not obtained because participants did not consider how the ideas they brainstormed added to or detracted from the overall quality of their compositions. In contrast to other studies in which brainstorming was more tightly related to each part of a story and overall quality subsequently improved (e.g., Graham & Harris, 1989; Sawyer et al., 1992), the brainstorming procedure applied in the present study and in the Troia et al. (1999) study was more open-ended, as students simply generated a list of writing ideas to use in their story. To enhance the power of this more open-ended approach to brainstorming in the present study, students were provided with feedback on how their use of the planning strategies affected overall story quality. This was not done in the previous study by Troia et al. (1999). As noted earlier, story quality in our study improved when students were taught how to use the three planning strategies. Although it is not possible to isolate the reasons for this improvement, as the present study and the one conducted by Troia et al. (1999) differ on more than one dimension, this finding does indicate that improvements in the overall quality of stories written by students with LD are possible when an open-ended approach to brainstorming is combined with feedback regarding the impact of advance planning on writing quality.

> Teaching students with LD three basic planning strategies via an explicit and highly teacher-directed approach had a positive, albeit modest, impact on their writing performance.

The findings from the present study and from several previous investigations (e.g., Danoff et al., 1993; MacArthur, Schwartz, & Graham, 1991) also raise some concerns about overreliance on instructional approaches to writing for students with LD that depend heavily on the use of incidental or informal methods of teaching, such as the process approach to writing. In the present study, the story writing performance of students assigned to the process writing condition declined over the course of the study, especially in terms of overall quality. In other studies, improvements in the writing performance of students with LD were obtained when more explicit instructional procedures were incorporated within this approach (Danoff et al., 1993; MacArthur et al., 1991). Additional research is needed, however, before any conclusions can be drawn about the general efficacy of writing approaches such as process writing for students with LD. Future investigations should include a more fully explicated model of process writing than was used in the present study. For example, we did not stress planning, include mini-lessons or conferencing activities, or foster the development of a writing community. In any event, we anticipate that both the informal or incidental methods underlying approaches such as process writing and the more explicit and direct instruction of skills and strategies are necessary components of an effective writing program for students with LD (Graham & Harris, 2001). Consider, for instance, the skill of spelling. In a recent review of the literature, Graham (2000) found that incidental and direct instructional approaches both contributed to the development of spelling competence in good and poor spellers.

Despite the positive impact of the strategy instruction procedures on the story writing performance of the participating students, the results concerning generalization and application of the inculcated strategies over time were discouraging. Although students in the strategy instruction group spent more time planning their posttest stories in advance than their peers in the process writing group, only half of the children who were taught planning strategies overtly used them at this point. Four weeks later, the two groups of students did not differ in the amount of time spent planning in advance, nor did children in the strategy instruction group overtly use any of the planning strategies they had been taught. When children in the two groups were asked to write a paper in an uninstructed genre, persuasive essay writing, there were no differences either in the amount of time spent planning in advance or in the length and quality of the resulting essays. Moreover, none of the students who were taught the three planning strategies overtly used them when writing a persuasive essay, despite having been given opportunities through assigned homework to generalize STOP & LIST to diverse tasks. One potential reason for the lack of advance planning for the uninstructed genre may be that only three homework exercises were actually completed by most students, which may have done little to deepen their appreciation of the broad utility of the planning strategies or to build their internal capacity for generalizing what they had learned.

> **We anticipate that both the informal or incidental methods underlying approaches such as process writing and the more explicit and direct instruction of skills and strategies are necessary components of an effective writing program for students with LD.**

The generalizability of our findings to special and general education classrooms is unclear. For example, the immediate, explicit, and individualized feedback regarding linkages between strategy use and writing performance provided to students in this study may be difficult to replicate in whole classes. However, there are several ways to modify the procedures we used so that this level of feedback could be easily incorporated into classroom planning strategy instruction. Students could be taught how to use a checklist as they are planning to indicate if and when they have completed each step of the strategy. In conjunction with such a checklist, students could work in pairs to evaluate each other's writing quality using a simplified scoring rubric that includes ratings for overall quality as well as genre-specific text structure elements. The rubric would serve to focus students' discussion on the most important aspects of their writing. Graphing the number of completed strategy steps alongside the quality rating for each composition could be a powerful method for increasing students' appreciation of the usefulness of the strategy.

> In conclusion, the present study demonstrated that the writing performance of students with LD can be improved by teaching them to set goals, brainstorm ideas, and organize their ideas in advance of writing.

When students share their writing with others, they could be asked to reflect on how well the strategy worked for them and to offer suggestions for improving the efficacy of the strategy. Thus, through the use of a procedural facilitator, scoring guidelines, peer conferencing, and performance monitoring, students could obtain beneficial feedback tailored to their personal writing needs with little teacher intervention.

In conclusion, the present study demonstrated that the writing performance of students with LD can be improved by teaching them to set goals, brainstorm ideas, and organize their ideas in advance of writing. This finding supports the hypothesis that students with LD benefit from explicit writing instruction designed to help them improve their planning behaviors. It also adds to a growing body of literature showing that the writing difficulties of students with LD are due at least in part to difficulties with planning (Graham & Harris, 2000), as instruction in planning resulted in improvements in these children's writing performance.

References

Arana-Ward, M. (1997, March 16). The lady in her labyrinth. *Washington Post Book World*, p. 10.

Brown, A. L., & Campione, J. C. (1990). Interactive learning environments and the teaching of science and mathematics. In M. Gardner, J. Green, F. Reif,

A. Schoenfeld, A. di Sessa, & E. Stage (Eds.), *Toward a scientific practice of science education* (pp. 112–139). Hillsdale, NJ: Erlbaum.

Calkins, L. (1981). Case study of a nine year old writer. In D. Graves (Ed.), *A case study observing the development of primary children's composing, spelling, and motor behavior during the writing process* (pp. 239–262). Durham: University of New Hampshire.

Calkins, L. (1986). *The art of teaching writing.* Portsmouth, NH: Heinemann.

Danoff, B., Harris, K. R., & Graham, S. (1993). Incorporating strategy instruction within the writing process in the regular classroom: Effects on the writing of students with and without learning disabilities. *Journal of Reading Behavior, 25*(3), 295–322.

De La Paz, S., & Graham, S. (1997). Effects of dictation and advanced planning instruction on the composing of students with writing and learning problems. *Journal of Educational Psychology, 89,* 203–222.

Deshler, D. D., & Schumaker, J. B. (1986). Learning strategies: An instructional alternative for low-achieving adolescents. *Exceptional Children, 52,* 583–590.

Englert, C. S., Raphael, T., Anderson, L., Anthony, H., Stevens, D., & Fear, K. (1991). Making strategies and self-talk visible: Cognitive strategy instruction in writing in regular and special education classrooms. *American Educational Research Journal, 28,* 337–373.

Flower, L., & Hayes, J. (1980). The dynamics of composing: Making plans and juggling constraints. In L. W. Gregg & E. R. Steinberg (Eds.), *Cognitive processes in writing: An interdisciplinary approach* (pp. 31–50). Hillsdale, NJ: Erlbaum.

Gould, J. D. (1980). Experiments on composing letters: Some facts, some myths, and some observations. In L. W. Gregg & E. R. Steinberg (Eds.), *Cognitive processes in writing: An interdisciplinary approach* (pp. 97–127). Hillsdale, NJ: Erlbaum.

Graham, S. (2000). Should the natural learning approach replace spelling instruction? *Journal of Educational Psychology, 92,* 235–247.

Graham, S., & Harris, K. R. (1989). A components analysis of cognitive strategy training: Effects on learning disabled students' compositions and self-efficacy. *Journal of Educational Psychology, 81,* 353–361.

Graham, S., & Harris, K. R. (1996). Self-regulation and strategy instruction for students who find writing and learning challenging. In M. Levy & S. Ransdell (Eds.), *The science of writing: Theories, methods, individual differences, and applications* (pp. 347–360). Hillsdale, NJ: Erlbaum.

Graham, S., & Harris, K. R. (1997a). Self-regulation and writing: Where do we go from here? *Contemporary Educational Psychology, 22,* 102–114.

Graham, S., & Harris, K. R. (1997b). It can be taught, but it does not develop naturally: Myths and realities in writing instruction. *School Psychology Review, 26,* 414–424.

Graham, S., & Harris, K. R. (2000). The role of self-regulation and transcription skills in writing and writing development. *Educational Psychologist, 35,* 3–12.

Graham, S., & Harris, K. R. (2001). Prevention and intervention of writing difficulties for students with learning disabilities. *Learning Disabilities Research & Practice, 16,* 74–84.

Graham, S., Harris, K. R., & Troia, G. A. (1998). Writing and self-regulation: Cases from the self-regulated strategy development model. In D. H. Schunk & B. J. Zimmerman (Eds.), *Developing self-regulated learners: From teaching to self-reflective practice* (pp. 20–41). New York: Guilford Press.

Graves, D. H. (1983). *Writing: Teachers and children at work.* Exeter, NH: Heinemann.

Harris, K. R., & Graham, S. (1996). *Making the writing process work: Strategies for composition and self-regulation.* Cambridge, MA: Brookline.

Kellogg, R. T. (1987). Effects of topic knowledge on the allocation of processing time and cognitive effort to writing processes. *Memory & Cognition, 15,* 256–266.

MacArthur, C. A., Schwartz, S. S., & Graham, S. (1991). Effects of a reciprocal peer revision strategy in special education classrooms. *Learning Disabilities Research & Practice, 6,* 201–210.

McCutchen, D. (1988). "Functional automaticity" in children's writing: A problem of metacognitive control. *Written Communication, 5,* 306–324.

Minzesheimer, B. (1997, August 28). Reichs' literary skulduggery: Forensic anthropologist digs into mysteries with "Deja Dead." *USA Today,* p. 6D.

Poplin, M. (1988). The reductionist fallacy in learning disabilities: Replicating the past by reducing the present. *Journal of Learning Disabilities, 21,* 389–400.

Sawyer, R., Graham, S., & Harris, K. R. (1992). Direct teaching, strategy instruction, and strategy instruction with explicit self-regulation: Effects on learning disabled students' composition skills and self-efficacy. *Journal of Educational Psychology, 84,* 340–352.

Stein, N., & Glenn, G. (1979). An analysis of story comprehension in elementary school children. In R. O. Freedle (Ed.), *New directions in discourse processing* (Vol. 2, pp. 53–120). Norwood, NJ: Ablex.

Thomas, C. C., Englert, C. S., & Gregg, S. (1987). An analysis of errors and strategies in the expository writing of learning disabled students. *Remedial and Special Education, 8*(1), 21–30.

Troia, G. A., Graham, S., & Harris, K. R. (1999). Teaching students with learning disabilities to mindfully plan when writing. *Exceptional Children, 65*, 235–252.

Wansart, W. (1988). The student with learning disabilities in a writing process classroom: A case study. *Reading, Writing, and Learning Disabilities, 4*, 311–319.

Wong, B. Y. L. (1994). Instructional parameters promoting transfer of learned strategies in students with learning disabilities. *Learning Disability Quarterly, 17*, 110–120.

Wong, B. Y. L. (1997). Research on genre-specific strategies for enhancing writing in adolescents with learning disabilities. *Learning Disability Quarterly, 20*, 140–159.

Zaragoza, N., & Vaughn, S. (1992). The effects of process writing instruction on three 2nd grade students with different achievement profiles. *Learning Disabilities Research & Practice, 7*, 184–193.

Excerpts From

Improving Fourth-Grade Students' Composition Skills: Effects of Strategy Instruction and Self-Regulation Procedures

Cornelia Glaser and Joachim C. Brunstein

Journal of Educational Psychology, Vol. 99, 2007, Pages 297–310.

Drawing on Graham and Harris's (2003) work on teaching cognitive and self-regulatory writing strategies to young and unskilled writers, in this study we sought to examine the potential benefits of integrating self-regulation procedures into writing strategies training designed to improve elementary schoolchildren's composition skills. Our aim was to demonstrate that self-regulation activities are effective in the sense that they augment performance effects of strategy instruction, ensure strategy maintenance, and facilitate transfer of the learned strategies to untrained tasks. To test these ideas, we taught fourth graders writing strategies in combination with self-regulation procedures and contrasted this treatment with two comparison conditions (teaching strategies alone and didactic lessons in composing) in a pretest, posttest, and follow-up test design.

Present Research

In this study...our aim was to demonstrate that explicit self-regulation instructions can indeed contribute to the acquisition of writing strategies and, thus, to the development of young students' writing skills. Different from previous studies that primarily used a dismantling strategy to remove from the multifaceted SRSD [self-regulated strategy development] package individual elements of self-reflective practice (e.g., self-instructions and self-assessment routines), we first created a strategy training aimed at improving fourth-grade students' composition skills and then added to it a set of interrelated self-regulatory activities that were explicitly taught to students.

The strategy training, which was inspired by the aforementioned work of Graham and Harris (2003), included methods of direct instruction and cognitive modeling as well as phases of guided and independent practice to help students acquire effective strategies (e.g., the widely used story grammar strategy) for planning and redrafting stories. To manipulate the presence versus absence of self-regulation procedures as an integral part of the strategy training, we adopted a self-regulatory model described by Zimmerman (1998). In this model, self-regulation is assumed to be organized within a learning cycle that capitalizes on three kinds of self-reflective thoughts: goal setting and strategic planning; self-monitoring of one's accuracy in implementing a selected strategy; and self-assessment of strategy outcome and task performance. These processes are considered to be cyclic or recursive because each process entails information that can lead to changes in a subsequent step of the cycle. In addition, these processes qualify as self-reflective cognitions in the sense that self-monitoring of learning activities and associated corrective processes are central features of each step included in the cycle.

> Self-regulation is assumed to be organized within a learning cycle that capitalizes on three kinds of self-reflective thoughts: goal setting and strategic planning; self-monitoring of one's accuracy in implementing a selected strategy; and self-assessment of strategy outcome and task performance.

To test these predictions, we used a pretest, posttest, follow-up test design that included three conditions: strategy instruction plus self-regulation, strategy instruction alone, and an active control group receiving didactic lessons in composing.

To test the effectiveness of the intervention conditions, we administered a genre-specific knowledge test and examined students' strategy-related skills when planning and revising a story. We expected students of both strategy conditions to attain higher knowledge scores than students in the control condition but expected only students taught to monitor and regulate their composing behavior to display superior performance when planning and revising a story. The idea underlying this expectation was that a self-regulated learning approach to composition should enable students to translate their newly acquired knowledge about good writing into an organized pattern of strategic behaviors when planning and revising their own stories (cf. Alexander, 1997).

Method

Participants and Design

Participants were 113 fourth graders attending six classes in three elementary schools serving middle-class neighborhoods in a medium-sized German town. The average age of the sample was 9.9 years

(SD = 0.58). German was the primary language of all children. Their ethnic identification was predominantly (96%) Caucasian.

The study involved a quasi-experimental pretest, posttest, follow-up test design with three conditions. We randomly assigned the six classes to the three conditions, with students from two intact classes participating in each condition: strategy plus self-regulation (22 girls and 19 boys), strategy-only (19 girls and 15 boys), and control (15 girls and 23 boys) conditions.

Strategy Plus Self-Regulation

Writing strategies. At the start of the intervention, students were taught a general planning strategy for working out writing material. The strategy consisted of three steps—planning, writing, and revising a self-constructed text—designed to help students guide and organize their writing activities and integrate them into a structured pattern of interconnected behaviors. To help students carry out these steps when composing a story, they were taught a set of three genre-specific strategies.

Strategy instruction. Strategy instruction involved the following techniques widely used in SRSD studies (Harris & Graham,1999; Harris & Pressley, 1991): activation of background knowledge; direct instruction and group discussions of strategies; cognitive modeling of each step involved in a strategy; reciting mnemonics to retrieve each step from memory; guided, collaborative, and independent practice in drafting and rewriting stories; progress feedback as to the quality of stories; and verbal scaffolding of instructional support during the training period.

Self-regulation procedures. This strategy instructional program was embedded in a number of self-regulation procedures taught exclusively to students in the strategy plus self-regulation condition. [See Table 1.]

Discussion

[The] pattern of findings [we observed] suggests that the combination of composing strategies with self-regulation procedures produces incremental effects on students' writing achievements and facilitates maintenance and generalization of these effects.

First, students of both strategy instructional interventions acquired substantial knowledge about composing. However, compared with students who were taught strategies alone, students in the strategy plus self-regulation condition were better able to use their knowledge when planning and revising a story.... This finding is consistent with the view that self-regulation activities

TABLE I. Characteristics of Strategies' Intervention Conditions

Instructional procedure	Strategy plus self-regulation	Strategy only
Preskill development: Explicit instruction and small-group discussion of story paragraphs, story grammar elements, and stylistic features of stories.	+	+
Strategy instruction: Explicit instruction, cognitive modeling, and small-group discussion of effective writing strategies (3-steps strategy, A-H-A, and 7-W questions).	+	+
Strategy retrieval: Using mnemonic charts to memorize story grammar elements and stylistic features of stories.	+	+
Practice in strategy use: Guided, collaborative, and independent practice in planning, composing, and redrafting stories.	+	+
Self-regulation procedures: Explicit instruction in and modeling of self-regulation procedures followed by guided and independent practice in		
(a) self-monitoring of strategic planning	+	
(b) self-assessment of writing performance	+	
(c) self-monitoring of revision activities	+	
(d) criterion setting and procedural goals	+	
Additional practice: Practicing compositional skills with didactic material.		+

NOTE: A-H-A = denoted in German the major sections of a story: beginning, main body, and ending; 7-W = a grammalogue that referred in German to the following questions: Who is the main character? Where does the story take place? When does the story take place? What is the goal or concern of the main character? What culminating point does the story aim at? What chain or sequence of action leads up to this point? How does the story end?

foster the translation of strategy-related knowledge into strategic task performance (see also Graham, Harris, & Mason, 2005).

Second, students who were taught strategies in combination with self-regulation practices improved in the completeness and quality of their stories from pretest to posttest to a greater extent than students who received strategy instruction alone. The finding that strategy-only students (who also improved from pretest to posttest) outperformed control students immediately after the training indicates that the strategy-only condition represented a conservative standard of comparison for the evaluation of the full self-regulatory intervention. Students who received didactic lessons in composing showed no improvement in their stories over the course of this study. It thus appears unlikely that extended practice in composing had by itself a substantial impact on students' writing performance (see also Graham et al., 2005).

Third, 5 weeks after the training, strategy-only students relapsed in their achievements to pretest levels. In contrast, strategy plus self-regulation students were able to maintain the superior level of performance they had reached at posttest and, thus, outperformed students of both comparison groups at maintenance. Hence, self-regulation procedures ensured that postinstructional improvements in story writing were maintained over the follow-up interval.

Fourth, these performance effects generalized to a task that required students to recall central parts of an orally presented story. At posttest and at maintenance, strategy plus self-regulation students scored higher on the written recall measure than students of either comparison group. A mediational analysis revealed that differences in story recall were accounted for by differences in the schematic completeness of students' compositions. From this result, it is tempting to conclude that instruction in self-regulation facilitates the generalization of writing strategies to related types of tasks (e.g., listening comprehension).

General Conclusion

Taken together, we believe these findings add to our understanding of how SRSD promotes the development of strategic writing among upper elementary grade children.

References

Alexander, P. A. (1997). Mapping the multidimensional nature of domain learning: The interplay of cognitive, motivational, and strategic forces. In M. L. Maehr & P. R. Pintrich (Eds.), *Advances in motivation and achievement* (Vol. 10, pp. 213–250). Greenwich, CT: JAI Press.

Graham, S. (2006b). Writing. In P. A. Alexander & P. H. Winne (Eds.), *Handbook of educational psychology* (2nd ed., pp. 457–478). Mahwah, NJ: Erlbaum.

Graham, S., & Harris, K. R. (2003). Students with learning disabilities and the process of writing: A meta-analysis of SRSD studies. In H. L. Swanson, K. R. Harris, & S. Graham (Eds.), *Handbook of learning disabilities* (pp. 323–344). New York: Guilford Press.

Graham, S., Harris, K. R., & Mason, L. (2005). Improving the writing performance, knowledge, and self-efficacy of struggling young writers: The effects of self-regulated strategy development. *Contemporary Educational Psychology, 30,* 207–241. Harris, K. R., & Graham, S. (1999). Programmatic intervention research: Illustrations from the evolution of self-regulated strategy development. *Learning Disability Quarterly, 22,* 251–262.

Harris, K. R., & Pressley, M. (1991). The nature of cognitive strategy instruction: Interactive strategy construction. *Exceptional Children, 57,* 392–405.

Zimmerman, B. J. (1998). Academic studying and the development of personal skill: A self-regulatory perspective. *Educational Psychologist, 33,* 73–86.

Excerpts From

Improving the Writing, Knowledge, and Motivation of Struggling Young Writers: The Effects of Self-Regulated Strategy Development With and Without Peer Support

Karen R. Harris, Steve Graham, and Linda H. Mason

American Educational Research Journal, Vol. 42, 2006, Pages 295–340.

One purpose of the current study...was to examine the effectiveness of an instructional program in improving the performance of young, struggling writers attending urban schools serving a high percentage of children from low-income families. A struggling writer was defined as a child who scored at or below the 25th percentile on a norm-referenced test of writing performance that measured the inclusion of specific thematic elements in a story and who was also identified as a poor writer by the classroom teacher. The experimental intervention, self-regulated strategy development (SRSD; Harris & Graham, 1996, 1999), is compatible with current theories on the development of competence in a subject-matter domain (Alexander, 1992, 1997; Chi, 1985; Harris & Alexander, 1998; Pintrich & Schunk, 1996). These conceptualizations emphasize that learning is a complex process that depends, in large part, on changes that occur in a learner's strategic knowledge, domain-specific knowledge, and motivation (Alexander, Graham, & Harris, 1996).

> Previous investigations have shown that SRSD has a strong impact on improving the writing performance of upper-elementary and middle school students.

Although the primary focus of SRSD is on teaching students strategies for successfully completing an academic task, students are also taught knowledge and self-regulatory procedures (e.g., goal setting, self-monitoring, and self-instruction) needed to carry out the target strategies and better understand the task. In addition, instructional procedures for fostering aspects of motivation, such as student effort, are embedded within the model.

Previous investigations have shown that SRSD has a strong impact on improving the writing performance of upper-elementary and middle school students (effect sizes typically exceed 0.80), including enhancing the writing of youngsters attending urban schools (Graham & Harris, 2003, in press). The effectiveness of SRSD with primary grade students, however, has been tested in only one study with third-grade children (Graham, Harris, & Mason, 2005), and data are limited on the effects of the model on writers' knowledge and motivation. In the study involving third-grade students, SRSD instruction in how to plan and write stories and persuasive essays had a strong impact on the writing performance of children who were experiencing difficulty learning to write. After treatment, SRSD-instructed students' stories and persuasive papers were longer, more complete, and qualitatively better than papers written by control students (effect sizes exceeded 1.78 for all of these measures).

Like the older students in the Graham et al. (2005) investigation, the second-grade students in this study were taught a general strategy that emphasized planning in advance....We decided to make planning the central focus of our instruction for three reasons. First, planning is an essential ingredient in skilled writing; skilled writers spend a considerable amount of time planning what to do and say (Flower & Hayes, 1980; Graham, in press; Kellogg, 1987), including setting goals, generating ideas, and organizing ideas into a writing plan (Hayes & Flower, 1980). Second, struggling writers are less knowledgeable about the strategies and processes involved in planning a paper than their peers who are better writers (Graham & Harris, 2000). For example, Englert, Raphael, Fear, and Anderson (1988) found that poor writers were less knowledgeable than good writers about how to develop and organize ideas for writing a paper. Third, young writers, including those who find writing difficult, do little planning in advance of writing (Cameron & Moshenko, 1996; MacArthur & Graham, 1987). Advanced planning may be especially advantageous for both novice and struggling writers. A written plan provides an external memory wherein a child can store ideas without the risk of losing them. It may further reduce the need to plan while writing, freeing resources to engage in other writing processes such as translating ideas into words and transcribing words into printed text (Kellogg, 1986, 1987).

> Advanced planning may be especially advantageous for both novice and struggling writers. A written plan provides an external memory wherein a child can store ideas without the risk of losing them.

The second purpose of this investigation was to determine whether social support through peer assistance would enhance SRSD-instructed students' performance, especially in terms of maintenance and generalization.... In the present study, therefore, we examined whether adding peers working together to support strategy use, maintenance, and generalization would augment performance effects. This concept of peer support draws upon theories of social learning that emphasize mental sharing and collective thinking in the undertaking of a demanding or complex task (Hastie & Pennington, 1991; Perkins, 1992; Salomon, 1993). The peer support component involved two peers working together to promote strategy use outside of the strategy instruction situation.

Writing instruction for children in the comparison condition was based on the Writers' Workshop model (Calkins, 1986; Graves, 1983). We selected this approach for two reasons. First, this is the model that teachers in the participating schools used to teach writing. Second, Writers' Workshop, or other variants of the process approach to writing instruction, has become the most prominent paradigm for the teaching of writing in the United States (Pathey-Chavez, Matsumara, & Valdes, 2004; Pritchard & Honeycutt, in press).

Method

Participants

Screening

At the end of October 2001, 273 second-grade children (from 11 classrooms) attending four schools in a single urban school district in the Washington, D.C., area were administered the Story Construction Subtest from the Test of Written Language 3 (TOWL-3; Hammill & Larsen, 1996). This subtest assesses a child's ability to write a complete and interesting story (by examining whether specific thematic elements are included in the story). To be identified as a struggling writer, a student had to have a score on this test that fell two thirds of a standard deviation or more below the mean for the normative sample.... Seventy children were identified as struggling writers according to the criteria just specified. The parents of 66 of these 70 children granted informed consent for their children to take part in the study.

Conditions

The 66 second-grade children were randomly assigned to three conditions: SRSD instruction only (n = 22), SRSD plus peer support (n = 22), and comparison (n = 22).

Specific Instructional Procedures

SRSD Only

SRSD (Harris & Graham, 1992) was used in teaching the general planning strategy, the two genre-specific strategies, and the accompanying knowledge and self-regulatory procedures needed to use these strategies and manage the writing task. With this approach, students are explicitly and systematically taught strategies for accomplishing specific writing tasks. They are also taught any information or skills needed to use these strategies. They further learn how to use the self-regulation procedures, including goal setting, self-monitoring, self-reinforcement, and self-instructions, to help them manage the writing strategies and task of writing as well as to obtain concrete and visible evidence of their progress. SRSD instruction is designed to promote students' independent use of the target strategies and accompanying self-regulation procedures. Instruction is scaffolded so that responsibility for applying and recruiting the target strategies, accompanying knowledge or skills, and self-regulation procedures gradually shifts from instructor to students. Children are viewed and treated as active collaborators in the learning process. The role of effort in learning is emphasized and rewarded. The level and type of feedback and instructional support are individualized by the instructor so that they are responsive to students' needs. Instruction is criterion rather than time based, in that children move through each instructional stage at their own pace and do not proceed to later stages of instruction until they have met initial criteria for doing so. Instructional stages are revisited and combined as necessary.

SRSD Plus Peer Support

The only differences between the instructional procedures in the SRSD-only condition and the SRSD with peer support condition were as follows. During the develop background knowledge stage, the concept that students would act as partners to help each other apply the strategies they were learning to other situations and in other classes was introduced. This included helping each other identify when, where, and how part or all of what they were learning could be applied in other classes; helping each other do so; and discussing at the next session their successes and difficulties in using these procedures in one or more situations.

Comparison Condition

Writing instruction was delivered to students in the comparison condition by their regular teacher. Before the start of the study, these teachers were interviewed to determine their approach to writing instruction (interviews were conducted by the second author). All of the teachers and their principals were asked to indicate what approach they used to teach writing. Each teacher as well as the principals indicated that they used a Writers' Workshop model (Calkins, 1986; Graves, 1983).

Assessing Writing Performance

Before the start of instruction (pretest), students' writing skills were assessed in four different genres: story, persuasive, personal narrative, and informative writing. After instruction in how to plan and write a story, students' story and personal narrative writing skills were again assessed. These posttest measures allowed us to examine whether SRSD instruction had a positive effect on children's story writing skills and to determine whether instructional effects transferred to a similar but different genre, personal narratives. Likewise, after students learned how to plan and write a persuasive essay, their persuasive and informative writing skills were assessed.

Writing Prompts

Assessments for each genre involved writing a composition in response to a writing prompt. As a means of increasing motivation, students were provided with a choice of two prompts (in the same genre) whenever they were asked to write a paper. The only exception involved the persuasive writing classroom generalization probe, in which students were asked to write about a single topic. This situation more closely resembled what teachers did when they assigned a writing topic.

Assessing Writing Knowledge

Before instruction started (pretest) and once instruction ended (posttest), students individually answered three open-ended questions. The first question was taken from a writing knowledge survey constructed by Graham, Schwartz, and MacArthur (1993). It assessed students' knowledge about planning: "When you are asked to write a paper for class or for homework, what kinds of things can you do to help you plan and write your paper?" The other two questions, developed by Graham et al. (in press), examined students' knowledge of the two genres taught in this study. The first asked students to tell a friend what kinds of things are included in a story, whereas the second made the same inquiry about writing to persuade.

Assessing Effort and Intrinsic Motivation

Through the use of procedures described by Gottfried (1990), classroom teachers were asked to rate students' intrinsic motivation before the start of the study and at the end of it.

Results

Students in both SRSD conditions worked together in small groups of two. Thus, the unit of analysis was the pair's mean performance. For the SRSD-only condition, there were 11 pairs of students. Likewise, the SRSD plus peer support condition initially included 11 pairs, but one student moved during the course of the study. Because neither the child who moved nor the one who replaced him completed all of the assessments, only the scores of the student who completed the full instructional regime in this pair were used in the analyses. There were also 11 pairs of students in the comparison condition at the start of the study, one pair for each classroom teacher. Two of these students, from different classrooms, moved before the experiment was completed. The remaining student's scores were used in the analyses in both of these instances.

We conducted a two-way analysis of variance (ANOVA) with repeated measures to test for statistically significant differences between conditions for each of the writing and motivation measures. The independent variable was condition, and the repeated measure was time of testing. For stories, time of testing included three levels: pretest, posttest, and maintenance. For all other writing and motivation variables, time of testing included two levels: pretest and posttest.

Writing Performance

Planning Time

Immediately after instruction, there was a statistically significant difference in the amount of time (in minutes) that students in the three treatment conditions spent planning their stories. As expected, students in the two SRSD conditions spent more time than comparison students planning their posttest stories. SRSD students in both conditions spent almost 5 minutes planning their stories, whereas comparison students spent less than one fourth of a minute planning.

Length

There was a statistically significant main effect for time of testing as well as a statistically significant interaction between condition and time of testing for length of students' stories. Tests of simple main effects for the interaction revealed that there was a statistically significant difference in the length of students' stories at posttest, $F(2, 30) = 3.74$, $MSE = 2,536.60$, $p = .036$, and maintenance, $F(2, 30) = 5.59$, $MSE = 1,348.46$, $p = .009$, but not at pretest. A follow-up posttest analysis indicated that students in the SRSD plus peer support condition wrote longer stories than did students in the comparison condition. There was no statistically significant difference between the length of posttest stories among comparison and SRSD-only students or between the two SRSD conditions.

Elements

There were statistically significant effects for time for testing, condition, and the interaction between the two in terms of the number of basic elements that students included in their stories. Tests of simple main effects for the interaction revealed that there was a statistically significant difference between the number of basic story elements at posttest, $F(2, 30) = 32.98$, $MSE = 31.24$, $p = .000$, and maintenance, $F(2, 30) = 16.50$, $MSE = 22.30$, $p = .000$, but not at pretest. A follow-up posttest analysis indicated that students in both SRSD conditions included more basic elements in their stories than did children in the comparison condition. These findings were replicated at maintenance as well.

> Students in the SRSD plus peer support condition wrote longer stories than did students in the comparison condition.

Quality

There was a statistically significant main effect for time of testing as well as a statistically significant interaction between condition and time of testing for quality of students' stories. Tests of simple main effects for the interaction revealed that there was a statistically significant difference in quality of stories at posttest, $F(2, 30) = 3.74$, $MSE = 2,536.60$, $p = .036$, and maintenance, $F(2, 30) = 2.67$, $MSE = 4.46$, $p = .042$, but not at pretest. A follow-up posttest analysis indicated that students in the SRSD plus peer support condition wrote qualitatively better stories than did students in the comparison condition. There was no statistically significant difference between the quality of posttest stories among comparison and SRSD-only students or between the two SRSD conditions. At

> Students in the SRSD plus peer support condition wrote qualitatively better stories than did students in the comparison condition.

maintenance, students in both SRSD conditions wrote qualitatively better stories than did the children in the comparison condition.

Writing Knowledge

When asked to indicate how they would plan a paper at posttest (Question 1), students primarily answered this question by describing substantive processes such as making a list, writing ideas down, webbing, planning, organizing notes, and so forth.... As predicted, students in both SRSD conditions identified more substantive processes for planning than their peers in the comparison condition. There was no statistically significant difference between the two SRSD conditions, however.

> Students in both SRSD conditions identified more substantive processes for planning than their peers in the comparison condition.

Intrinsic Motivation and Effort

There were no statistically significant effects of condition, time of testing, or their interaction for either of these measures. Thus, contrary to predictions, SRSD instruction did not influence teachers' perceptions of these two measures of children's motivation.

Conclusion

The present results demonstrate that, as early as second grade, the writing performance and knowledge of young struggling writers can be improved substantially by teaching them general and genre-specific strategies for planning in conjunction with the knowledge and self-regulatory procedures needed to use these strategies effectively. These findings provide further verification that explicit and systematic strategy instruction can enhance students' writing performance (e.g., see De La Paz, 1999, 2001; Englert, Raphael, Anderson, Anthony, & Stevens, 1991; Graham, 2006; Wong, 1997; Yeh, 1998), including the writing of children in the primary grades (Beal, Garrod, & Bonitatibus, 1990) as well as children attending urban schools primarily serving low-income families (Graham et al., 2005). Finally, our results show that a common procedure in clinical psychology, peers helping each other maintain and generalize gains (Brownell & Jeffrey, 1987; Jacobson, 1989), can be applied successfully to academic learning with young children.

The findings of this study have several important educational implications. First, they support the contention that it is beneficial to explicitly and systematically teach struggling writers specific strategies for carrying out writing processes such as planning. Although we did not examine whether such instruction is also effective with average and above-average writers, the findings from a recent meta-analysis suggest that this is the case. Graham (2006) examined effect sizes for studies in which strategies for planning, revising, or both were explicitly taught to school-aged students. In terms of overall writing quality, mean effect sizes were 0.82 (based on 13 calculated effect sizes) for average writers and 1.15 (based on 9 calculated effect sizes) for above-average writers. It must be noted that these strategy studies involving average and above-average writers were conducted with children in Grade 4 and above. Thus, additional research is needed to determine whether strategy instruction in writing is effective with these primary-grade children.

Second, the findings of this study raise important issues as to whether Writers' Workshop or other process approaches to writing instruction are powerful enough for students who experience difficulty learning to write. Although students in the comparison condition did evidence growth in their writing development during the 6 months of this experiment, they made significantly less progress than their peers in the two SRSD conditions. Several other studies with struggling writers have yielded similar results (e.g., Graham et al., 2005; Saddler, Moran, Graham, & Harris, 2004; Troia & Graham, 2002).

> The writing performance and knowledge of young struggling writers can be improved substantially by teaching them general and genre-specific strategies for planning in conjunction with the knowledge and self-regulatory procedures needed to use these strategies effectively.

Although additional research is needed to determine the overall effectiveness of process approaches such as Writers' Workshop with struggling writers, investigators should also examine how such approaches can be made more effective for these students. One possibility is to integrate more explicit strategy instruction directly into Writers' Workshop. This was done in a study conducted by Danoff, Harris, and Graham (1993) and had a positive effect on the writing performance of both average and poor writers.

Finally, an important issue is how strategy instruction procedures such as SRSD can be implemented in schools where writing practices are strongly driven by high-stakes testing. If high-stakes assessments focus more on mechanical concerns, such as spelling or usage, then instructional practices that promote the development of planning, revising, and other self-regulatory processes will probably be ignored by school officials looking to increase test scores. Many high-stakes assessments, however, are designed to assess writing more broadly, including evaluation of organization, ideation, vocabulary, and overall quality (Johnston, Penny, & Gordon, 2001). De La Paz (1999, 2001) applied the SRSD model to the teaching of writing strategies designed to improve performance on the mandatory writing competency test used by the state of Tennessee. This instruction had positive effects on the writing of students who were both good and poor writers.

References

Alexander, P. (1992). Domain knowledge: Evolving issues and emerging concerns. *Educational Psychologist, 27,* 33–51.

Alexander, P. (1997). Mapping the multidimensional nature of domain learning: The interplay of cognitive, motivational, and strategic forces. In M. Maehr & P. Pintrich (Eds.), *Advances in motivation and achievement* (Vol. 10, pp. 213–250). Greenwich, CT: JAI Press.

Alexander, P., Graham, S., & Harris, K. R. (1996). A perspective on strategy research: Progress and prospects. *Educational Psychology Review, 10,* 129–154.

Beal, C., Garrod, A., & Bonitatibus, G. (1990). Fostering children's revision through training in comprehension monitoring. *Journal of Educational Psychology, 82,* 275–280.

Brownell, K., & Jeffery, R. (1987). Improving long-term weight loss: Pushing the limits of treatment. *Behavior Therapy, 18,* 353–374.

Calkins, L. (1986). *The art of teaching writing.* Portsmouth, NH: Heinemann.

Cameron, C., & Moshenko, B. (1996). Elicitations of knowledge transformational reports while children write narratives. *Canadian Journal of Behavioural Science, 28,* 271–280.

Chi, M. (1985). Interactive roles of knowledge and strategies in the development of organized sorting and recall. In S. Chipman, J. Siegel, & R. Glasser (Eds.), *Thinking and learning skills: Research and open questions* (Vol. 2, pp. 457–483). Hillsdale, NJ: Erlbaum.

Danoff, B., Harris, K. R., & Graham, S. (1993). Incorporating strategy instruction into the school curriculum: Effects on children's writing. *Journal of Reading Behavior, 86,* 363–368.

De La Paz, S. (1999). Self-regulated strategy instruction in regular education settings: Improving outcomes for students with and without learning disabilities. *Learning Disabilities Research and Practice, 14,* 92–106.

De La Paz, S. (2001). Teaching writing to students with attention deficit disorders and specific language impairments. *Journal of Educational Research, 95,* 37–47.

Englert, C., Raphael, T., Anderson, L., Anthony, H., & Stevens, D. (1991). Making strategies and self-talk visible: Writing instruction in regular and special education classrooms. *American Educational Research Journal, 28,* 337–372.

Englert, S., Raphael, T., Fear, K., & Anderson, L. (1988). Students' metacognitive knowledge about how to write informational texts. *Learning Disability Quarterly, 11,* 18–46.

Flower, L., & Hayes, J. (1980). The dynamics of composing: Making plans and juggling constraints. In L. Gregg & E. Steinberg (Eds.), *Cognitive processes in writing* (pp. 31–50). Hillsdale, NJ: Erlbaum.

Gottfried, A. (1990). Academic intrinsic motivation in young elementary school children. *Journal of Educational Psychology, 82,* 525–538.

Graham, S. (2006). Strategy instruction and the teaching of writing: A meta-analysis. In C. MacArthur, S. Graham, & J. Fitzgerald (Eds.), *Handbook of writing research* (pp. 187–207). New York: Guilford Press.

Graham, S. (in press). Writing. In P. Alexander & P. Winne (Eds.), *Handbook of educational psychology.* Mahwah, NJ: Erlbaum.

Graham, S., & Harris, K. (2000). The role of self-regulation and transcription skills in writing and writing development. *Educational Psychologist, 35,* 3–12.

Graham, S., & Harris, K. R. (2003). Students with learning disabilities and the process of writing: A meta-analysis of SRSD studies. In L. Swanson, K. Harris, & S. Graham (Eds.), *Handbook of learning disabilities* (pp. 323–344). New York: Guilford Press.

Graham, S., Harris, K. R., & Mason, L. (2005). Improving the writing performance, knowledge, and motivation of struggling young writers: The effects of self-regulated strategy development. *Contemporary Educational Psychology, 30,* 207–241.

Graham, S., Schwartz, S., & MacArthur, C. (1993). Knowledge of writing and the composing process, attitude toward writing, and self-efficacy for students with and without learning disabilities. *Journal of Learning Disabilities, 26,* 237–249.

Graves, D. (1983). *Writing: Teachers and children at work.* Exeter, NH: Heinemann.

Hammill, D., & Larsen, S. (1996). *Test of Written Language 3.* Austin, TX: Pro-Ed.

Harris, K. R., & Alexander, P. (1998). Integrated, constructivist education: Challenge and reality. *Educational Psychology Review, 10,* 115–128.

Harris, K. R., & Graham, S. (1992). *Helping young writers master the craft: Strategy instruction and self-regulation in the writing process.* Cambridge, MA: Brookline Books.

Hastie, R., & Pennington, N. (1991). Cognitive and social processes in decision making. In L. Resnick, J. Levine, & S. Teasley (Eds.), *Perspectives on socially shared cognition* (pp. 308–327). Washington, DC: American Psychological Association.

Hayes, J., & Flower, L. (1980). Identifying the organization of writing processes. In L. Gregg & E. Steinberg (Eds.), *Cognitive processes in writing* (pp. 3–30). Hillsdale, NJ: Erlbaum.

Jacobson, N. (1989). The maintenance of treatment gains following social learning-based marital therapy. *Behavior Therapy, 20,* 325–336.

Johnston, R., Penny, J., & Gordon, B. (2001). Score resolution and the interrater reliability of holistic scores in rating essays. *Written Communication, 18,* 229–249.

Kellogg, R. (1986). Designing idea processors for document composition. *Behavior Research, Methods, Instruments, and Computers, 18,* 118–128.

Kellogg, R. (1987). Effects of topic knowledge on the allocation of processing time and cognitive effort to writing processes. *Memory & Cognition, 15,* 256–266.

MacArthur, C., & Graham, S. (1987). Learning disabled students' composing under three methods of text production: Handwriting, word processing, and dictation. *Journal of Special Education, 21,* 22–42.

Pathey-Chavez, G., Matsumara, I., & Valdes, R. (2004). Investigating the process approach to writing instruction in urban middle schools. *Journal of Adolescent and Adult Literacy, 47,* 442–476.

Perkins, D. (1992). *Smart schools: Better thinking and learning for every child.* New York: Free Press.

Pintrich, P., & Schunk, D. (1996). *Motivation in education.* Englewood Cliffs, NJ: Prentice Hall.

Pritchard, R., & Honeycutt, R. (in press). The process approach to writing instruction: Examining its effectiveness. In C. MacArthur, S. Graham, & J. Fitzgerald (Eds.), *Handbook of writing research.* New York: Guilford Press.

Saddler, B., Moran, S., Graham, S., & Harris, K. R. (2004). Preventing writing difficulties: The effects of planning strategy instruction on the writing performance of struggling writers. *Exceptionality, 12,* 13–17.

Salomon, G. (1993). *Distributed cognition: Psychological and educational considerations.* Cambridge, England: Cambridge University Press.

Troia, G., & Graham, S. (2002). The effectiveness of highly explicit and teacher-directed strategy instructional routine: Changing the writing performance of students with learning disabilities. *Journal of Learning Disabilities, 35,* 290–305.

Wong, B. (1994). Instructional parameters promoting transfer of learned strategies in students with learning disabilities. *Learning Disability Quarterly, 17,* 110–119.

Yeh, S. (1998). Empowering education: Teaching argumentative writing to cultural minority middle-school students. *Research in the Teaching of English, 33,* 49–84.

Excerpts From

Explicitly Teaching Strategies, Skills, and Knowledge: Writing Instruction in Middle School Classrooms

Susan De La Paz and Steve Graham

Journal of Educational Psychology, Vol. 94, 2002, Pages 687–698.

The present study examined the effectiveness of an instructional program designed to improve the writing performance of middle school students. Although the program primarily focused on teaching students strategies for planning, drafting, and revising text, the knowledge and skills needed to support these processes were also emphasized. This emphasis included knowledge about the characteristics of good writing, criteria for evaluating writing, and the structure of expository essays that involved explanation and persuasion (the writing task emphasized in this study). Writing skills that were addressed included constructing a thesis statement and using mature vocabulary, transition words, and different types of sentences. These skills are not only important in constructing a good essay but were also stressed on a statewide writing competency exam taken by students.

> The key element of the instructional program was a strategy that organized and directed the processes for planning and writing an essay.

The key element of the instructional program was a strategy that organized and directed the processes for planning and writing an essay. The students developed a plan in advance of writing that involved analyzing the demands of the writing assignment, setting goals for writing, and generating and organizing material to write about. The strategy also prompted students to use their plan while writing; revise and upgrade their plan as needed; and include transition words, interesting or mature vocabulary, and varied (error-free) sentence types.

Method

Setting and Participants

Setting. The study took place in two middle schools in a suburban school district in the Southeast. The two middle schools had similar demographic characteristics.

Teachers. Five seventh- and eighth-grade teachers agreed to participate in this study. We randomly assigned the 10 language arts classes taught by these teachers to the experimental and control conditions as follows: 6 were randomly assigned to the experimental condition (i.e., strategy instruction). Three of these classes were at the eighth-grade level and 3 of these classes were at the seventh-grade level. We assigned the 4 remaining classes to the control condition (with 2 classes at each grade level). Thus, teachers taught both experimental and control classes.

Students. The students in this investigation included 58 seventh and eighth graders; 30 students participated in the experimental condition and 28 students participated in the control condition. Whereas classes had been randomly assigned to the experimental and/or control conditions, students were drawn from intact classes, resulting in a quasi-experimental design.

General Procedures

Table 2 provides a visual outline of the instruction for students in the experimental and comparison group.

TABLE 2. Summary of Procedures for Experimental and Control Groups

Stage	Group	
	Experimental	Control
Preinstruction	Students were taught the characteristics of expository essays.	Students were taught the characteristics of expository essays.
	Students were taught the basic (5-paragraph) essay form.	Students were taught the basic (5-paragraph) essay form.
	Students were taught terminology for understanding writing prompts.	Students were taught terminology for understanding writing prompts.
Pretesting	Single 35-min session to plan and compose an essay.	Single 35-min session to plan and compose an essay.
Instruction Similarities	Students composed 5 essays (the same essay topics were used in both conditions, and 35 min were allotted for composing each essay).	Students composed 5 essays (the same essay topics were used in both conditions, and 35 min were allotted for composing each essay).
	Students selected 1 of their essays for a class portfolio.	Students selected 1 of their essays for a class portfolio.
	Teachers reviewed the different types of sentences.	Teachers reviewed the different types of sentences.
	Students were retaught the basic (5-paragraph) essay form.	Students were retaught the basic (5-paragraph) essay form.

Stage	Group	
	Experimental	Control
Instruction Differences	Students were taught to independently use the PLAN and WRITE strategy to compose an essay (this included establishing the purpose and the benefits of the strategy and its steps, describing it, modeling its use, memorizing the mnemonic and the strategy steps, and providing adjusted teacher and peer assistance until the strategy could be applied independently).	Teachers directed the generation and organization of writing ideas, using either webbing or Power Writing, before students composed essays (students were periodically reminded to use these procedures when writing the essay).
	Students were taught the knowledge and skills needed to use the PLAN and WRITE strategy (this included instruction in composing a thesis sentence and introductory paragraph; use of varied sentence types, interesting vocabulary, and transition words; maintaining control of the topic; and procedures for evaluating the quality of an essay).	Students were taught a variety of discrete writing skills (this included vocabulary, spelling, and grammar instruction).
	Students were taught to use self-regulatory procedures to facilitate the acquisition and the use of the PLAN and WRITE strategy (this included goal setting, self-monitoring, self-evaluation, and self-instructional statements).	Teachers graded students' essays, providing them with feedback on the quality of their writing (essays were not revised by students, however).
	Students were provided with temporary procedural support to help them initially use the PLAN and WRITE strategy (this included a brainstorming sheet for organizing ideas as well as an essay sheet and cue cards that reminded them to include basic essay and paragraph components).	Students read assigned books during class time.
	Students revised their essays after receiving feedback from a peer (this was facilitated by teaching them how to use a revising checklist to provide and receive feedback).	Students were provided homework to reinforce skills taught in class.
	Students were administered a quiz to test their knowledge of the steps of the PLAN and WRITE strategy.	Students were administered tests and quizzes to assess their knowledge of material taught in class.
Posttesting	Single 35-min session to plan and compose an essay.	Single 35-min session to plan and compose an essay.
Maintenance	One month after posttesting, a single 35-min session to plan and compose an essay.	One month after posttesting, a single 35-min session to plan and compose an essay.

Results

Table 3 presents planning scores for students in each group at pretest, posttest, and maintenance. The means and standard deviations for length, vocabulary, and quality for the two instructional conditions at pretest, posttest, and maintenance are presented in Table 4.

TABLE 3. Percentage of Students Engaging in Specific Types of Planning

		Type of planning			
Condition	1	2	3	4	5
Experimental					
Pretest	80	17	0	3	0
Posttest	3	3	3	77	13
Maintenance	0	7	3	50	40
Control					
Pretest	80	10	7	3	0
Posttest	23	40	7	27	3
Maintenance	8	23	3	37	28

NOTE: Percentages do not always add up to 100 because of rounding. Planning scores are as follows: 1 = no advanced planning; 2 = listing ideas; 3 = topics given with emerging subordination; 4 = three subtopics, each with two or more details; 5 = accurate, fully developed map or outline.

TABLE 4. Means and Standard Deviations for Length, Vocabulary, and Quality by Condition

	Experimental		Control	
Condition	M	SD	M	SD
Length				
Pretest	184.33	59.02	183.39	63.92
Posttest	236.17	67.43	190.82	55.61
Maintenance	229.67	77.01	179.68	46.80
Vocabulary				
Pretest	13.60	6.73	12.32	6.03
Posttest	17.23	8.03	11.17	5.36
Maintenance	18.50	6.89	13.25	5.60
Quality				
Pretest	3.13	0.94	3.21	0.88
Posttest	3.63	0.89	2.86	0.45
Maintenance	3.73	1.01	3.14	0.80

Discussion

This study examined the effects of an integrated writing program on middle school students' essay-writing abilities. The intervention applied in this study taught students strategies for planning, drafting, and revising an expository essay involving explanation and persuasion. Students were also taught the knowledge and skills needed to carry out these strategies as well as to write effectively. Students learned to apply the inculcated processes, skills, and knowledge in a flexible but coordinated manner. We anticipated that such instruction would have a salutary impact on students' writing performance, because it addressed aspects of composing (i.e., planning, producing, revising text as well as self-regulation in the writing process) that

> **Students learned to apply the inculcated processes, skills, and knowledge in a flexible but coordinated manner.**

are challenging for developing writers (Scardamalia & Bereiter, 1986).

Writing Behavior

As expected, the writing program had a positive effect on the writing performance of the participating middle school students. Immediately following instruction, students in the experimental group produced essays that were longer, contained more mature vocabulary, and were qualitatively better than the essays generated by youngsters in the control classrooms. These effects were maintained on an essay written 1 month after instruction ended.

Application of SRSD in the Regular Classroom

The present study provides additional verification that the SRSD model can be applied successfully with developing writers in traditional classrooms. Most of the students who have participated in studies using the SRSD model were students with writing disabilities, and they often received instruction from a specially trained tutor (see Harris & Graham, 1999). The present study, along with two previous investigations (Danoff et al., 1993; De La Paz, 1999), dem-

> **The present study provides additional verification that the SRSD model can be applied successfully with developing writers in traditional classrooms.**

onstrate that SRSD also provides an effective means for teaching normally developing writers and that this instruction can be delivered in the regular classroom.

Educational Implications

The present study provides support for the educational practice of directly teaching writing strategies, along with the skills and knowledge needed to apply them. Other studies (Danoff et al., 1993; De La Paz, 1999; Englert et al., 1991; Yeh, 1998) have also shown that such instruction improves the writing performance of normally developing students. In these studies, teachers modeled how to use writing strategies (and accompanying skills and knowledge), providing extensive instruction, practice, and assistance until students could apply them independently. This method differs considerably from the classroom practices of many teachers in which there is little evidence of extended or even explicit instruction in writing strategies and many writing skills (Anthony & Anderson, 1987; Graham & Harris, 1996).

> ## Why is explicit and more extended instruction in writing not more prominent in schools?

Why is explicit and more extended instruction in writing not more prominent in schools? One reason is because many teachers rely on informal or incidental methods of learning (i.e., the natural learning approach) to promote writing development (see Graham & Harris, 1997). Proponents of the natural learning approach believe that explicit instruction is not necessary, as strategies, skills, and knowledge are best learned through real use in meaningful and authentic contexts. Several studies, however, challenge this assumption, by showing that students who participate in writing programs based on these principles benefit when more extensive, structured, and explicit instruction is included (Danoff et al., 1993; MacArthur et al., 1991; Yeh, 1998). For example, Danoff et al. (1993) found that children in process-writing classrooms, where informal and incidental learning methods were emphasized, made considerable gains

> ## Students who participate in writing programs based on these principles benefit when more extensive, structured, and explicit instruction is included.

in writing when SRSD instruction in planning was provided through an extended series of mini-lessons.

Another possible reason why explicit instruction in writing is not more prominent is that some educators believe that directly teaching writing strategies, skills, and knowledge is counterproductive and may even be harmful (Elbow, 1981; Freedman, 1993; Petraglia, 1995). In the area of planning, for instance, preplanning is viewed by some experts as potentially harmful because it attempts to circumvent the nonlinear and recursive nature of writing and keeps writers from exploiting ideas or opportunities that might otherwise arise while writing (see Kellogg,

1990). Others argue that explicit teaching is counterproductive because rhetorical behavior is not rule governed or independent of the context in which it is applied (Petraglia, 1995). As this and other studies (Danoff et al., 1993; De La Paz, 1999; Englert et al., 1991; Harris & Graham, 1999; Yeh, 1998) have demonstrated, however, such instruction is beneficial. Following explicit strategy instruction, for example, students' knowledge of writing increases, they use more sophisticated writing strategies, and the quality of their writing improves (Graham & Harris, 1993).

References

Alexander, P., Graham, S., & Harris, K. R. (1998). A perspective on strategy research: Progress and prospect. *Educational Psychology Review, 10,* 129–154.

Anthony, H., & Anderson, L. (1987, April). The nature of writing instruction in regular and special education classrooms. Paper presented at the annual meeting of the American Educational Research Association, Washington, DC.

Danoff, B., Harris, K. R., & Graham, S. (1993). Incorporating strategy instruction within the writing process in the regular classroom: Effects on the writing of students with and without learning disabilities. *Journal of Reading Behavior, 25,* 295–319.

De La Paz, S. (1999). Self-regulated strategy instruction in regular education settings: Improving outcomes for students with and without learning disabilities. *Learning Disabilities Research & Practice, 14,* 92–106.

Elbow, P. (1981). *Writing with power.* New York: Oxford University Press.

Englert, C., Raphael, T., Anderson, L., Anthony, H., Steven, D., & Fear, K. (1991). Making writing and self-talk visible: Cognitive strategy instruction writing in regular and special education classrooms. *American Educational Research Journal, 28,* 337–373.

Freedman, A. (1993). Show and tell? The role of explicit teaching in the learning of new genres. *Research in the Teaching of English, 27,* 222–251.

Graham, S., & Harris, K. R. (1993). Self-regulated strategy development: Helping students with learning problems develop as writers. *Elementary School Journal, 94,* 169–181.

Graham, S., & Harris, K. R. (1996). Self-regulation and strategy instruction for students who find writing and learning challenging. In M. Levy & S. Ransdell (Eds.), *The science of writing: Theories, methods, individual differences, and applications* (pp. 347–360). Mahwah, NJ: Erlbaum.

Graham, S., & Harris, K. R. (1997). It can be taught, but it does not develop naturally: Myths and realities in writing instruction. *School Psychology Review, 26,* 414–424.

Harris, K. R., & Graham, S. (1999). Programmatic intervention research: Illustrations from the evolution of self-regulated strategy development. *Learning Disability Quarterly, 22,* 251–262.

Kellogg, R. (1990). Effectiveness of prewriting strategies as a function of task demands. *American Journal of Psychology, 103,* 327–342.

MacArthur, C., Schwartz, S., & Graham, S. (1991). The effects of a reciprocal peer revision strategy in special education classrooms. *Learning Disability Research and Practice, 6,* 201–210.

Petraglia, J. (1995). Writing as an unnatural act. In J. Petraglia (Ed.), *Reconceiving writing: Rethinking writing instruction* (pp. 79–100). Mahwah, NJ: Erlbaum.

Scardamalia, M., & Bereiter, C. (1986). Written composition. In M. Wittrock (Ed.), *Handbook of research on teaching* (3rd ed., pp. 778–803). New York: MacMillan.

Yeh, S. (1998). Empowering education: Teaching argumentative writing to cultural minority middle-school students. *Research in the Teaching of English, 33,* 49–84.

Chapter 4

Grammar, Genre, and Skills in Teaching Writing

"The narrative seems contrived."

Introduction

Within early process-based instruction, grammar and genre skills were thought to arise naturally from deep immersion into and exposure to speaking, listening, reading, and writing; the more one engages in these activities, the more one takes in language rules and syntactic structures almost instinctively. But research over the past 30 years suggests, instead, that students benefit from particular ways of teaching language skills, such as mini-lessons on grammar, that are grounded in the task they are asked to perform, such as writing, while they are performing it. That important insight establishes one of the sources of strategy instruction.

For example, decades of research show that teaching grammar in isolation from writing does little to help students write—drills on parts of speech do not translate into flawless prose. But as researchers have discovered, teaching grammar within and at the time of composing can make a difference. **Constance Weaver,** a leader in promoting this approach, provides a broad view of this research in the chapter's first article; at the same time, she identifies the catch-22 of grammar instruction for teachers: although traditional grammar instruction is ineffective, standardized and high-stakes tests often assess grammar in isolated, multiple-choice questions rather than within student writing. Weaver advocates that teachers stuck in this situation find ways of "teaching less grammar but teaching it more effectively for writing," and she provides 10 ways to incorporate grammar that are "smarter" strategies for writing than having students remember lists of prepositions or the rules of adjective order.

In a related argument, other researchers point out that having students memorize the features of genres is much less effective than allowing them to learn about genre as a strategy for writing *while* they are writing. The study by **Roger Beard** and **Andrew Burrell,** the second article in the chapter, shows that children's writing development can include increasingly higher quality narratives in one school year. Beard and Burrell's work helpfully tracks the specific features of students' stories that improved during that year, and they also suggest that one outcome of this study is providing research-based language that can be used to identify achievement and point out room for improvement with students. Using genre as the investigative lens "provided indications of development in the children's writing that could not be ascertained from the use of more numerical or impressionistic judgments." Their study provides a pathway to a clearer understanding of writing development within the narrative form.

Turning to another genre, nonfiction writing, the authors of the next study, **Richard Andrews, Carole Torgerson, Graham Low,** and **Nick McGuinn,** update a 2006 review of literature with more recent research to identify the best "conditions" for this genre-based instruction. More specifically, they highlight the research-proven practices that contribute to student achievement in argumentative writing: a strategy-based approach that specifically focuses on planning, the use of oral debate to inform argumentative writing, explicit goals for writing, teacher modeling, and teacher coaching. This study indicates that oral debate and discussion seem to be important components of preparing students to write persuasive/opinion papers. As **Scott Beers** and **William Nagy** point out in the next article, children easily use a variety of genres in daily speech, but until recently they encountered mostly narrative as they learned to read. Beers and Nagy identify that genres have micro-level differences in both oral and written work. In their study, they compare the writing that students completed in four different genres—narrative, descriptive, compare/contrast, and persuasive—and show that persuasive essays had more clauses per T-unit[1] than did the other genres at each grade level and descriptive texts had more words per clause than did the other genres. The authors speculate that genre-specific instruction might usefully incorporate syntax as a way to promote student achievement in the kind of writing they will be asked to complete in high school and beyond.

In the last article, **Thierry Olive, Monik Favart, Caroline Beauvais,** and **Lucie Beauvais** compare students' effort in writing narrative versus argumentative text and also identify how handwriting skills contribute to writing. Their study reiterates the importance of handwriting to writing production: handwriting fluency frees up working memory, which can then be used in the writing process. They also find that with more familiarity in a genre, students expend less effort on basic writing processes and engage more in planning and revising. The researchers show that by fifth grade, students easily produce narratives but are less able to produce argumentative writing—writing a reasoned argument entails drawing on more working memory to create a text. But by ninth grade, producing written prose has become automatic, making students' writing process more efficient regardless of genre. The researchers conclude that "not only children's early exposure to genres, but also the explicit teaching of genres is important as young writers' cognitive effort varies with the type of text they are writing."

---

[1]A T-unit is the smallest group of words that can form a complete thought; it can be composed of a main clause and its subordinate clauses and often is a sentence. Linguists use the number of clauses in a T-unit as a measure of complexity in written and oral language. The concept of T-units also allows linguists to compare speaking and writing development across languages.

Excerpts From

Grammar to Enrich and Enhance Writing: A Smart Perspective

Constance Weaver

The Grammar Plan Book, Pages 3–9, ©2007 Heinemann.

What's the weather report? "Cloudy with a chance of meatballs," as in Judi Barrett's picture book by the same title? Hardly. How about "Sunny, with a chance of little yellow grammar modules falling from the sky?" No, not that either.

What is "grammar" anyway?

Fundamentally, the grammar of a language is its *structure*. It's the elements of the language and the structural "rules" for combining them—whether or not anybody understands those rules consciously. The term *grammar* is also used for *descriptions* of its structure—whether reasonably accurate or not. The best known but least helpful descriptions are those of traditional school grammar, which have persisted with little change for literally hundreds of years. When people talk about "teaching grammar," they commonly mean teaching traditional grammar, often in isolation from its practical uses.

The major problem with those little grammar modules—yellow or not—is this: They present grammar in isolation, which is not the most productive or efficient way to get students to use grammar more effectively in their writing. While hardly any experimental research has directly addressed this question, the predominant conclusion from a century of research shows that teaching grammar in isolation, as a school subject, has little or no effect on most students' writing.

Again and again, researchers have summarized the research and come to essentially the same conclusion about the ineffectiveness, for writing, of teaching grammar in isolation. The latest of these studies was conducted at the University of York, in England, and published in 2004. The researchers conclude:

> In terms of practice, the main implication of our findings is that there is no high quality evidence that the teaching of grammar, whether traditional or generative/transformational, is worth the time if the aim is the improvement of the quality and/or accuracy of written composition. (Andrews et al., 2004b, p. 4)

Let me emphasize: Teaching grammar in isolation does not do much to enrich the quality of students' writing, nor does it do much to enhance its accuracy. In other words, isolated teaching of grammatical concepts associated with "standard" English does not make much of a difference in the forms students use when they write. Teachers need to make the connection explicit as they guide students in editing.

Hardly any experimental research has been done on the effects on students' writing of teaching grammar in isolation compared with teaching it in the context of writing. Perhaps the only substantial study is one conducted over several months in six schools, grades four through six. As reported by DiStefano and Killion (1984), the aim of the study was to see whether students would apply writing conventions better if these were taught in conjunction with students' writing instead of in isolation. At the end of the study, the only significant differences favored the classes that were taught grammatical conventions in the context of their use in writing.

Unfortunately, teachers are currently under increased pressure to prepare students for standardized tests of grammar. Politicians and the public don't know the research; they only know what they want: better writing that reflects the conventions of mainstream edited American English, or "standard" English as it's popularly called. Smart teachers, knowing that extensive isolated grammar instruction isn't very effective even for taking tests (McQuade, 1980), will teach grammar intertwined with writing, and, if necessary, separately help students prepare for such tests by teaching additional skills in the context of practice tests (keeping in mind that the better students can often teach themselves, using a practice-test book). This is certainly the most efficient use of instructional time and probably the most effective as well, with skills taught in the context of their use.

And indeed, after reiterating their conclusion that there is "no high quality evidence" that teaching any kind of grammar in isolation "is effective with regard to writing development," the authors of the York study advise:

> Having established that much, we can now go on to research what is effective, and to ask clearer and more pertinent questions about what works in the development of young people's literacy. (p. 5)

Meanwhile, what is the smart teacher to do?

What do smart teachers do about teaching grammar?

An obvious first question is, "What do you mean by a smart teacher?" In my opinion, smart teachers are those who, from research and experience,

- know kids and the different ways they learn best,
- know their subject, and
- know "best practice"—specifically, the best practices for accomplishing their instructional goals.

Smart teachers, in other words, operate from solid knowledge.

But I'd like to suggest that, at their best, smart teachers are also

- risk-takers and experimenters,
- innovators, and
- integrators within and across subject areas.

This means that smart teachers heed the research on teaching grammar in isolation. If their primary purpose for teaching grammar is to strengthen student writing, they do the best they can—under current political and administrative circumstances—to move away from teaching grammar in isolation and experiment instead with ways of teaching less grammar but teaching it more effectively for writing—often by drawing on literary and other published texts for examples and by incorporating selected aspects of grammar into the teaching of writing. Some smart teachers and language arts consultants are even affecting how grammar is taught in their schools—and in their states!

Grammar and good writing

Good writing is not produced by grammar study in isolation from writing, as research has shown again and again. In fact, George Hillocks (1986) found in his statistical analysis of research that the teaching of grammar as a method of improving writing actually had negative effects, perhaps mainly because it replaced time that teachers could have spent actually guiding students through the writing process. Historically, most students have not learned grammar well, fewer have remembered much after being tested on it, and fewer still have independently applied the relevant aspects of grammar study to their own writing. If improving writing is our primary goal, it's time for a major change in how we teach grammar.

—Excerpted and paraphrased from *Grammar to Enrich and Enhance Writing*, by Constance Weaver

---

Teaching certain kinds of grammatical constructions to enrich writing can strengthen students' writing by

- encouraging the addition of details (ideas) to make the writing more interesting;
- clarifying the relationships between and among ideas and enhancing organizational flow;
- helping create a particular style or voice; and
- promoting variety, fluency, and rhythm within sentences and paragraphs.

By first attending to such issues, we can help students produce pieces of writing that are worthy of being edited, proofread, and shared with an audience beyond just the teacher or just the teacher and classmates. In other words, as we help students edit their writing, we can also teach the grammar needed for understanding and applying the key conventions of grammar, usage (including word choices), punctuation, and spelling (the internal grammar of words) that are appropriate to purpose and audience. In the forthcoming *Grammar to Enrich and Enhance Writing*, attention to details, style/voice, and sentence fluency are generally considered to be part of *grammar to enrich writing*, while reserving the phrase *grammar to enhance writing* for attention to editing conventions. In this chapter I follow the same practice.

Attention to the various aspects of grammar and related skills can strengthen—to a greater or lesser degree—all six of the "6 traits of writing" that are commonly taught and addressed:

- Ideas
- Organization
- Voice
- Word choice
- Sentence fluency
- Conventions

See, for example, Ruth Culham's *6+1 Traits of Writing* (2003) and Vicki Spandel's *Creative Writers Through 6-Trait Assessment and Instruction* (2005). Whether phrased the same or not, whether separate or combined, the topics in many of the current rubrics for assessing writing—in state writing assessments and in standardized tests, as well as in local classrooms—are typically similar, and most can be addressed by selective attention to grammar during the process of writing.

Principles to guide the smart teaching of grammar for writing

Drawn from research and experience, the following observations about the teaching of grammar may be taken as principles to guide the smart teaching of grammar for improving writing. Because of the intended brevity of this [chapter], the principles are not discussed in much detail but simply offered for your consideration.

Ten observations and principles drawn from research, observation, and experience

1. Grammar taught in isolation from writing does not produce significant improvements in writing (with the exception of sentence combining, which is a technique for writing sentences, not teaching grammar). It is both more motivating and more practical to teach selected aspects of grammar in conjunction with the writing process by providing examples of good writing and mini-lessons, and by conferencing with students.

2. It is better to teach a few things repeatedly and well than a lot of grammatical terms that have little or no practical relevance to writing. Equally important: We must realize that by no means all the constructions that students use in their writing need to be taught. More and more students spontaneously demonstrate command of grammatical options when they have rich opportunities to read and discuss the craft of good literature.

> Whether phrased the same or not, whether separate or combined, the topics in many of the current rubrics for assessing writing...are typically similar, and most can be addressed by selective attention to grammar during the process of writing.

3. It is not realistic to expect students to master something that is taught just once. Many repetitions may be necessary, in different meaningful contexts and over several school months and years.

4. Whenever possible, students who have already mastered a construction or skill should be taught something they have not yet mastered rather than what other classmates still need to learn. Grammatical constructions, revision techniques, and editing skills should be taught as students are developmentally ready for them and have practical need for them, not according to an arbitrary scope-and-sequence chart.

5. Grammatical constructions and skills that are important for writing should be taught in conjunction with writing and reinforced over several grade levels, allowing for more and more students to achieve at least a reasonable level of competence in their use.

6. In many schools and classrooms, grammatical constructions and skills can be first taught at earlier grade levels than specified in the average scope-and-sequence chart. Early teaching to students who appear ready allows them to progress faster and offers the possibility of earlier "mastery," as well as greater progress toward mastery over time by more students.

7. Repeatedly teaching editing skills in conjunction with the editing process is more effective in producing independent application than teaching the skills in isolation (a variation of item 1). Marking up

> ## Grammar taught in isolation from writing does not produce significant improvements in writing.

student papers with corrections is not a productive way of teaching editing skills.

8. English language learners (those learning English as a second or subsequent language) should be taught ways of making their sentences more interesting, not just ways of making their sentences more correct. The same is true for other students who may need explicit help in using "standard" English forms when they edit and write.

9. When we teach the use of new kinds of grammatical constructions in writing, many students may at first make new kinds of errors. Their risk taking needs to be honored and celebrated for them to continue to progress. And then we need to reteach the concept as many times as necessary.

10. We teachers need to serve as role models, sharing our own drafts and revision/editing strategies as well as final pieces. Teacher-written models for imitation are also a strong motivator.

You might reread these principles, deciding which are the most important for guiding your own teaching of grammar in smarter and smarter ways.

References

Andrews, R., Togerson, C., Beverton, S., Locke, T., Low, G., Robinson, A., & Zhu, D. (2004b). The effect of grammar teaching (syntax) in English on 5 to 16 year olds' accuracy and quality in written composition. In *Research evidence in education library*. London, EPPI-Centre, Social Science Research Unit, Institute of Education.

Culham, R. (2003). *6 + 1 traits of writing: The complete guide grades 3 and up*. New York: Scholastic.

DiStefano, P., & Killion, J. (1984). Assessing writing skills through a process approach. *English Education, 16*, 203–209.

Hillocks, G., Jr. (1986). *Research on written composition: New directions for teaching*. Urbana, IL: National Council of Teachers of English.

McQuade, F. (1980). Examining a grammar course: The rationale and the result. *English Journal, 69*, 26–30.

Spandel, V. (2005). *Creative writers through 6-trait assessment and instruction*. Boston: Allyn & Bacon.

Excerpts From

Investigating Narrative Writing by 9–11-Year-Olds

Roger Beard and Andrew Burrell

Journal of Research in Reading, Volume 33, 2010, Pages 77–93.

Some previous work in the field

Large-scale studies in the United Kingdom and the United States have found total text length (word count) to be a crude but valid measure of writing development (e.g. Chall, Jacobs & Baldwin, 1990; Mortimore, Sammons, Stoll, Lewis & Ecob, 1988). Other studies of the development of the constituents of writing have included the influential work in the United States of Loban (1963) and Hunt (1965). In the United Kingdom, a substantial study by Harpin (1976) was also in this tradition. Harpin investigated samples of creative and factual writing from nearly 300 junior schoolchildren (7–11-year-olds) over six terms. The analysis focused on word counts, vocabulary and syntactical structures, providing indications of the general direction and rate of development in this age range. In a later paper, Harpin (1986) acknowledges the need for quantitative studies to be refined by the inclusion of broader textual assessments, which also take account of the situational demands made on the writer. Cameron & Besser (2004), investigating the writing skills of pupils for whom English is an additional language, analysed 264 scripts from 13 schools in eight Local Authorities in order to identify key features of language that pupils learning English as an additional language appeared to handle less confidently than English mother tongue speakers. Other studies have examined the occurrence of specific features, such as subordination in different genres of children's writing (Allison, Beard & Willcocks, 2002) and features of sentence structure in different key stages (Hudson, 2009).

None of these studies, however, has used repeat designs and standardised tasks that allow developments in specific constituents of writing to be investigated over a specific timescale. The study reported in this paper addresses this gap in the literature on writing through a rigorous analysis of children's narrative writing at the end of the primary school age range. The core research questions were as follows: what features are found in Year 5 narrative writing? How does the profile of features change when the same writing tasks are undertaken in Year 6?

Methods

Design

A repeat design was used. The National Foundation for Educational Research *Literacy Impact Test B* was administered to 112 Year 5 children near the end of the spring term and again 1 year later. The test comprises a 10-minute persuasive description writing task and a 30-minute narrative writing task (both continuous prose), using content that is likely to appeal equally to boys and girls: an advertisement for a new dessert and a narrative about a surprise reward, in the form of a gift, from collecting cereal tokens. Both tasks are supported with teacher introductions that are set out in the *Literacy Impact Teachers' Guide* (Twist & Brill, 2000).

Participants

The participants were all the Year 5 pupils (60 boys, 52 girls) from five schools representing a range of socioeconomic catchments from two English Local Authorities.

Results

Quantitative data

Both the mean and the median of the *Literacy Impact* raw scores increased between Year 5 and Year 6 (see Table 2).

TABLE 2. Summary statistics for Year 5 and Year 6 *Literacy Impact* tests

	Year 5 (n = III)	Year 6 (n = II2)
Mean	15.80	19.07
Median	14.00	19.00

Of the 111 pupils in the sample who completed the tasks in both years, 27 (24.3%) achieved a lower score in the second year, 13 (11.7%) showed no change and 71 (64.0%) showed an improvement in their score. The proportion achieving a lower score in Year 6 may appear surprising. However, when the 13 highest gain children are compared with the 15 children whose scores had decreased the most, the mean differences for the scores on the tests as a whole were 13.5 and 6.1, respectively. Of the 15 children whose scores had decreased, the range was smaller, 3–11, compared with a range of 11–19 in the 13 highest gain children. Eight of the 15 came from one class, perhaps indicating that the narrative task had been rushed for some reason.

Two of these children had only managed to write an introductory, albeit reasonably coherent, paragraph.

Table 3 shows that, across the sample as a whole, there was an improvement in all categories.

TABLE 3. Mean score in each category for Year 5 and Year 6 (*n* = III for Year 5 and II2 for Year 6)

Category	Mean score for Year 5	Mean score for Year 6
Purpose and organisation	4.66	5.54
Grammar, vocabulary, style	3.28	3.87
Punctuation	1.26	1.94
Spelling	1.71	1.96
Handwriting	1.35	1.57

Qualitative data

Given the current concern about writing that was referred to earlier, this section will report some of the findings that illustrate narrative features in which there were significant developments. In order to provide some 'conceptual calibration', this section will also report and briefly summarise and illustrate the features that characterised the texts of the high and low attainment subgroups.

Table 4 summarises the features that generally characterised the texts of the high attainment subsample.

TABLE 4. Imaginative narrative: what characterised high attainment?

Textual element	Features
Overall effectiveness of imaginative narrative	Consistent narrative structure Frequent use of dialogue Series of paragraphs
Content	Attention to the specified story prompt Focus on Alex's [main character] anticipation and subsequent reaction to the free gift
Language use	Third person/past tense used consistently Dialogue in different tense Stylistic choices used to draw the reader into events Appropriate and adventurous vocabulary to emphasise actions, thoughts, and feelings
Other	Length often about 300 words Handwriting joined and usually fluent Punctuation reasonably secure

Table 5 summarises the features that generally characterised low attainment in narrative texts.

TABLE 5. Imaginative narrative: what characterised consistently low attainment?

Textual element	Features
Overall effectiveness of imaginative narrative	Limited information about setting and characters Little attempt to organise the narrative into paragraphs No/limited use of dialogue Incomplete/rather abrupt ending
Content	Lack of attention to specified story prompt
Language use	Third person/past tense used inconsistently Only time-related connectives
Other	Length often below 200 words Handwriting a mixture of print and joined Punctuation often missing/limited in use

When the texts of the 13 children in the 'high gains' subsample were considered, a range of features and explanations were evident. It is also interesting to note that all five schools were represented in this subsample. Where characterisations could be derived, they are shown in Table 6.

TABLE 6. Imaginative narrative: what characterised high gains?

Textual element	Features
Overall effectiveness of imaginative narrative	More features of narrative structure (e.g. initial setting with sequence of events in chronological order) Greater use of paragraphing More direct speech More developed interaction between characters
Content	Improved attention to specified story prompt Greater focus on Alex's reaction to the gift
Language use	Third person/past tense used more consistently Greater use of connectives Vocabulary used more to emphasise action, thoughts or feelings
Other	Increase in word length Improved handwriting—mostly joined and fluent Improved and increased use of punctuation

Discussion

This study is, to the best of our knowledge, the first to have used a repeat design and standardised tasks that allow developments in specific constituents of primary schoolchildren's writing to be investigated over a specific timescale. The data reported here provide some indications of the features of children's narrative writing in the 9–11 age range and how these changed over a 12-month period in which the five schools all reported following the same national curriculum and national strategy guidance. Given the circumstances of the test administration, it seems unlikely that any of the schools provided any specific preparation or support for the writing tasks used in the study. The range of individuality of the texts seems to bear this out.

While the raw data from the *Literacy Impact* and technical accuracy ratings provided some indications of development (Beard, Burrell, Swinnerton & Pell, 2007), a more specific range of results were found from the use of the genre-specific rating scale that was an original part of this project. The use of this scale provided indications of development in the children's writing that could not be ascertained from the use of more numerical or impressionistic judgements. Looking across the sample as a whole, the findings reflected a substantial amount of significant data capture. As well as reflecting

> It may also be testimony to the teaching that the children had experienced that, in the 12 months between the two tasks, they had learned to translate greater attention into clear evidence of purpose, through attempts to engage the reader.

positively on a range of dimensions of pupil learning, the data may be of value in replication studies and could in time contribute to international comparative studies, when cultural and cross-national issues might be addressed. It may also be testimony to the teaching that the children had experienced that, in the 12 months between the two tasks, they had learned to translate greater attention into clear evidence of purpose, through attempts to engage the reader. This engagement was extended into portraying key events from the main character's point of view, allocating more narrative structure to the main event and elaborating on the resolution through dialogue. More specifically, there was greater use of action to develop character and main event, connectives to inject suspense, exclamations for impact, adventurous vocabulary to add interest and verbs to emphasise action, thoughts or feelings.

Overall the findings provide evidence of the multiplicity of narrative techniques used by the children in the sample and the variation in the means by which development was achieved. Nearly all the texts contained elements of individuality and many of the children in the sample had drawn upon considerable ingenuity in the 30 minutes that they had for the task. This was evident in the qualitative analysis.

The qualitative analysis of the subsamples also underlines the large range of attainment that is evident in this age range. Comparison of the texts of accomplished writers…with those of children…clearly struggling with written language at a number of levels, underlines the challenges that teachers face. Such comparisons could be used to support the greater use of layered curriculum provision and early interventions that have recently been endorsed across the principal UK political parties (Gross, 2008).

> Nearly all the texts contained elements of individuality and many of the children in the sample had drawn upon considerable ingenuity in the 30 minutes that they had for the task.

The immediate contribution of this paper may be to add to what is known about narrative development in primary and elementary schoolchildren. It may also contribute to practice, although not by using the identified features of narrative as notional curriculum content to be applied in practice tasks…. Rather, the findings from the study may add to the language of literacy, especially in informing dialogue between teachers and learners and perhaps, in time, between learners and learners. If the latter is achieved, then the study may further contribute to what Bereiter and Scardamalia (1987) have suggested is a key issue in writing development—reading with a writer's alertness to technique.

References

Allison, P., Beard, R. & Willcocks, J. (2002). Subordination in children's writing. *Language and Education, 16*(2), 97–111.

Beard, R., Burrell, A., Swinnerton, B. & Pell, G. (2007). Investigating development in writing in 9–11 year olds. In M. Conrick & M. Howard (Eds.), *From applied linguistics to linguistics applied: Issues, practices, trends. British studies in applied linguistics.* (Vol. 22, pp. 56–75). University of Birmingham, British Association for Applied Linguistics.

Bereiter, C. & Scardamalia, M. (1987). *The psychology of written composition.* Hillsdale, NJ: Lawrence Erlbaum.

Cameron, L. & Besser, S. (2004). *Writing in English as an additional language at Key Stage 2*. Research Report RR586. London: Department for Education and Skills.

Chall, J., Jacobs, V. A. & Baldwin, L.E. (1990). *The reading crisis: Why poor children fall behind*. Cambridge, MA: Harvard University Press.

Gross, J. (Ed.) (2008). *Getting in early: Primary schools and early intervention*. London: The Smith Institute/ The Centre for Social Justice.

Harpin, W. (1976). *The second R: Writing development in the junior school*. London: Allen and Unwin.

Harpin, W. (1986). Writing counts. In A. Wilkinson (Ed.), *The writing of writing*. (pp. 158–176). London: Open University Press.

Hudson, R. (2009). Measuring maturity. In R. Beard, D. Myhill, J. Riley & M. Nystrand (Eds.), *Handbook of writing development*. (pp. 349–362). London: Sage.

Hunt, K.W. (1965). *Grammatical structures written at three grade levels*. Research Report No. 3. Champaign, IL: National Council of Teachers of English.

Loban, W. (1963). *The language of elementary school children. NCTE Research Report No.1*. Champaign, IL: National Council of Teachers of English.

Mortimore, P., Sammons, P., Stoll, L., Lewis, D. & Ecob, R. (1988). *School matters: The junior years*. Wells: Open Books.

Twist, L. & Brill, F. (2000). *Literacy impact*. Slough: National Foundation for Educational Research.

Excerpts From

Teaching Argument Writing to 7- to 14-Year-Olds: An International Review of the Evidence of Successful Practice

Richard Andrews, Carole Torgerson, Graham Low, and Nick McGuinn

Cambridge Journal of Education, Volume 39, 2009, Pages 291–310.

Abstract

A systematic review was undertaken in 2006 to answer the question 'What is the evidence for successful practice in teaching and learning with regard to non-fiction writing (specifically argumentational writing) for 7- to 14-year-olds?', using EPPI-Centre methodology. Results showed that certain conditions have to be in place. These include: a writing process model in which students are encouraged to plan, draft, edit and revise their writing; some degree of cognitive reasoning training in addition to natural cognitive development; peer collaboration, thus modelling a dialogue that will become internal and constitute 'thought'; and explicit explanations of the learning processes. Specific strategies include: 'heuristics'; planning; oral argument, counterargument and rebuttal to inform written argument; explicit goals (including audiences) for writing; teacher modelling of argumentational writing; and 'procedural facilitation'. This article confirms the results of the 2006 study in the light of recent research. Implications for policy, practice and further research are considered.

Review question and methods

Research question, scope and inclusion criteria

The core research question for the 2006 review was: 'What is the evidence for successful practice in teaching and learning with regard to non-fiction writing (specifically argumentational writing) for 7- to 14-year-olds?'

The review question looked for evidence of successful practice in teaching and learning with regard to argumentational non-fiction writing for 7- to 14-year-olds. Therefore the relevant literature included studies that could be used to draw causal inferences, i.e., inferences that various practices (strategies and methods) in the teaching and learning of argumentational non-fiction writing can improve pupils' nonfiction writing.

Case studies, explorations of relationships and other non-experimental designs were included only where there was an evaluation.

TABLE I. Main characteristics and overall weights of evidence of studies included in the synthesis

Author, date, country	Study design	Age of participants	Overall weight of evidence
Englert *et al.* 1991 USA	RCT	9–11 (Grades 4 and 5)	High
Ferretti *et al.* 2000 USA	RCT	9–12 (Grades 4 and 6)	High
De La Paz and Graham 1997 USA	RCT	10–13 (Grades 5, 6 and 7)	High to medium
Troia and Graham 2002 USA	RCT	9–11 (Grades 4 and 5)	High to medium
De La Paz and Graham 2002 USA	RCT	12–14 (Grades 7 and 8)	Medium to high
Graham *et al.* 2005 USA	RCT	8–9 (Grade 3)	Medium to high
Crowhurst 1990 Canada	RCT	11–12 (Grade 6)	Medium
Knudson 1991 USA	RCT	9–13 (Grades 4, 6 and 8)	Medium
Knudson 1992, 1994 USA	RCT	8–11 (Grades 3 and 5)	Medium
Reznitskaya *et al.* 2001 USA	CT	9–11 (Grades 4 and 5)	Medium
Yeh 1998 USA	CT	12–13 (Grade 7)	Medium

[**NOTE:** RCT = randomized controlled trial; CT = controlled trial.]

Table 1 shows the main characteristics of the studies included in the synthesis, ranked by their overall weights of evidence. All six studies rated 'medium to high' or above were randomized controlled trials. Three of the five studies rated 'medium' were randomized controlled trials and two were controlled trials.

Summary of results

From consideration of the eleven studies in the 2006 review, it appeared that certain conditions were either assumed or had to be in place to create a climate for successful practice. Recent research simply reinforces the position set out here. Overall then, these conditions are not specific to argumentational writing but include:

- A writing process model in which students are encouraged to plan, draft, edit and revise their writing (De La Paz & Graham, 2002; Englert *et al.*, 1991; Troia & Graham, 2002).
- Self-motivation (in the form of personal target-setting—one aspect of self-regulated strategy development) (Graham *et al.*, 2005).
- Some degree of cognitive reasoning training in addition to the natural cognitive development that takes place with maturation (Englert *et al.*, 1991; Ferretti *et al.*, 2000), for example the self-

regulated strategy development suggested by Mason and Shriner (2008).

- Peer collaboration, thus modelling a dialogue that (it is hoped) will become internal and constitute 'thought' (Englert *et al*. 1991).
- Explicit and very clear explanations for students of the processes to be learned, though there is a suggestion in Reznitskaya *et al*. (2001) that these are less important than peer discussion.

More specifically and more relevantly to the present article, a number of strategies were identified in the 2006 review that have contributed to successful practice in teaching and learning with regard to argumentational writing for 7- to 14-year-olds. They have been supported by recently published articles:

- 'Heuristics', i.e., scaffolding of structures and devices that aid the composition of argumentational writing—in particular, planning, which can include examining a question, brainstorming, organizing and sequencing ideas and evaluating (De La Paz & Graham, 1997, 2002; Englert *et al.*, 1991; Troia & Graham, 2002). Planning that is extensive, elaborated and hierarchical can make for more effective argumentational drafting and completion of essays (De La Paz & Graham, 2002). Yeh (1998) used heuristics based on Toulmin (1958) and classical rhetoric.
- The use of oral argument, counterargument and rebuttal to inform written argument (De la Paz & Graham 1997; Reznitskaya *et al.* 2001).
- The identification of explicit goals (including audiences) for writing (Ferretti *et al.*, 2000, Midgette, Haria, & MacArthur, 2008).
- Teacher modelling of argumentational writing (Englert *et al.*, 1991).
- 'Procedural facilitation', i.e., coaching by the teacher through the process of writing argument (De La Paz & Graham, 2002).

Discussion and implications
Recent research literature

Since the technical report of our review was completed three other experimental research studies, that we are aware of, have been published. …The foci of these three studies are: social and cognitive processes underlying the development of argumentational knowledge (Reznitskaya, Anderson, & Kuo, 2007); the effects of content and audience awareness goals for revision of persuasive essays (Midgette *et al.*, 2008); and self-regulated strategy development instruction for writing an opinion essay (Mason & Shriner, 2008).

Strengths and limitations

The recent research reinforces, in a limited way, some of the findings of the 2006 review, as detailed above. There are both strengths and limitations to our study. First, our focus in the 2006 review was tightly on *effective* and successful practice in the teaching of argumentational writing for 7- to 14-year-olds, with a consequent emphasis on randomized and controlled trials. Although confining ourselves to experimental research enables us to address an effectiveness question, there is little description in these articles of the contextual factors that make for a successful writing climate, though we *have* identified key conditions that have to be in place to make writing pedagogy stick. We would argue, though, that the tight focus and subsequent identification of these conditions and of writing heuristics makes an original contribution to knowledge on the topic of argumentational writing, albeit via review and synthesis. Second, we acknowledge that all the studies discussed originate in the US, with the exception of one from Canada. Transferability to the curricular and school context in England should not be taken for granted. However, we think it is important to learn from studies undertaken overseas where it is possible to identify successful practice.

Practice

Further development of practice with regard to the teaching and learning of argumentational writing must take on board what has been said above about the links between conditions for learning and specific 'heuristics' for improving such writing. To use a gardening metaphor, the ground needs to be well prepared for new practices to take root, and for sustained and vigorous growth to take place within a framed curriculum plan.

Our knowledge of textbooks and practices in the field suggests that few programmes for teaching argument address both aspects of the problem. The 'critical thinking' movement has spawned a variety of approaches, as have innovations in learning styles and strategies. Neither of these traditions has been linked specifically to the teaching of argumentational writing in English, nor across the curriculum. There has also been little in the way of transfer of argumentational skills across the transition from primary to secondary schools in the UK.

There is every indication, however, that practitioners and policy makers working within the context of the National Curriculum for

English in England would be receptive to the recommendations made in this study. The genre-based approach to English pedagogy introduced with the National Literacy Strategy in the final years of the twentieth century challenged the perceived dominance of narrative within the classroom by encouraging a focus upon so-called non-fictional genres such as 'discursive writing'. The genre-based approach also brought with it an explicit concern not only for the ways in which texts are structured but also for how they seek to position their readers at word, sentence and whole text level.

Most significantly, perhaps, 'argument' is now firmly embedded within the assessment procedures of the English National Curriculum than it was in earlier versions of the National Curriculum. At Key Stage 3, for example, several of the Assessment Focuses for EN3 (Writing) examine pupils' ability to attend to 'deep' and 'surface' structural features of their writing, with a particular emphasis upon 'composition'

> **Planning that is extensive, elaborated and hierarchical can make for more effective argumentational drafting and completion of essays.**

and the ability to gauge requirements of audience and purpose. Typical national examination assignments at Key Stages 3 (when statutory tests were still in operation) and 4 might be to argue a case for the retention of a public park as a recreational space for young people, to write a letter to a head teacher, arguing for a change in a school's curriculum, or to write in role as a character from a play by Shakespeare, urging a particular course of action. For EN1 (Speaking and Listening) assessment, pupils might be encouraged—and again this is an effective strategy highlighted by the 2006 report—to work as a team on the creation of a poster designed to argue a particular case.

In terms of 'curriculum backwash', this shift in assessment focus has encouraged a corresponding classroom emphasis upon the structures and strategies associated with argumentational writing. At a lexical and syntactical level, for example, pupils might be taught how to use a 'discursive marker' such as the word 'however' within a sentence. They might be encouraged to learn and consolidate argumentational strategies through the acquisition of mnemonics such as 'a forest': *alliteration, facts, opinion, repetition, emotive language* and *three (rule of)*.

Practitioners—particularly those new to teaching—need the kind of guidance that this study can give on how to model good argumentational writing practice themselves, on how to coach their pupils in the most effective and proven writing procedures and on how to establish engaging learning opportunities in which the skills of written argument

142

might be developed and incrementally honed across the key stages and across all four modalities currently defined as constituting 'English'.

Conclusion

In the light of continued problems with writing performance in England, particularly at ages 7–11, and specifically with argumentational writing because of its conceptual and structural demands, we feel that the results of the 2006 review and consideration of more recent studies are significant. The key finding is that there is a need to distinguish between the conditions that have to be in place for successful writing of argument on the one hand; and the writing heuristics that are successful in these conditions on the other. We therefore feel we have gone some way to identifying the context for successful argumentational writing, though admit there is more work to do on defining the range of nature of these contexts.

References

Crowhurst, M. (1990). Teaching and learning the writing of persuasive/ argumentative discourse. *Canadian Journal of Education, 15,* 348–359.

De La Paz, S., & Graham, S. (1997). Effects of dictation and advanced planning instruction on the composing of students with writing and learning problems. *Journal of Educational Psychology, 89,* 203–222.

De La Paz, S., & Graham, S. (2002). Explicitly teaching strategies, skills, and knowledge: Writing instruction in middle school classrooms. *Journal of Educational Psychology, 94,* 687–698.

Englert, C.S., Raphael, T.M., Anderson, L.M., Anthony, H.M., & Stevens, D.D. (1991). Making strategies and self-talk visible: Writing instruction in regular and special education classrooms. *American Educational Research Journal, 28,* 337–372.

Ferretti, R.P., MacArthur, C.A., & Dowdy, N.S. (2000). The effects of an elaborated goal on the persuasive writing of students with learning disabilities and their normally achieving peers. *Journal of Educational Psychology, 92,* 694–702.

Graham, S., Harris, K.R., & Mason, L. (2005). Improving the writing performance, knowledge, and self-efficacy of struggling young writers: The effects of self-regulated strategy development. *Contemporary Educational Psychology, 30,* 207–241.

Knudson, R.E. (1991). Effects of instructional strategies, grade, and sex on students' persuasive writing. *Journal of Experimental Education, 59,* 141–152.

Knudson, R.E. (1992). *An analysis of persuasive discourse: Learning how to take a stand.* Paper presented at the Annual Meeting of the National Reading Conference, San Antonio, TA. ERIC document ED353581.

Knudson, R.E. (1994). An analysis of persuasive discourse: Learning how to take a stand. *Discourse Processes, 18,* 211–230.

Mason, L.M., & Shriner, J.G. (2008). Self-regulated strategy development instruction for writing an opinion essay: Effects for six students with emotional/behavior disorders. *Reading and Writing: An Interdisciplinary Journal, 21*(1–2), 71–93.

Midgette, E., Haria, P., & MacArthur, C. (2008). The effect of content and audience awareness goals for revision on the persuasive essays of fifth- and eighth-grade students. *Reading and Writing: An Interdisciplinary Journal, 21*(1–2), 131–151.

Reznitskaya, A., Anderson, R., & Kuo, L.J. (2007). Teaching and learning argumentation. *Elementary School Journal, 17*(5), 449–472.

Reznitskaya, A., Anderson, R.C., McNurlen, B., Nguyen Jahiel, K., Archodidou, A., & Kim, S. (2001). Influence of oral discussion on written argument. *Discourse Processes, 32,* 155–175.

Toulmin, S. (1958). *The uses of argument.* Cambridge: Cambridge University Press.

Troia, G.A., & Graham, S. (2002). The effectiveness of a highly explicit, teacher-directed strategy instruction routine: Changing the writing performance of students with learning disabilities. *Journal of Learning Disabilities, 35,* 290–305.

Yeh, S.S. (1998). Empowering education: Teaching argumentational writing to cultural minority middle-school students. *Research in the Teaching of English, 33,* 49–83.

Excerpts From

Writing Development in Four Genres from Grades Three to Seven: Syntactic Complexity and Genre Differentiation

Scott F. Beers and William E. Nagy

Reading & Writing, Volume 24, 2011, Pages 183–202.

Introduction

To succeed in school, students must be able to read and write in a variety of genres. Written language itself, even in the simplest texts beginning readers encounter, differs substantially from spoken language in its structure; so at its outset, learning to write necessarily involves the acquisition of a new genre. However, written language does not consist of a single genre. Even in the elementary grades, students are at least implicitly required to distinguish among narratives, descriptions, and an increasing range of expository genres, including explanation, persuasion, and compare/contrast.

Of course, young children can recognize and produce a variety of genres in oral language (Hudson & Shapiro, 1991; Purcell-Gates, 1988). However, facility in understanding and producing written genres is acquired gradually, and for many students, only with difficulty (Snow & Uccelli, 2009). Part of the difficulty students face may stem from the relative paucity of exposure to informational texts, at least in the primary grades (Christie, 1987; Duke, 2000). However, exposure to informational texts alone is likely not sufficient for a student to become a skilled reader and writer of academic genres. Students must also learn the communicative purposes of different genres, along with their organizational structures. Additionally, students must acquire the linguistic resources to compose in academic genres, including the use of more sophisticated word forms and syntactic structures (Berman, 2009). Certain syntactic structures, such as subordinate clauses, relative clauses, and complex noun phrases allow writers to express more complex ideas.

Despite the relative lack of syntax-focused instruction in current writing curricula, students do seem to acquire the ability to compose more complex sentences and clauses. Research on syntactic complexity has shown that students use increasingly complex syntactic structures as they gain familiarity and skill with school-related writing (Reilly, Zamora, & McGivern, 2005; Schleppegrell, 2004). However, little research has focused on how this development occurs during early grade levels and in different text genres (Purcell-Gates, 1988; Tower, 2003), and when different genres are compared, they usually focus only on narratives and expository texts (Berman & Nir-Sagiv, 2007; Berman & Verhoeven, 2002; Crowhurst, 1980; Stewart & Grobe, 1979). Descriptive texts are rarely included (for an exception, see Crowhurst & Piche, 1979), and compare/contrast texts have not, to our knowledge, been included in studies comparing the development of syntactic complexity. This study replicates and extends previous research by exploring the development of syntactic complexity in student writing from grades three, five, and seven in four common school-related genres: narrative, descriptive, compare/contrast, and persuasive essay.

Later syntactic development

This study focuses upon the syntactic level of linguistic and discursive literacy development, using two well-established measures of syntactic complexity to examine differences across four genres at three grade levels. These measures, words per clause and clauses per T-unit, serve as broader measures of syntactic complexity than other approaches, and using them offers several advantages. First, measures of syntactic complexity have proven to be sensitive to genre differences for adolescent writers (Beers & Nagy, 2009; Crowhurst & Piche, 1979) and elementary-age students (Scott & Windsor, 2000). As this study includes writers as young as eight, who are not likely to use sophisticated linguistic devices such as nominalizations, participles, and past perfect forms (which typically emerge in high school), broader syntax measures are more likely to detect emerging differences for younger writers. Second, using these measures situates this study within the long trajectory of research on syntactic complexity, allowing for replication, clarification, and expansion of previous findings. Third, these measures of syntactic complexity are still considered reliable indices of syntactic density (Berman, 2009).

> **Despite the relative lack of syntax-focused instruction in current writing curricula, students do seem to acquire the ability to compose more complex sentences and clauses.**

Young writers, syntax, and genre

As explained earlier, beginning writers need to acquire a first strand of linguistic literacy, and developing writers, a second strand of discursive literacy, which involves using more advanced linguistic resources in genre-appropriate ways. Genres are viewed as socially constructed language practices serving specific social purposes (Halliday & Hasan, 1985), each of which may differ in their micro-level aspects (linguistic features) as well as their macro-level characteristics (overall organizational principles and text structures) to express different ways of making meaning. Children develop an initial sensitivity to genre differences at a young age. For example, primary grade children can distinguish between storytelling and pretend play (Benson, 1993), and between fictional narratives and descriptions (Tolchinsky & Sandbank, 1994). Additionally, several research studies have found that primary-age students can produce oral language samples that demonstrate basic levels of genre differentiation (Duke & Kays, 1998; Pappas 1991, 1993; Purcell-Gates, 1988).

> **Student writers also appear to differentiate between genres in their compositions, especially when the linguistic features of narrative and non-narrative (expository) genres are compared.**

Student writers also appear to differentiate between genres in their compositions, especially when the linguistic features of narrative and non-narrative (expository) genres are compared. Compared to narratives, expository texts composed by student writers have been reported to have longer clauses (Malvern, Richards, Chipere, & Duran, 2004), more complex noun phrases (Ravid & Berman, 2010), more nominalized forms (Schleppegrell, 2004), more relative and adverbial clauses (Scott & Windsor, 2000; Scott, 2004), and more passive voice constructions (Reilly et al., 2005). Few of these marked syntactic structures are used by younger school-aged students; many are only mastered in high school or later (Berman & Nir-Sagiv, 2007). At younger ages, students appear to differentiate between narrative and expository genres on the syntactic level, with differences in clauses per T-unit emerging as early as age nine and in words per clause by age twelve (Crowhurst & Piche, 1979; Scott & Windsor, 2000).

Based on previous research, we hypothesized that the persuasive essays, with the subordinating devices required for argumentation, would have more clauses per T-unit than the other three genres being examined at each grade, although we expected that these differences would become more pronounced with each grade as students acquire more syntactic resources. For words per clause, we expected that the clause-lengthening devices such as attributive adjectives and prepositional phrases would be more apparent in the descriptive and compare/contrast texts, at least at grades five and seven, than in the persuasive essays and narratives. Since clause-lengthening structures used in essays tend to develop in later grades, we hypothesized that the persuasive essays would be similar to the narratives at each grade level, but that the descriptive and compare/contrast texts would have more words per clause than persuasive essays at grades five and seven.

Method

This analysis was part of a five-year longitudinal study of writing and its connections with reading and oral language development. Phase two (in progress) has focused upon linguistic analyses of experimenter-designed writing tasks to assess different genres of writing at different levels of language and transcription modes.

Procedures

The study was conducted at a university laboratory in the Pacific Northwest. Each year, participants were brought to the university to complete a variety of reading, writing, and other language-related assessments.

Writing tasks

Students composed texts in four school-related genres (narrative, descriptive, compare/contrast, and persuasive essay). All student texts were handwritten upon a sheet of paper with the title of the text (indicating the genre) at the top.

Coding and scoring

The primary data sources for this study were the texts from Cohort 1 (grades three and five) and Cohort 2 (grades five and seven). Each text was coded for three linguistic variables; overall text length in words, T-unit boundaries, and clause boundaries. Clauses and T-units were defined using the criteria set by Hunt (1965). Non-finite constructions (such as gerunds and participles) were not coded as separate clauses.

Results

Clauses per T-unit

The simple contrasts between genres showed that persuasive essays had more clauses per T-unit than the narratives at each grade level (all p values < .001), the descriptive texts at each grade level (all p values < .001), and the compare/contrast texts at each grade level (all p values < .001) (Table 4).

TABLE 4. Tests of simple contrasts for clauses per T-unit: persuasive versus other genres

Cohort	Grade	Genre contrast					
		Persuasive/narrative		Persuasive/descriptive		Persuasive/comp/con	
		F	p	F	p	F	p
I	3	57.85	.000	58.82	.000	40.77	.000
I	5	116.00	.000	215.47	.000	110.28	.000
2	5	138.43	.000	169.52	.000	125.97	.000
2	7	143.28	.000	141.53	.000	95.01	.000

Words per clause

The simple contrasts showed that the persuasive texts had fewer words per clause than the narratives at grade seven ($p < .001$), with the differences approaching significance at grade five ($p = .007$ for cohort one, and $p = .003$ for cohort two). The persuasive texts also had fewer words per clause than the descriptive texts at all grade levels ($p = .004$ for grade three, for grades five and seven all p values $< .001$). There were no differences found between the persuasive texts and the compare/contrast texts for words per clause (Table 5).

TABLE 5. Tests of simple contrasts for words per clause: persuasive versus other genres

Cohort	Grade	Genre contrast					
		Persuasive/narrative		Persuasive/descriptive		Persuasive/comp/con	
		F	p	F	p	F	p
I	3	.13	.722	8.88	.004	.19	.667
I	5	7.68	.007	45.92	.000	.01	.937
2	5	9.22	.003	34.22	.000	.18	.674
2	7	34.24	.000	41.59	.000	4.67	.033

Text length in words

For the simple contrasts, the difference between the persuasive essays and narratives was not significant at third grade, but was significant at fifth grade for both cohorts ($p = .001$ for cohort one, $p < .001$ for cohort two), and at seventh grade ($p < .001$). The difference between persuasive essays and descriptive texts was significant only for seventh grade ($p < .001$). The difference between persuasive essays and compare/contrast texts was significant for both cohorts at all grade levels ($p = .001$ for grade three, all ps $< .001$ for grades five and seven) (Table 6).

TABLE 6. Tests of simple contrasts for text length in words: persuasive versus other genres

Cohort	Grade	Genre contrast					
		Persuasive/narrative		Persuasive/descriptive		Persuasive/comp/con	
		F	p	F	p	F	p
1	3	1.836	.179	1.920	.169	11.902	.001
1	5	12.386	.001	8.139	.005	33.420	.000
2	5	16.627	.000	.661	.418	76.220	.000
2	7	55.276	.000	44.024	.000	54.891	.000

Qualitative analyses

To gain more insight into the main effects of genre for these measures, and to identify cases to illustrate these findings, we re-examined selected subsets of the data, identifying students who had typical values for each variable—within a standard deviation and a half of the mean—but who also showed a large difference in syntactic complexity between the non-narrative genres. In the case of clauses per T-unit, we were interested in finding out how and why students used greater subordination in persuasive essays than in the other genres. In the case of words per clause, we paid special attention to identifying what clause-lengthening constructions were used by students.

Conclusion

We found that the third-, fifth-, and seventh-grade students in our study did, for the most part, make distinctions among the four genres examined, in ways that showed up clearly for two measures of syntactic complexity. These broad measures of syntactic complexity provided a lens through which differences in student writing across genres could be viewed, and helped us identify examples of these differences in syntax use. Clearly, there is more research to be done, to identify more specifically the genre-specific syntactic constructions required by school-based writing and how students acquire them.

> We found that the third-, fifth-, and seventh-grade students in our study did, for the most part, make distinctions among the four genres examined, in ways that showed up clearly for two measures of syntactic complexity.

Grammar, Genre, and Skills

Consistent with previous research, students at these grade levels used relatively few clause-lengthening constructions characteristic of *linguistic literacy,* many of which appear to be acquired in high school or later. Notably, these students appeared to recognize the different communicative purposes associated with each genre, which indicates some development of *discursive literacy.* However, their ability to write effectively in them (especially compare/contrast and persuasive texts) was likely compromised by their limited knowledge of the syntactic structures needed to carry out these communicative purposes effectively.

If so, these findings raise several compelling questions. First, what accounts for the relatively slow acquisition of genre-appropriate syntactic constructions? There are at least three possibilities, all of which may influence students' developmental trajectories. One possibility may be that there are cognitive limitations upon students at younger ages, such that students are not fully capable of creating adequate mental representations of the discourse types they are asked to write (Berman & Nir-Sagiv, 2007). If so, students may have sufficient linguistic resources to compose academic texts, but lack the ability to marshal these resources to meet the organizational and communicative demands of the specific genre. A second possibility may be that most students' linguistic capacities simply develop along a relatively slow trajectory that, with few exceptions, prevents them from using more complex syntactic structures until high school, even if they understand clearly the structure and purpose of the genres assigned. A third possibility, however, may involve the instructional approaches used to teach writing in different genres. Should syntax be taught as a school subject? Would genre-specific writing instruction that included a focus upon the syntactic tools required perhaps accelerate the acquisition of these syntactic structures? If so, how might this be instruction be combined with authentic literacy practices?

> Notably, these students appeared to recognize the different communicative purposes associated with each genre, which indicates some development of *discursive literacy.*

References

Beers, S. F., & Nagy, W. E. (2009). Syntactic complexity as a predictor of adolescent writing quality: Which measures? Which genre? *Reading and Writing: An Interdisciplinary Journal, 22,* 185–200.

Benson, M. S. (1993). 4-and 5-year olds' narratives in pretend play and storytelling. *First Language, 13,* 203–224.

Berman, R. A. (2009). Developing linguistic knowledge and language use across adolescence. In E. Hoff & M. Shatz (Eds.), *Blackwell handbook of language development* (pp. 347–367). Malden, MA: Wiley-Blackwell.

Berman, R. A., & Nir-Sagiv, B. (2007). Comparing narrative and expository text construction across adolescence: A developmental paradox. *Discourse Processes, 43,* 79–120.

Berman, R. A., & Verhoeven, L. (2002). Developing text-production abilities across languages, genre, and modality. *Written Languages and Literacy, 5,* 1–22.

Christie, F. (1987). Genres as choice. In I. Reid (Ed.), *The place of genre in learning: Current debates* (pp. 22–34). Geelong, VIC, Australia: Deakin University Centre for Studies in Literary Education.

Crowhurst, M. (1980). Syntactic complexity and teachers' quality ratings of narrations and arguments. *Research in the Teaching of English, 14,* 223–231.

Crowhurst, M., & Piche, G. L. (1979). Audience and mode of discourse effects on syntactic complexity in writing at two grade levels. *Research in the Teaching of English, 13,* 101–109.

Duke, N. K. (2000). 3.6 Minutes per day: The scarcity of informational texts in first grade. *Reading Research Quarterly, 35,* 202–224.

Duke, N. K., & Kays, J. (1998). Can I say 'Once upon a time?': Kindergarten children's developing knowledge of information book language. *Early Childhood Research Quarterly, 13,* 295–318.

Halliday, M. A. K., & Hasan, R. (1985). *Language, context, and text: Aspects of language in social-semiotic perspective.* Geelong, VIC, Australia: Deakin University Press.

Hudson, J. A., & Shapiro, L. R. (1991). From knowing to telling: The development of children's scripts, stories, and personal narratives. In A. McCabe & C. Peterson (Eds.), *Developing narrative structure* (pp. 89–135). Hillsdale, NJ: Lawrence Erlbaum Associates, Inc.

Hunt, K. W. (1965). *Grammatical structures written in three grade levels.* Research report no. 3. National Council of Teachers of English, Champaign, IL.

Malvern, D. D., Richards, B. J., Chipere, N., & Duran, P. (2004). *Lexical diversity and language development: Quantification and assessment.* Basingstoke, Hampshire: Palgrave Macmillan.

Pappas, C. C. (1991). Young children's strategies in learning the "book language" of information books. *Discourse Processes, 14,* 203–225.

Pappas, C. C. (1993). Is narrative "primary"? Some insights from kindergarteners' pretend readings of stories and information books. *Journal of Reading Behavior, 25,* 97–129.

Purcell-Gates, V. (1988). Lexical and syntactic knowledge of written narrative held by well-read-to kindergartners and second graders. *Research in the Teaching of English, 22,* 128–157.

Ravid, D., & Berman, R. (2010). Developing noun phrase complexity at school age: A text-embedded cross-linguistic analysis. *First Language, 30,* 3–26.

Reilly, J. S., Zamora, A., & McGivern, R. F. (2005). Acquiring perspective in English: The development of stance. *Journal of Pragmatics, 37,* 185–208 (Special issue on Developing Discourse Stance across Adolescence).

Schleppegrell, M. J. (2004). *The language of schooling: A functional linguistics perspective.* Mahwah, NJ: Lawrence Erlbaum Associates.

Scott, C. M. (2004). Syntactic contributions to literacy learning. In C. A. Stone, E. R. Silliman, B. J. Ehren, & K. Apel (Eds.), *Handbook of language and literacy: Development and disorders* (pp. 340–362). New York: The Guilford Press.

Scott, C. M., & Windsor, J. (2000). General language performance measures in spoken and written narrative and expository discourse of school-age children with language learning disabilities. *Journal of Speech, Language, and Hearing Research, 43,* 324–339.

Snow, C. E., & Uccelli, P. (2009). The challenge of academic language. In D. R. Olson & N. Torrance (Eds.), *The Cambridge handbook of literacy* (pp. 112–133). Cambridge: Cambridge University Press.

Stewart, M. F., & Grobe, C. H. (1979). Syntactic maturity and mechanics of writing: Their relationship to teachers' quality ratings. *Research in the Teaching of English, 13,* 207–213.

Tolchinsky, L., & Sandbank, A. (1994). Text production and text differentiation: Developmental changes and educational influences. In S. Strauss (Ed.), *Learning environments and psychological development.* Norwood, NJ: Ablex.

Tower, C. (2003). Genre development and elementary students' informational writing: A review of the literature. *Reading Research and Instruction, 42,* 14–39.

Excerpts From

Children's Cognitive Effort and Fluency in Writing: Effects of Genre and of Handwriting Automatisation

Thierry Olive, Monik Favart, Caroline Beauvais, and Lucie Beauvais

Learning and Instruction, Volume 19, 2009, Pages 299–308.

I. Introduction

Learning to write efficiently a text is a long process that requires explicit and formal instruction. For students who have not yet acquired all the skills needed to translate their ideas into a coherent text, writing is difficult and effortful. Students have to integrate resource-demanding processes ranging from idea conceptualization to motor execution (Flower & Hayes, 1980; Hayes & Flower, 1980), while the working memory capacity required for such integration is limited (Baddeley, 1986, 2007; McCutchen, 1996). With instruction and practice, however, some of these processes become less costly (e.g., motor execution, spelling or reading). This frees up working memory resources that allow children to take into account constraints related to the writing task itself and the situation. For example, students acquire discourse schemata and genre knowledge that guide textual organization and coherence, making text composition easier to manage and writing less effortful. Yet, it is important to notice that even after several years of practice and instruction, composing a text remains a complex task; even in literate adults, all writing processes continue to place large demands on working memory (Kellogg, 1996; Olive, 2004).

> Composing a text remains a complex task; even in literate adults, all writing processes continue to place large demands on working memory.

The present study investigated how cognitive effort of students who write a text changes between Grades 5 and 9. More specifically, we compared cognitive effort related to writing narrative and argumentative texts. A second aim of the study was to assess the extent to which students' handwriting skills contributed to cognitive effort and writing fluency.

I.I. Cognitive effort in writing

[C]ognitive effort refers to the fraction of working memory resources that are momentarily allocated to the writing task, and more precisely to the resources that are needed to implement the writing processes in a particular writing task (Kellogg, 1996; McCutchen, 2000). Thus, cognitive effort is a function of the demands of the writing situation, the individual's genre knowledge and writing skills, and the extent to which the writing processes have been automatised.

> Cognitive effort is a function of the demands of the writing situation, the individual's genre knowledge and writing skills, and the extent to which the writing processes have been automatised.

Regarding the writing processes, irrespectively from the writing situation and the task, planning and revision are always more effortful than translating (Olive, 2004). In a review of cognitive effort in text writing Piolat and Olive (2000) (see also Olive, Kellogg, & Piolat, 2002) showed that factors related to writers' skills and to the writing situation differently affect the cognitive effort of text writing. In the present study, we studied one situation-specific factor, that is, genre knowledge, and one writer-specific factor, namely level of handwriting automatisation.

I.2. Genre knowledge

Acquisition of genre knowledge is often assumed to begin before writing instruction takes place (Donovan & Smolkin, 2006; Halliday, 1975). Very young children (before six years of age) demonstrate emerging awareness of the different genres because they are exposed to a variety of genres very early in their life (Smolkin & Donovan, 2001).

Because of this early acquisition, it is usually assumed that narratives are easier to write than argumentative texts. From Grade 5, students already use the narrative schema in their writing (Fayol, 1985). Consequently, to organize their text, they simply need to fill the different slots of this schema with the content knowledge they have retrieved from their long-term memory, according to a "schema-driven" strategy (Flower, Schriver, Carey, Hass, & Hayes, 1989) or a knowledge-telling strategy (Scardamalia & Bereiter, 1987). ...By contrast, no such schema exists for argumentative texts where the organization of content is constructed by writers who organize by themselves the textual frame as they generate their arguments (Andriessen & Coirier, 1999). In this case, students have to use the knowledge-transforming strategy (McCutchen, 2000; Scardamalia & Bereiter, 1987) that requires them to (re-)organize the conceptual content with respect to the rhetorical and pragmatic goals. Argumentative texts are also considered more difficult to write than narratives because they involve logical and coherent reasoning, which are acquired late in cognitive development (Siegler, 1996). Interestingly, Kellogg (1994, 2001) showed that even in undergraduates, cognitive effort when writing a narrative is lower than when writing an argumentative text.

I.3. Handwriting demands in children

In the initial stages of writing, handwriting indeed uses up most of the resources of working memory and its cognitive demands might compromise the use of other writing processes (Bourdin & Fayol, 2002). Practising handwriting is thus indispensable to allow students to reduce as soon as possible its demands on working memory.

> When attention is freed up from the lower-level processes of text generation and transcription, it can be devoted to the higher-level processes, such as planning or revising.

Graham and Weintraub (1996) precisely described how the mechanical demands of handwriting might interfere with the higher-level processes involved in writing a text. First, if children's handwriting is very slow, they may not be able to keep up with their thoughts and ideas and so they may forget their ideas and intentions before they get them on paper. Second, switching attention from planning to handwriting may affect the coherence and complexity of the product. Third, competing attention demands may make it difficult for the child to translate his or her intentions into text. Accordingly, when attention is freed up from the lower-level processes of text generation and transcription, it can be devoted to the higher-level processes, such as planning or revising (Bourdin & Fayol, 2002). Planning and translating can then be more efficiently coordinated in working memory (Alves, Castro, & Olive, in press; Olive & Kellogg, 2002), ensuring that text writing fully meets the requirements of discourse structure.

Berninger and Swanson (1994) have also found that transcription skills are critical in the development of all writing processes. Transcription and text generation skills account for a decreasing proportion of variance of writing fluency (in terms of number of words written down in a limited time) and quality as students develop from elementary to junior high school. However, even if their influence declines, as children

156

grow older, transcription continues to contribute to both writing fluency and quality across junior high school.

I.4. The present study—hypotheses

[T]he present study aimed at comparing the cognitive effort of 5th and 9th graders in two different writing tasks: narrative and argumentative text writing. The second aim of the study was to analyze the contribution of handwriting in students' cognitive effort and writing fluency.

Students from Grades 5 and 9 were selected because each of these grades is associated with a specific step in writing acquisition in relation to the two variables we focused on in this study: genre and level of handwriting automatisation. According to Berninger and Swanson's (1994) model of writing development, planning is not yet established in Grade 5 and handwriting is just becoming automatised. Conversely, in Grade 9, handwriting is automatised and allows cognitive resources to be allocated to planning and setting out of ideas in appropriate textual structures.

Students' cognitive effort during writing was assessed by means of a secondary reaction time task. This task has been shown to be non-intrusive with writing but, of major interest, it has been successfully applied to study cognitive effort of skilled writers in different writing tasks (Olive et al., 2002). Students were asked to write their texts while responding as quickly as possible to auditory signals that were randomly distributed across the writing task. The latency of responses indicated the cognitive effort of writing: the longer the responses to the auditory signals, the greater the cognitive effort in the writing task. We expected less cognitive effort in Grade 9 than in Grade 5 (Hypothesis 1), and in the narrative than in the argumentative text (Hypothesis 2). We also expected the writing of an argumentative text to be especially difficult and costly in terms of working memory demands for 5th graders as compared to the 9th graders (Hypothesis 3).

To investigate how handwriting contributes to cognitive effort and fluency in writing, we first assessed handwriting skills and then used this measure of handwriting as a predictor of cognitive effort by means of regression analysis. Overall, we expected handwriting skills to explain higher percentage of variance of cognitive effort (Hypothesis 4) and of fluency (Hypothesis 5) in writing in Grade 5 than in Grade 9. It was also expected that handwriting skills should explain higher percentage of variance in narrative than in argumentative text writing (Hypothesis 6) because when writing requires more complex and effortful processes (as it is the case with argumentative texts) cognitive effort would result mainly from the implementation of these effortful high-level writing processes. By contrast, when the high-level writing processes are less demanding during writing (as it is the case with narratives) cognitive effort would result mainly from the implementation of handwriting processes.

Finally, students' difficulty in writing the texts was assessed with textual structuring through the use of connectives. Management of cohesion through connectives is a good indicator of the development of text structuring (for a review see Favart, 2005). Several studies show that the number and diversity of connectives are related to the acquisition of planning (Favart & Passerault, in press) and vary according to the genre (see Favart & Chanquoy, 2007, for a comparison between narrative and argumentative texts). For instance, conceptual organization is more difficult to achieve in an argumentative text than in a narrative one, for both 5th and 9th graders, and improves between these two grades (Favart & Coirier, 2006). Accordingly, we expected argumentative texts to be more structured by connectives than narratives ones (Hypothesis 7). We also expected that 9th graders would handle connectives in a more efficient way than 5th graders to improve the structure of their argumentative texts thus reflecting a more efficient conceptual organization of this genre between Grades 5 and 9 (Hypothesis 8). According to Favart and Chanquoy (2007) the strong chronological order of narrative events bypassed the need to use a large number of diversified connectives to express narrative relations, whereas connectives have to be more numerous and more specifically produced in order to sustain content in the argumentative texts.

4. Discussion

The present study investigated cognitive effort of 5th and 9th graders in writing a text. Because cognitive effort directly results from the knowledge and skills that are involved in a particular writing task, we examined whether genre and grade affected their cognitive effort. Students wrote two texts of different genres: one narrative, the other argumentative. We also examined if handwriting demands contributed to students' fluency and cognitive effort in writing.

> Higher grade level was associated with decreased cognitive effort, improved handwriting, increased fluency in writing, and higher percentage and diversity of connectives than lower grade level.

The findings regarding developmental differences are as follows: higher grade level was associated with decreased cognitive effort, improved handwriting, increased fluency in writing, and higher percentage and diversity of connectives than lower grade level. The findings on text structure, as defined by the number and categories of connectives used, support the idea that writing a text is more difficult for young students. Overall, 9th graders used greater number of, and more diversified, connectives. The increase in the number and diversity of connectives between Grade 5 and 9 reflects acquisition of planning (Favart & Passerault, in press). Indeed, connectives are linguistic markers that contribute to text organization: the more sophisticated the planning, the more diversified and appropriate use of connectives. According to Hypothesis 8, older students structure the argumentative text in a more efficient way than younger students. The former used more connectives, which were also more diversified, suggesting that these students were able to take into account the specific relations between the ideas they provided in their text. It is, however, worth noticing that other measures of text structure or quality might have revealed, with age, other differences in the texts that were composed. However, as describing how text characteristics change with age was not the purpose of the present study, we did not further analyze the text students produced. It is only important to remember that the changes we observed in text structure imply that the differences in cognitive effort we found can be interpreted, at least partially, in terms of the difficulty the younger students have to plan and organize their text. Finally, it must be pointed out that the argumentative texts produced by the younger students do not represent real argumentation: they are only premises of argumentative texts.

> **With age, students' revision skills also improve and important changes in revision occur across elementary and high school years.**

> **Several studies have shown the importance of automatised handwriting in writing acquisition. For instance, individual differences in handwriting skills have been shown to be related to writing achievement.**

As expected, the cognitive effort in text writing decreased as grade increased: 9th graders experienced less cognitive effort than 5th graders when writing their texts, thus validating Hypothesis 1. This presumably resulted from more automatised writing processes in Grade 9, that is, not only handwriting but also the higher-level writing processes. For instance, with age, students acquire more factual knowledge that is also more structured in their long-term memory. Accessing this information is more rapid, and as this knowledge is more organized in schemas, writing requires less costly planning (McCutchen, 2000). With age, students' revision skills also improve and important changes in revision occur across elementary and high school years (Allal, 2004). However, planning and revision processes of older students are more complex (Scardamalia & Bereiter, 1987). Older students use the knowledge-transforming strategy; they also revise the semantic and organizational aspects of their text. Accordingly, there should be increase of cognitive effort. Yet, there was decrease of cognitive effort in Grade 9, and this seems to be a paradox. This paradox is actually only apparent. Students' practice of writing at school makes the writing processes more efficient and more fluent, with some of the writing sub-processes becoming more automatised (e.g., spelling, reading and handwriting). This fluency and automatisation result in reduced demands on working memory and explain why the total cognitive effort in text writing decreased between grades in the present study.

> If handwriting is enough automatised, more working memory resources are available for the high-level writing process related to planning and revision, which are most critical for writing achievement.

The idea that some writing sub-processes, and particularly the low-level ones, become more automatised in higher grades is observed in the case of handwriting. As expected, handwriting was more automatised and contributed less to cognitive effort, in Grade 9 than in Grade 5 supporting Hypothesis 4. Indeed, the older students wrote down almost twice as many letters as the younger ones at the Alphabet task. This finding is in line with others showing that transcription becomes less costly from Grade 5 onwards (Berninger, 1999; Bourdin & Fayol, 1994; Graham & Weintraub, 1996; Sassoon et al., 1989). Several studies have shown the importance of automatised handwriting in writing acquisition. For instance, individual differences in handwriting skills have been shown to be related to writing achievement (Graham & Harris, 2000). Jones and Christensen (1999) observed that handwriting skills accounted for 50% of the variance in text quality of 2nd graders. Graham et al. (1997) also found that handwriting contributed to writing skills of students in Grades 1–6. This remains true even for undergraduate students (Connelly, Dockrell, & Barnett, 2005; Peverly, 2006). Therefore, if handwriting is enough automatised, more working memory resources are available for the high-level writing process related to planning and revision, which are most critical for writing achievement.

The general decrease in the demands of writing processes in Grade 9 is also supported by the lower fluency in writing of the 5th graders relative to the 9th graders. As fluency in writing is the end product of all the writing processes (McCutchen, 1988), an increased fluency in writing indicates more efficient writing processes. Interestingly, but conversely to Hypothesis 5, handwriting demands did not explain any variance of the fluency in writing neither in 5th graders nor in 9th graders. In sum, the increase in writing fluency between the two grades seems to result mainly from larger efficiency of the high-level writing processes than from a more automatised handwriting.

> **Students' earlier exposure to narratives results in greater mastery of that genre.**

Although most genre differences were not significant, genre affected the structure of the text as indicated by the use of connectives, thus validating Hypothesis 7. There were fewer and less varied and specific connectives in the narrative than in the argumentative text, giving support to Hypothesis 8. This finding is consistent with that of Favart and Chanquoy (2007) for 5th graders and adults: even in adults, the strong chronological order of narrative events limits the need to use a large number of diversified connectives to express narrative relations, whereas connectives have to be more numerous and more specifically produced in order to sustain cohesion of content in the argumentative text. This specificity is mainly observed in Grade 9. The difficulty that students encounter when writing such texts comes from the fact that they are less exposed to this genre but also to the inherent characteristics of argumentative texts, which have a self-sustained structure, requiring logical and formal reasoning, needing knowledge not only in favour, but also against the writers' opinion or ideas (Andriessen & Coirier, 1999).

Across grades, and by contrast to Hypothesis 2, students' cognitive effort did not vary with the genre of the text they had to write. This finding may mean low performance on the argumentative text if other criteria of text structure or quality were used. Moreover, this absence of effect of genre on cognitive effort may be due to the fact that the texts produced by children, and particularly the youngest ones, were not really argumentative with articulated arguments. Thus, it is possible that students composed their text using a knowledge-telling strategy, which is less costly than the knowledge-transforming strategy required for producing a strong argumentation. Thus, at least for the students involved in the present study, difficulties in writing narrative and argumentative texts were not manifested in cognitive effort as measured by interference RT. It is highly probable that students devoted all their working memory capacity in writing texts of both genres. However, the interaction between grade and genre indicated that cognitive effort of only argumentative text decreased from Grade 5 to Grade 9, with less cognitive effort in Grade 9, verifying Hypothesis 3. This finding confirms, first, that students continue to improve their skills related to writing argumentative texts between Grade 5 and 9 and, second, that writing narrative texts is well mastered in Grade 5. One possible explanation of such difference in mastering the writing of narrative and argumentative texts lies in students' exposure to these two genres. As was mentioned above (Donovan & Smolkin, 2006), students' earlier exposure to narratives results in greater mastery of that genre. According to Berninger and Swanson (1994), in Grade 5, planning is just emerging whereas it is established in Grade 9. Because planning is more involved in argumentative than in narrative composition, students' cognitive effort in writing argumentative texts probably reflects changes in planning ability across grades. Finally, handwriting did not contribute differently to cognitive effort of argumentative and narrative texts, thus falsifying Hypothesis 6.

> High-level writing processes, despite being more complex, were overall less demanding in working memory denoting more automatisation of other high-level processes, particularly in the writing of argumentative texts.

As expected, and despite the fact that students encountered more difficulty to write argumentative texts, no difference in writing fluency was observed between narrative and argumentative texts....

To summarize the present findings, 9th graders encountered less difficulty in writing their texts and exhibited less cognitive effort than 5th graders. Cognitive effort in 9th graders presumably resulted from the demands of only the high-level writing processes since handwriting was automatised and did not affect cognitive effort. These high-level writing processes, despite being more complex, were overall less demanding in working memory denoting more automatisation of other high-level processes, particularly in the writing of argumentative texts. By contrast, the larger cognitive effort of 5th graders came to some extent from the handwriting demands and, mainly, by the demands of high-level processes involved in writing. Writing a narrative or an argumentative text did not affect fluency in writing (i.e., number of words used), but it did affect students' cognitive effort. Gaining experience through instruction leads to the easing of cognitive effort later on in Grade 9.

4.1. Implications and limitations of the study

The educational implications of these findings relate to at least two aspects of learning and teaching to write. First, they underline that not only children's early exposure to genres, but also the explicit teaching of genres is important as young writers' cognitive effort varies with the type of text they are writing. Second, this study showed the role of level of handwriting automatisation in writing. Recently, Graham et al. (2008) surveyed how handwriting is taught in American primary schools. They observed that despite the fact that handwriting is being taught by the majority of teachers of primary grades, the recommended instructional procedures are applied unevenly in classrooms. Educational interventions focusing on handwriting, however, succeed in improving handwriting automatisation and writing achievement. In addition, teachers may also be attentive to children with poor handwriting skills in order to remediate their difficulty. Jones and Christensen (1999) showed that instructions aimed at improving handwriting fluency and letter formation of 1st graders with poor handwriting enhanced their performance when writing a story.

To conclude, this study complements experiments of cognitive effort in text writing by adults, and is the first one to address the issue of children's cognitive effort associated with text writing. It must be noticed that the decrease in cognitive effort we observed between Grade 5 and 9 does not fit with the idea of performance amplification in writing (Kellogg, 1994). Performance amplification refers to the fact that in order to compose a high-quality text, writers need to devote their full working memory capacity to writing. So it may be expected that students, as adults, devote all the working memory resources on writing an argumentative text and that no difference is observed between age groups. Actually, it is highly probable that the reduction in cognitive effort we observed in the 9th graders ceases after a certain time and increases again when students use more elaborated writing strategies later on. Accordingly, variations in cognitive effort along with age may indicate shifts in acquisition of writing processes. To deepen our understanding of acquisition of writing in relation to working memory, more systematic studies of age-related changes in the cognitive effort of different writing situations in different writing tasks need to be carried out.

References

Allal, L. (2004). Integrating writing instruction and the development of revision skills. In L. Allal, L. Chanquoy, & P. Largy (Eds.), *Revision: Cognitive and instructional processes* (pp. 139–156). Dordrecht, The Netherlands: Kluwer.

Alves, R. A., Castro, S. L., & Olive, T. Execution and pauses in writing narratives: processing time, cognitive effort and typing skill. *International Journal of Psychology*. doi:1080/00207590701403850, in press.

Andriessen, J., & Coirier, P. (1999). *Foundations of argumentative text processing.* Amsterdam: Amsterdam University Press.

Baddeley, A. D. (1986). *Working memory.* Oxford, England: Oxford University Press.

Baddeley, A. D. (2007). *Working memory, thought and action.* Oxford, England: Oxford University Press.

Berninger, V. W. (1999). Coordinating transcription and text generation in working memory during composing: automatic and constructive processes. *Learning Disability Quarterly, 22*(2), 99–112.

Berninger, V. W., & Swanson, H. L. (1994). Modifying Hayes and Flower's model of skilled writing to explain beginning and developing writing. In J. S. Carlson, & E. C. Butterfly (Eds.), Children's writing: Toward a process theory of the development of skilled writing. *Advances in cognition and educational practice,* Vol. 2 (pp. 57–81). Greenwich, CT: JAI Press.

Bourdin, B., & Fayol, M. (1994). Is written language production more difficult than oral language production? A working memory approach. *International Journal of Psychology, 29,* 591–620.

Bourdin, B., & Fayol, M. (2002). Even in adults written production is still more costly than oral production. *International Journal of Psychology, 37,* 219–227.

Connelly, V., Dockrell, J., & Barnett, J. (2005). The slow handwriting of undergraduate students constrains overall performance in exam essays. *Educational Psychology, 25,* 99–107.

Donovan, C. A., & Smolkin, L. B. (2006). Children's understanding of genre and writing development. In C. A. MacArthur, S. Graham, & J. Fitzgerald (Eds.), *Handbook of writing research* (pp. 131–143). New York: Guilford.

Favart, M. (2005). Les marques de cohesion: Leur rôle fonctionnel dans l'acquisition de la production écrite de texte. [Cohesion devices: their functional role in the acquisition of text production]. *Psychologie Française, 50*(3), 305–322.

Favart, M., & Chanquoy, L. (2007). Les marques de cohésion comme outils privilégiés de la textualisation: une comparaison entre élèves de CM2 et adultes experts. [Cohesion devices as crucial tools of text composition: a comparison between 5th graders and expert adults]. *Langue Française, 155*(3), 51–58.

Favart, M., & Coirier, P. (2006). Acquisition of the linearization process in text composition in third to ninth graders: effects of textual superstructure and macrostructural organization. *Journal of Psycholinguistic Research, 35*(4), 305–328.

Favart, M., & Passerault, J. M. Acquisition of relations between the conceptual and the linguistic dimensions of linearization in descriptive text composition in grades five to nine: a comparison with oral production. *British Journal of Educational Psychology*, doi:10.1348/000709908X289981, in press.

Fayol, M. (1985). *Le récit et sa construction*. [Narratives and their construction]. Neuchâtel, Switzerland: Delachaux & Niestlé.

Flower, L. S., & Hayes, J. R. (1980). The dynamics of composing: Making plans and juggling constraints. In L. W. Gregg, & E. R. Steinberg (Eds.), *Cognitive processes in writing* (pp. 31–50). Hillsdale, NJ: Erlbaum.

Flower, L. S., Schriver, K., Carey, L., Haas, C., & Hayes, J. R. (1989). *Planning in writing: The cognition of a constructive process*. Tech. Rep. No. 4. Berkeley, CA/Pittsburgh, PA: Center for the Study of Language.

Graham, S., Berninger, V. W., Abbott, R. D., Abbott, S. P., & Whitaker, D. (1997). The role of mechanics in composing of elementary students: A new methodological approach. *Journal of Educational Psychology, 89,* 170–182.

Graham, S., & Harris, K. (2000). The role of self-regulation and transcription skills in writing and writing development. *Educational Psychologist, 35,* 3–12.

Graham, S., Harris, K. R., Mason, L., Fink-Chorzempa, B., Mora, S., & Saddler, B. (2008). How do primary grade teachers teach handwriting? A national survey. *Reading and Writing, 21*(1), 49–69.

Graham, S., & Weintraub. (1996). A review of handwriting research: progress and prospects from 1980 to 1994. *Educational Psychology Review, 8,* 7–87.

Halliday, M. A. K. (1975). *Learning how to mean: Explorations in the functions of language*. London: Arnold.

Hayes, J. R., & Flower, L. S. (1980). Identifying the organization of writing processes. In L. W. Gregg, & E. R. Steinberg (Eds.), *Cognitive processes in writing: An interdisciplinary approach* (pp. 3–30). Hillsdale, NJ: Erlbaum.

Jones, D., & Christensen, C. A. (1999). The relationship between automaticity in handwriting and students' ability to generate written text. *Journal of Educational Psychology, 91,* 44–49.

Kellogg, R. T. (1994). *The psychology of writing*. New York: Oxford University Press.

Kellogg, R. T. (1996). A model of working memory in writing. In C. M. Levy, & S. E. Ransdell (Eds.), *The science of writing: Theories, methods, individual differences and applications* (pp. 57–71). Mahwah, NJ: Erlbaum.

Kellogg, R. T. (2001). Competition for working memory among writing processes. *American Journal of Psychology, 114*(2), 175–192.

McCutchen, D. (1988). "Functional automaticity" in children's writing: A problem of metacognitive control. *Written Communication, 5,* 306–324.

McCutchen, D. (1996). A capacity theory of writing: Working memory in composition. *Educational Psychology Review, 8*(3), 299–325.

McCutchen, D. (2000). Knowledge, processing and working memory: Implications for a theory of writing. *Educational Psychologist, 35,* 13–23.

Olive, T. (2004). Working memory in writing: Empirical evidence from the dual-task technique. *European Psychologist, 9,* 32–42.

Olive, T., & Kellogg, R. T. (2002). Concurrent activation of high-and low-level production processes in written composition. *Memory and Cognition, 30,* 594–600.

Olive, T., Kellogg, R. T., & Piolat, A. (2002). Studying text production with the triple task technique: Why and how? In T. Olive, & C. M. Levy (Eds.), *Contemporary tools and techniques for studying writing* (pp. 31–58) Dordrecht, The Netherlands: Kluwer.

Peverly, S. T. (2006). The importance of handwriting speed in adult writing. *Developmental Neuropsychology, 29,* 197–216.

Piolat, A., & Olive, T. (2000). Comment étudier le coût et le déroulement de la rédaction de textes? Bilan méthodologique. [How to study the cost and unfolding of text production? Methodological assessment]. *L'Année Psychologique, 100,* 465–502.

Sassoon, R., Nimmo-Smith, I., & Wing, A. M. (1989). Developing efficiency in cursive handwriting: an analysis of "t" crossing behavior in children. In R. Plamondon, C. Y. Suen, & M. L. Simner (Eds.), *Computer recognition and human production of handwriting* (pp. 287–297). Singapore: World Scientific.

Scardamalia, M., & Bereiter, C. (1987). Knowledge telling and knowledge transforming in written composition. In S. Rosenberg (Ed.), *Reading, writing and language learning. Advances in psycholinguistics, Vol. 2* (pp. 143–175). Cambridge, UK: Cambridge University Press.

Siegler, R. S. (1996). *Emerging minds: The process of change in children's thinking.* New York: Oxford University Press.

Smolkin, L. B., & Donovan, C. A. (2001). Comprehension acquisition and information book read aloud in a first grade classroom. *Elementary School Journal, 102,* 97–122.

Chapter 5

Writing Traits: Rubrics and Assessment

"My teacher said the school has tough new standards and I need to improve my vocabulary. What's 'vocabulary'?"

Reprinted with permission. www.CartoonStock.com

Introduction

Along with process-based instruction and a focus on strategies for writing, the 6+1 Trait® rubric-based model became an important component of writing instruction across the country in the last decade yet had scant research to back up its claims. But now a new study from the Institute of Education Sciences demonstrates that the 6+1 Trait model has important benefits for students. As study authors **Michael Coe, Makoto Hanita, Vicki Nishioka,** and **Richard Smiley** describe, grade 5 students' writing scores increased during the first year of the 6+1 Trait implementation in their classroom: three of six outcome measures had "statistically significant" increases in the scores between the treatment and control group of students, and the other three measures were higher in the treatment group compared to the control group. The pedagogy of the 6+1 Trait model has made it popular with teachers, and this important experimental study demonstrates that trait-based writing instruction can have a major impact on student writing even during the first year of its use. More reports from this study in later years may confirm increasing benefits for student writing.

The 6+1 Trait model is based on a rubric that incorporates six components of writing in addition to the "plus one" of presentation. Teachers use the trait-based model and other rubrics in two distinct ways in the classroom: as a guide for students and as an assessment tool for teachers. As **Regie Routman** points out in the second article of this chapter, rubrics can be useful lists for the criteria of good writing. However, she is more cautious about their use; she urges teachers to keep a focus on effective writing, not on checking off boxes: "Rubrics, like checklists, can disrupt the flow of teaching and learning," she writes, because teachers can focus too much on the rubric and not enough on what the student is trying to do with his or her writing.

The next article provides a rebuttal to this concern; **Vicki Spandel,** one of the creators of the 6+1 Trait approach, proposes, "When thoughtfully crafted and used with discretion and understanding, rubrics can be among the most useful instructional tools we have." The problem with rubrics, in her opinion, is their misuse. She does not see them as static but as a jumping off point for instruction, especially when teachers try to push students into true revision of their papers: rubrics, she says, can show students what writers do when they revise, giving students a purpose and a tool for deeper revision. Against critics who argue that rubrics result in standardized and homogenized student writing, Spandel validates the teacher's role and his or her professional expertise in helping students find their voice.

Similarly, **Susan De La Paz** emphasizes the strategic use of rubrics in the writing classroom by teachers who transform them into planning strategies. In her essay, she creates a four-step process for incorporating a rubric into the instruction for a particular essay; in this case, she uses a compare-contrast essay in social studies as the example. Like Spandel, De La Paz focuses on the conversation a teacher develops with the rubric in order to turn it into classroom content; she proposes that this process also allows for differentiated instruction because it gives teachers the opportunity to monitor particular sub-goals created for specific students or groups of students.

Students can also make rubrics their own by generating content and criteria that help them self-assess their writing. In the next study, **Heather Andrade, Ying Du,** and **Xiaolei Wang** find that both "using a model to generate criteria for an assignment and using a rubric for self-assessment can help elementary school students produce more effective writing." Using the study results, the authors explain that student grades would increase by about one-third with the implementation of the study's instructional model. In contrast to critics of rubrics, they conclude that "[t]he fact that rubric-referenced self-assessment was associated with higher scores on important qualities like ideas and content testifies to the potential of such processes to help students master significant, meaningful aspects of writing." Rubrics assist students by providing them with a concrete approach to revising their writing in terms of specific and articulated qualities of successful writing.

Rubrics are also used to assess the final products of writing; they provide teachers with a way to grade student writing that is based on criteria already provided to students within the rubric. In the last article of this chapter, researchers **Aliz Reza Rezaei** and **Michael Lovorn** compare the results of experiments designed to evaluate the objectivity of grading with and without rubrics. Their findings show that the application of a rubric for grading does not translate into consistent, objective grading of essays by trained evaluators. These conclusions show that assessing writing with a rubric may be much less helpful than providing that rubric for student learning. They conclude that to be most effective, "rubrics should be well-designed, topic-specific (contextual), analytic, and complemented by exemplars," and they also support teachers' professional judgment in using them in the classroom.

Excerpts From

An Investigation of the Impact of the 6+1 Trait Writing Model on Grade 5 Student Writing Achievement

Michael Coe, Makoto Hanita, Vicki Nishioka, Richard Smiley

Washington, DC: National Center for Education Evaluation and Regional Assistance, Institute of Education Sciences, U.S. Department of Education.

Summary

Reading, writing, and arithmetic have long been considered the foundation, or "basics," of education in the United States. Writing skills are important for an increasing number of jobs (National Commission on Writing 2004; Executive Office of the President 2009). Poor writing skills are a barrier to hiring and promotion for many individuals, and remediation of problems with writing imposes significant operational and training costs on public and private organizations (Casner-Lotto, Rosenblum, and Wright 2009; National Commission on Writing 2004, 2005). Writing is also important for the development of reading skills (Graham and Hebert 2010) and can improve learning in other academic content areas (Bangert-Drowns, Hurley, and Wilkinson 2004).

> A recent meta-analysis of research on writing instruction in grades 4–12 finds support for 11 "elements of effective adolescent writing instruction." …These elements are core components of the intervention examined in this study.

In response to the perceived neglect of writing in U.S. education, the National Commission on Writing proposed a set of recommendations for making writing a central element in school reform efforts (National Commission on Writing 2006). These concerns were echoed in regional needs assessment studies conducted by Regional Educational Laboratory (REL) Northwest, in which educators in the region placed a high priority on writing and literacy education (Gilmore Research Group 2006, 2009).

A growing body of research is beginning to shed light on classroom strategies and practices that improve the quality of student writing. For example, a recent meta-analysis of research on writing instruction in grades 4–12 finds support for 11 "elements of effective adolescent writing instruction" (Graham and Perin 2007a, 2007b). These recommended practices, synthesized from the findings of experimental studies, include having students analyze models of good writing; explicitly teaching students strategies for planning, revising, and editing their work; involving students in collaborative use of these writing strategies; and assigning specific goals for each writing project. These elements are core components of the intervention examined in this study.

Box I. The 6+1 Traits

I. Ideas Ideas are the main message, the content of the piece, the theme, together with the details that enrich and develop that theme.

2. Organization Organization is the internal structure, the thread of central meaning, the logical and sometimes intriguing pattern of the ideas within a piece of writing.

3. Voice Voice is the heart and soul, the magic, the wit, along with the feeling and conviction of the individual writer coming out through the words.

4. Word Choice Word choice is the use of rich, colorful, precise language that moves and enlightens the reader.

5. Sentence Fluency Sentence fluency is the rhythm and flow of the language, the sound of word patterns, the way in which the writing plays to the ear and not just to the eye.

6. Conventions Conventions refer to the mechanics of writing: spelling, paragraph formatting, grammar and usage, punctuation, and use of capitals.

+I. Presentation Presentation zeros in on the form and layout of the text and its readability; the piece should be pleasing to the eye.

SOURCE: 6+1 Trait Writing Summer Institute training agendas and records.

The 6+1 Trait® Writing model (Culham 2003) emphasizes writing instruction in which teachers and students analyze writing using a set of characteristics, or "traits," of written work: ideas, organization, voice, word choice, sentence fluency, conventions, and presentation [see Box 1]. The Ideas trait includes the main content and message, including supporting details. Organization refers to the structure and logical flow of the writing. Voice includes the perspective and style of the individual writer and his or her orientation toward the audience. Word Choice addresses the variety, precision, and evocativeness of the language. Sentence Fluency includes the rhythm, flow, and sound patterns in the construction of sentences that may make them pleasant and interesting to read. The Conventions trait, sometimes called mechanics, includes spelling, punctuation, grammar, capitalization, and other rule-based language forms. The trait of Presentation (the "+1" of the 6+1 Trait Writing model), which is focused on page layout and formatting issues, is related to the visual aspects of publishing writing. This trait might not be applied unless the writing project is carried through to publication or presentation in a classroom or public forum. Presentation is not typically measured in large-scale assessments of student achievement, which require students to use particular formatting.

What is the impact of 6+1 Trait Writing on grade 5 student achievement in writing?

This framework and the associated terminology for characterizing the qualities of writing may be used to study the writing of others, to plan or revise one's own writing, or to discuss the qualities of a piece of writing with others. The 6+1 Trait Writing model includes many of the features recommended in the Graham and Perin (2007a) meta-analysis. This approach has been widely disseminated: the publisher of the model reports having distributed professional development materials in all 50 states and conducted professional development institutes or workshops in 48 states and several countries.

The model has not been adequately studied using experimental methods. In order to provide evidence on the effectiveness of this approach, the study reported here was designed as a large-scale effectiveness trial (Flay 1986). The model was not applied under ideal laboratory conditions, with frequent supervision by program developers to ensure optimal implementation. Instead, professional development was provided to teachers who worked in 74 Oregon schools that were randomly assigned to the study conditions. The professional development approach allowed teachers to implement the model in their classrooms according to their own style and preferences.

The study addressed the following confirmatory research question:

- What is the impact of 6+1 Trait Writing on grade 5 student achievement in writing?

It also investigated two exploratory research questions:

- What is the impact of 6+1 Trait Writing on grade 5 student achievement in particular traits of writing?

• Does the impact of 6+1 Trait Writing on grade 5 student achievement vary according to student gender or ethnicity?

[G]rade 5 students were chosen as the target population because the development of academic writing skills is key in this grade level—a time when students focus on learning expository and persuasive writing, which is used in much of their subsequent academic careers (Common Core State Standards Initiative 2010). Subgroup analyses by gender and ethnicity were deemed to be of interest because of the variation in student assessment outcomes based on these factors (Cole 1997; Nowell and Hedges 1998; U.S. Department of Education 2003a, 2003b).

Study sample and methods

Data for the cluster-randomized experimental study were collected from participating grade 5 teachers and students in 74 Oregon schools. Two cohorts of schools participated in the study across two consecutive years. The intervention and data collection occurred in 54 schools during 2008/09 and in an additional 20 schools in 2009/10. Schools were first screened to ensure that they were not already using a trait-based writing instruction model, that they had an adequate number of grade 5 students to provide a reliable estimate of student performance, and that they were willing to participate. All procedures were the same in both cohorts of schools, and all data were combined for analyses (except for a specific analysis of cohort differences). Except where otherwise noted, this report describes the combined procedures and results of both cohorts of schools.

> Grade 5 students were chosen as the target population because the development of academic writing skills is key in this grade level—a time when students focus on learning expository and persuasive writing.

After administrators and teachers had been informed about the study and agreed to participate, each school was randomly assigned to either the treatment or control condition. Random assignment was done within pairs of schools that had been matched within each participating district to ensure that the treatment and control groups had similar percentages of students eligible for free or reduced-price lunch. (In districts with an odd number of participating schools, unpaired schools remaining after all paired schools were assigned were randomly assigned to the treatment or control condition.) Of the 74 schools in the study, 39 were randomly assigned to the treatment condition and 35 were randomly assigned to the control condition. As schools were the unit of random assignment, all participating grade 5 teachers in each school were assigned to the same condition.

Teachers in treatment group schools were offered training in the 6+1 Trait Writing model the summer before the data collection year and during that year. They learned how to apply the model and used it with students for the first time during the year in which student outcome data were gathered. Teachers in control group schools were not asked to change the instructional methods they would have used had they not participated in the study. The control condition thus represented a "business as usual" counterfactual in schools not already using trait-based writing instruction, with which the first-year implementation among treatment group schools was compared.

Teachers in both groups were asked to complete a survey at three points during the data collection year in order to report the extent to which they were using classroom practices recommended as part of the 6+1 Trait model. These self-report surveys were the only method used to determine whether treatment group teachers implemented the model with students or whether the practices recommended by the model were used by treatment group teachers more than they were used by control group teachers. Teachers in the two groups reported similar levels of use of these practices at the beginning of the study. By the end of the study, treatment group teachers reported greater use of these practices than did the control group teachers, but the newly developed survey instrument does not provide easily interpretable information about the magnitude of this difference or the specific level of implementation of these practices in treatment group or control group classrooms.

> Teachers in both groups were asked to complete a survey at three points during the data collection year in order to report the extent to which they were using classroom practices recommended as part of the 6+1 Trait model.

Within each school, all data for the study were collected during a single school year. Before the beginning of the year, teachers were asked to complete a questionnaire about their use of specific classroom writing instruction practices during the previous school year. Teachers in both the treatment and control groups reported that the classroom practices emphasized by the intervention were already in use at the outset of the study; this was part of the existing school environment into which the intervention was introduced. Teachers in the treatment group then attended a three-day summer institute that provided comprehensive training, planning time, and resource materials to help them learn and apply the 6+1 Trait Writing model. During the following school year, teachers in treatment schools attended three additional one-day workshops to further their understanding of the approach and to plan trait-based writing activities for their students. Teachers in both the treatment and control groups completed a survey on classroom practices at midyear and again at the end of the school year.

Students in both control and treatment classrooms wrote essays at the beginning of the school year, which were scored and used as baseline measures of student writing performance. Students completed essays again at the end of the school year. Scores on this essay test were used as the outcome measures for the study. Each essay was rated using a single "holistic" score for overall writing quality. It was also rated on each of the six core characteristics of writing quality included in the 6+1 Trait Writing model. The holistic score was used for the confirmatory analysis and the second exploratory analysis; the trait scores were used for the first exploratory analysis.

Because the research team was employed by Education Northwest, the organization that developed and markets the 6+1 Trait Writing model, care was taken to maintain the transparency of all research processes and to limit the possibility of introducing intentional or unintentional bias at key phases of the research. The research team at Education Northwest was kept blind to key aspects of the data during the scoring of student essays, and they operated and were supervised independently of the individuals in a different organizational unit who provided the professional development. The teams of essay raters did not know whether a particular essay was a pretest or a posttest or whether it came from a treatment or a control school. Details of the methods used to prevent bias are provided in the [full] report.*

Summary of findings

The sample included 102 teachers and 2,230 students in the treatment condition and 94 teachers and 1,931 students in the control condition. The confirmatory research question was addressed by comparing the mean difference between posttest student essay scores in the two conditions, using a benchmark statistical model that accounted for students' baseline (pretest) writing performance at the beginning of the school year, the poverty level of their school, and preexisting baseline differences between schools on three teacher-reported characteristics: the school average for the weekly teacher-reported hours students spend in

---

* Available from http://ies.ed.gov/ncee/edlabs/projects/project.asp?ProjectID=52

class practicing writing, the school average for teacher years of teaching experience, and the school average for teacher years of experience teaching writing. The statistical model also took into account the fact that students were clustered within schools and therefore were more likely to be similar to one another than would have been the case had students rather than schools been randomly assigned to conditions.

> ## Use of the 6+1 Trait Writing model significantly increased student writing scores during the year in which it was introduced to schools.

Following a plan defined prior to implementing the study, the benchmark estimates of effectiveness were based on a statistical analysis that imputed the outcome measures in cases where they were missing (5.5 percent of all cases). The effectiveness of the professional development was also estimated using a more common approach of deleting cases with missing values of the outcome measure. Another alternative analysis used a different statistical model to examine the data.

The benchmark estimates indicate that use of the 6+1 Trait Writing model significantly increased student writing scores during the year in which it was introduced to schools. After controlling for baseline writing scores, the estimated average score of students in the treatment group was 0.109 standard deviations higher (p = .023) than the estimated average score of students in the control group. An intervention with this effect size would be expected to increase the average level of achievement from the 50th to the 54th percentile.

The findings remained stable when tested using alternative choices for the analytic sample and the model specification. When students with missing data were excluded from the analysis sample, the estimated effect was 0.110 standard deviations (p = .018). Use of an analytic model that did not adjust for baseline measures of teacher experience and instructional practices resulted in an estimated effect size of .081 (p = .048).

In addition to the analysis of holistic writing scores, exploratory analyses found statistically significant differences between control and treatment group students on three of the six specific outcome measures of particular writing traits—organization, voice, and word choice—with effect sizes ranging from 0.117 to 0.144 (p = .031 to .018). For the other three traits—ideas, sentence fluency, and conventions—the mean outcome score of students in the treatment condition was higher than that of students in the control condition, but these differences were too small to be considered statistically significant given the size and sensitivity of the experiment.

TABLE 13. Estimated impact of 6+1 Trait Writing on individual trait scale scores, adjusted for exogenous differences in schools at baseline, pretest score, and pair fixed effect

Outcome measure: adjusted posttest score	Treatment group (n = 2,230)	Control group (n = 1,931)	Difference: treatment effect (SE)	Summary treatment effect[c] (SE)	Test statistic	95% confi-dence interval	Effect size[d]
Ideas							
Paired[a]	4.176	4.070	0.106 (0.041)	0.039 (0.038)	z = 1.03 p = .302	−0.035 to 0.113	0.070
Singleton[b]	4.462	4.802	−0.340 (0.097)				
Organization							
Paired[a]	3.953	3.873	0.080 (0.029)	0.060 (0.028)	z = 2.15 p = .031	0.005 to 0.114	0.117
Singleton[b]	4.055	4.335	−0.280 (0.116)				
Voice							
Paired[a]	4.403	4.311	0.092 (0.028)	0.062 (0.027)	z = 2.28 p = .023	0.009 to 0.116	0.132
Singleton[b]	4.429	4.761	−0.332 (0.103)				
Word Choice							
Paired[a]	4.069	3.983	0.086 (0.025)	0.055 (0.023)	z = 2.37 p = .018	0.009 to 0.101	0.144
Singleton[b]	4.128	4.298	−0.170 (0.068)				
Sentence Fluency							
Paired[a]	4.008	3.917	0.091 (0.032)	0.053 (0.030)	z = 1.77 p = .076	−0.006 to 0.111	0.112
Singleton[b]	4.138	4.385	−0.247 (0.088)				
Conventions							
Paired[a]	3.980	3.914	0.066 (0.035)	0.028 (0.033)	z = 0.864 p = .388	−0.036 to 0.092	0.054
Singleton[b]	4.062	4.276	−0.214 (0.090)				

NOTE: All the trait scale score outcome measures are covariate adjusted.

a. The covariate-adjusted posttest score for the treatment (control) group represents the predicted posttest score of a student who had a pretest score at the grand mean and who attended a treatment (control) school in the referent pair, under the condition that the school aggregates of the exogenous teacher variables were set to zero.

b. The covariate-adjusted posttest score for the treatment (control) group represents the predicted posttest score of a student who had a pretest score at the grand mean and who attended a treatment (control) school in which no students were eligible for free or reduced-price lunch, under the condition that the school aggregates of the exogenous teacher variables were set to zero.

c. The summary treatment effect is a pooled estimate combining the treatment effect among paired schools (those randomly assigned within matched pairs based on district and percentage of students eligible for free or reduced-price lunch) and singleton schools (those randomly assigned to experimental condition after all other schools in their district had been assigned as part of matched pairs).

d. Glass's *delta* (standardized difference using the control group standard deviation of the posttest scores).

Source: Authors' analysis, based on data described in text.

Results on measures of particular writing traits

Table 13 compares the covariate-adjusted posttest scores on each of the trait scales for the treatment and control groups. The difference between the two groups represents the treatment effect. The standard error of the estimate is adjusted to reflect the nesting of students within schools.

For all six trait scales, the estimated mean for the treatment group exceeded that for the control group. (The trait of presentation was not scored or analyzed, because students did not have the opportunity to address presentation issues during the assessment.) Three of these differences reached statistical significance at $p < .05$. For these three writing traits (organization, voice, and word choice) effect sizes ranged from 0.117 to 0.144. For the other three traits (ideas, sentence fluency, and conventions) the mean outcome score of students in the treatment condition was higher than that of students in the control condition, but these differences were too small to be considered statistically significant.

References

Bangert-Drowns, R.L., Hurley, M.M., and Wilkinson, B. (2004). The effects of school-based writing-to-learn interventions on academic achievement: a meta-analysis. *Review of Educational Research, 74*(1), 29–58.

Casner-Lotto, J., Rosenblum, E., and Wright, M. (2009). *The ill-prepared U.S. workforce: exploring the challenges of employer-provided workforce readiness training.* New York: Conference Board. Retrieved April 10, 2010, from http://www.shrm.org/Research/SurveyFindings/Articles/Documents/BED09Workforce_RR.pdf

Cole, N.S. (1997). *The ETS gender study: how females and males perform in educational settings.* Princeton, NJ: Educational Testing Service. (ERIC ED424337)

Common Core State Standards Initiative. (2010). *Common core state standards for English language arts & literacy in history/social studies, science, and technical subjects.* Retrieved February 10, 2011, from http://www.corestandards.org/assets/CCSSI_ELA%20Standards.pdf

Culham, R. (2003). *6+1 traits of writing: The complete guide, grades 3 and up.* New York: Scholastic Professional Books.

Executive Office of the President of the United States, Council of Economic Advisers. (2009). *Preparing the workers of today for the jobs of tomorrow.* Retrieved April 10, 2010, from http://www.whitehouse.gov/administration/eop/cea/Jobs-of-the-Future/

Flay, B.R. (1986). Efficacy and effectiveness trials (and other phases of research) in the development of health promotion programs. *Preventive Medicine, 15*(5), 451–474.

Gilmore Research Group. (2006). *Summary of proceedings from the 2006 state education forums.* Portland, OR: Northwest Regional Educational Laboratory.

Gilmore Research Group. (2009). *2007/2009 regional needs assessment summary of findings.* Portland, OR: Northwest Regional Educational Laboratory.

Graham, S., and Hebert, M. (2010). *Writing to read: evidence for how writing can improve reading. A report from Carnegie Corporation of New York.* Washington, DC: Alliance for Excellent Education.

Graham, S., and Perin, D. (2007a). A meta-analysis of writing instruction for adolescent students. *Journal of Educational Psychology, 99*(3), 445–476.

Graham, S., and Perin, D. (2007b). *Writing next: Effective strategies to improve writing of adolescents in middle and high schools. A report to Carnegie Corporation of New York.* Washington, DC: Alliance for Excellent Education.

National Commission on Writing. (2004). *Writing: A ticket to work...or a ticket out. A survey of business leaders.* Retrieved April 10, 2010, from http://www.collegeboard.com/prod_downloads/writingcom/writing-ticket-to-work.pdf

National Commission on Writing. (2005). *Writing: A powerful message from state government.* Retrieved April 10, 2010, from http://www.collegeboard.com/prod_downloads/writingcom/powerful-message-from-state.pdf

National Commission on Writing. (2006). *Writing and school reform.* Retrieved April 10, 2010, from http://www.collegeboard.com/prod_downloads/writingcom/writingschool-reform-natl-comm-writing.pdf

Nowell, A., and Hedges, L.V. (1998). Trends in gender differences in academic achievement from 1960 to 1994: an analysis of differences in mean, variance, and extreme scores. *Sex Roles, 39*(1/2), 21–43.

U.S. Department of Education, National Center for Education Statistics. (2003a). *The Nation's Report Card: state writing 2002. Snapshot report: Oregon grade 4, public school* (NCES 2003-532OR4). Retrieved February 11, 2011, from http://nces.ed.gov/nationsreportcard/pdf/stt2002/writing/2003532OR4.PDF

U.S. Department of Education, National Center for Education Statistics. (2003b). *The Nation's Report Card: state writing 2002. Snapshot report: Oregon grade 8, public school* (NCES 2003-532OR8). Retrieved February 11, 2011, from http://nces.ed.gov/nationsreportcard/pdf/stt2002/writing/2003532OR8.pdf

Make Assessment Count

Regie Routman

Writing Essentials: Raising Expectations and Results While Simplifying Teaching,
Pages 238–242, ©2004 Heinemann.

If assessments of learning provide evidence of achievement for public reporting, then assessments for learning serve to help students learn more.

—Richard J. Stiggins

There is lots of writing assessment going on these days, but little of it actually improves the quality of students' writing. Assessment of learning includes but is not limited to standardized measures such as state and district writing tests. While this type of assessment is necessary to check whether or not students are progressing—commonly called *accountability*—it is seldom used to improve daily instruction. As clarified by NCTE:

> Furthermore, standardized tests tend to focus on readily accessed features of the language—on grammatical correctness and stylistic choice—and on error, on what is wrong rather than on the appropriate rhetorical choices that have been made. Consequently the outcome of such assessments is negative: students are said to demonstrate what they do "wrong" with language rather than what they do well.

More troubling, standardized test results are often used to make inaccurate statements about students' learning, especially minority students.

While assessment of learning is legitimate (we must, after all, inform the public where our students stand), it must be balanced with assessment *for* learning, which is often classroom based (we must also inform ourselves, our students, and their caregivers about their progress for the specific purpose of improving student writing). In my experience, assessment to improve instruction and learning are too often absent.

A word of caution. While the National Assessment of Educational Progress, also known as the "nation's report card," publishes claims about the status of writing in the United States, these conclusions come from impromptu writing completed in fifteen minutes. Looking at students' writing over time, for purposeful communication to real audiences, is far more valid.

Become More Knowledgeable About Assessment

Think about the last piece you read that was memorable. Was it because the writing had correct grammar, punctuation, and spelling? Certainly those elements were necessary so you could read the piece with ease and focus on the message. But wasn't it the language, the way the author used words, that gripped you? At least that's how it is for me and most readers I know. Of course we depend on correct conventions and form. That's a given. But the inspiration isn't in that; it's in the language, the way the piece flows and is organized, the way the words grab the reader.

Good intentions around assessment can come to naught if we teachers have scant knowledge about teaching writing. For example, spending time examining students' writing—an admirable activity—does not guarantee writing improvement, even when it's done by every teacher in the school and across grade levels. If teachers sit down and look at student writing with a mind-set of correct conventions, without any concern for communicating with the reader through organization, voice, clear intention, and so on, the writing isn't going to improve much.

> **It is our job to ensure that assessment practices lead to targeted teaching and improved writing.**

Likewise, placing students on a writing continuum has the potential to be helpful or a waste of time, based on teachers' knowledge. For example, knowing expected writing behavior at different developmental stages can encourage professional conversations, suggest specific language to use when talking with parents and preparing report cards, and help us choose minilessons and establish standards. But unless teachers know how to teach writing well, student writing will not improve. Take care that most of your time and effort is spent teaching effectively, not matching students with writing stages.

It is our job to ensure that assessment practices lead to targeted teaching and improved writing. "Assessment to improve instruction requires active learning communities that sustain productive conversations about teaching and learning that are based on data." As a staff, you will need to write together, study together, converse together, gather schoolwide data, analyze these data, and set goals for improving writing instruction. There is no shortcut to helping students become effective writers, and there is no program you can buy that will do it for you.

Put Rubrics in Perspective

In many schools in which I work, the teaching of writing is being driven by six traits—ideas and content, organization, sentence fluency, voice, word choice, and conventions. Teaching these specific traits and judging writing on their basis is understandable, since most states' high-stakes writing tests are scored against these traits.

These six traits are a rubric—an evaluation tool. A rubric lists the criteria and/or the qualities expected in a piece of writing. ("Traits are the qualities—ideas, organization, voice, etc.—that define good writing. Criteria are the language we use to define how those traits look at various levels—beginning, developing, proficient—along a continuum of performance.") A rubric...lets the writer know what is expected in order for the writing to be judged excellent (or poor). In theory, embracing the six traits is a good idea, because we know what to look for in writing to assess it; in practice, it can be constraining, because teaching the traits in isolation often becomes the writing program and approach to all writing, especially when teachers are not knowledgeable about how to teach writing effectively.

> **At its most complex, a rubric can delineate many separate qualities and many levels of performance, from high to low.**

While students' test scores may be higher when their teachers adhere strictly to a set of writing traits, the writing is often "vacuous"—simplified and homogenized. Rubrics often fail to measure the development of ideas, overall coherence, and relevance of evidence presented, which sends a message to students that writing to the formula matters, not the content. Rubrics also "fail to provide a *demonstration* of the reading process that can later be internalized by the writer." For example, the writer learns he needs to improve his organization or voice or sentence fluency, but what does that mean? He may work to improve the trait because he's expected to, but he doesn't necessarily become a better writer.

Understand How Rubrics Work

Rubrics are a lot like checklists or guidelines. At its simplest, a rubric is a set of criteria for what needs to be included in a piece of writing.... The criteria can be general, as in the six traits mentioned previously, applying to all writing, or specific to a writing genre or form.... At its most complex, a rubric can delineate many separate qualities and many levels of performance, from high to low.

A rubric can be used to guide text content and/or evaluate text quality:

- A **content rubric** provides explicit criteria to frame the writing and define the task (lets students, teachers, administrators, and parents know what is expected; helps guide the writing).

- An **evaluation rubric** provides criteria explaining how the writing will be rated or scored, often on a scale of numbers (such as from 1 to 4) or words (such as *limited, competent, excellent*).

Rubrics can be *holistic* (one score for the whole piece) or *analytic* (separate scores for each trait); formal or informal; and created by state, district, school, or classroom.

The rubric, like a checklist, helps teachers evaluate writing, decide what minilessons to teach, and what goals to set. It helps students know what to include in a writing assignment, what constitutes quality, and how they will be evaluated.

Keep Your Focus on Effective Writing

Don't overdo it. When you focus on a checklist (or rubric) instead of the child, you miss a lot of what the child is trying to do. Rubrics, like checklists, can disrupt the flow of teaching and learning. When you read a piece of writing, you lose the meaning of what the child is trying to do if, at the same time, you're trying to keep a whole list of criteria in mind. "Although rubrics promote reliability, they may simultaneously undermine validity, the more important determinant of the quality of an assessment." In other words, groups of people scoring papers can be trained to do so against a rubric in a similar, consistent manner (reliability), but whether or not those scores are an accurate representation of the skills and abilities of effective writers (validity) is another question entirely.

> When you focus on a checklist (or rubric) instead of the child, you miss a lot of what the child is trying to do.

Assessments must be both reliable and valid. I worry that conscientious teachers will spend hours scoring papers against a rubric only to have writing remain stagnant because they are looking primarily at word choice or skills in isolation, such as spelling or sentence fluency, and not at the big picture, at what the writer is trying to say. Teachers may agree on what they see (reliability), but if they are looking with a narrow lens focused on skills, those scores do not accurately assess effective writing (validity). The latter is a critical point; if students' writing is to improve, what we are teaching and expecting must be valid.

In Defense of Rubrics

Vicki Spandel

English Journal, Vol. 96, 2006, Pages 19–22.

Rubrics—particularly writing rubrics—have come under some criticism lately, some of it justified, much of it not. When thoughtfully crafted and used with discretion and understanding, rubrics can be among the most useful instructional tools we have. They give us direction and a basis for conversation. They cause us to go deep inside performance and question our traditional beliefs about what we define as proficient. They keep us honest, for when we put our thinking on paper, there is no longer a place to hide. Best of all, they serve as a guide to revision, giving student writers an insider's view of what makes writing work.

A rubric captures the essence of performance at various levels. Good writing may go beyond the rubric, or reflect qualities a rubric cannot capture in simple terms. No assessment (score, grade, narrative description, or conference) reveals *everything*—but each offers useful insights.

Like any instructional tool or strategy, rubrics can be misused, even wielded as weapons to justify the closing of a door; a *good* rubric, however, shows a writer how to open that door and come inside. And therein lies the key: It has to be good.

Rubrics are not all alike. Some are vaguely written, shrouded in jargon, more accusatory than helpful. Some emphasize a formulaic approach to writing or focus on trivia at the expense of substance, and to the extent they influence instruction, this can have devastating ramifications. The quality of voice, for instance, is omitted from many rubrics because it is thought too difficult to define. Yet Donald M. Murray tells us that "voice is the quality, more than any other, that allows us to recognize excellent writing" (21). Surely a quality that gives us a reason to read in the first place should be at the center of our writing assessment and instruction. Good rubrics embrace what we value most deeply, always.

> Sketchy, formulaic rubrics are created by critics whose primary concern is the rapid scoring of someone *else's* work; instructionally useful rubrics are created by readers who think reflectively about how to make their own and others' writing better.

Because it demands reflecting on and describing performance with some precision, creating a rubric teaches us to think. For this reason, whenever possible, we should include students in the process, encouraging them to examine writing from a reader's point of view. Writing is, after all, the making of reading. Sketchy, formulaic rubrics are created by critics whose primary concern is the rapid scoring of someone else's work; instructionally useful rubrics are created by readers who think reflectively about how to make their own and others' writing better.

> **Because it demands reflecting on and describing performance with some precision, creating a rubric teaches us to think.**

As we become increasingly proficient at reading like writers, our rubrics change to mirror that new thinking. Lucy McCormick Calkins has said that rubrics drafted by others work best as "starting points from which we make our own rubrics" (325). I agree. As anyone who has developed (or revised) a rubric will tell you, the journey is a gradually unfolding revelation, during which we continually discover new ways to express what we think and feel. A fifth-grade student began with one rubric's definition of voice as "passion" and "flavor," then added her personal touch: "It's when you feel the exclamation point even though it's not there."

Over time, all reflective readers personalize rubrics. For me, voice is a moment of truth, or what I sometimes call "the chill factor." Some years ago, an eighth-grade student wrote an alternately poignant and comical story about an orphaned 4-H calf, Ginweed, that he had raised to show in the state fair—where she won three ribbons. On show day, Ginweed wore the expensive leather halter the writer's parents had bought for his birthday. The night following the show, fate and the story

> **It is easy to be dismissive about rubrics if we view them as mere lists of expectations.**

took a turn. Ginweed became entangled in the rope that bound her, fell backward, and hanged herself. The writer tells us, "I buried her with the halter and two of the three ribbons she had won. Later that night I went back to her grave. 'Ginweed,' I said, 'we had a heck of a good time together.' And I walked away from the grassless patch of earth" (Spandel, *9 Rights* 75). Those simple lines haunt me still. I have kept the paper for twenty-two years, and "a piece I choose to keep" is part of my personal definition for voice.

When students design and use their own rubrics, they read, process text, and view their writing differently. They come to see those rubrics less as rigid requirements and more as *writing guides*. They take charge of their writing process and no longer depend on us to choreograph their revision.

Writing *is* revision, after all. If we cannot teach students to revise, we cannot, in the truest sense, teach them to write. If students think that revision consists of "fixing the spelling" or "making a paper longer," they may never write a piece that will cause someone to gasp or cry or shout, "You've got to hear this." Without hope of such response, why write at all? Students who learn to think about such issues as clarity and detail, leads and conclusions, voice and audience are in a much better position to revise their writing with purpose and skill. Rubrics that address these issues in clear language show students the *kinds of things* writers do when they revise. Students hunger for and need this information. Donna Flood, director of professional development for ESU#3 in Omaha, asks, "Would you ever invite someone to dinner and not provide them with directions? That's what we were doing...we were inviting children to the learning buffet and telling them that if they could find their way, they were welcome to join us. But if they didn't happen to have the skills necessary to find their way, then—too bad for them. They were out of luck."

> When students ask what makes writing successful, we need to not only describe it but also show them—through modeling or written text—how effective writing can *look*. This is an issue of fairness.

It is easy to be dismissive about rubrics if we view them as mere lists of expectations. They are much more than that. In reality, a writing guide has *three* parts: (1) the written criteria we commit to paper, (2) the examples that show our criteria in action and serve as models for students, and (3) the reader who acts as an interpreter. All are critical.

Consider examples. Often I have asked teachers in workshops, "How helpful would it have been to you *as a writer* if your teachers had given you two samples of writing—one showing what they were looking for in, say, a research paper, and one showing problems to avoid?" The room invariably comes alive with nods and verbal assents. When students ask what makes writing successful, we need to not only describe it but also show them— through modeling or written text—how effective writing can *look*. This is an issue of fairness. Further, if we do not put our thinking on paper, let's not kid ourselves into believing that we are not using rubrics. We're just keeping them "tucked away in our mind's eye" (Flood). All of us look for *something* in writing. If we do not make that something known, we say to students, "I can't describe it," "I prefer not to reveal what I am looking for," or "You figure it out." None is a very satisfying answer to a struggling writer.

Alfie Kohn has said that "[r]ubrics are, above all, a tool to promote standardization, to turn teachers into grading machines or at least allow them to pretend that what they are doing is exact and objective" (12). I could not disagree more. Using a rubric well is an interactive, interpretive process, in which a teacher's wisdom, insight, experience, and judgment play an important role. Far from becoming robotlike in their response, good readers use criteria as reminders, then look diligently for the tiniest sparks of voice, an unexpected phrase or connection, the trail of the writer's thinking.

> Using a rubric well is an interactive, interpretive process, in which a teacher's wisdom, insight, experience, and judgment play an important role.

It is ridiculous to imagine that we are somehow ruled by the very rubrics we create. Rubrics cannot inhibit our understanding of writing any more than a precise map can tell us where and when to travel. They record what we know *now*, but they cannot preclude exploration of new territory. True, rubrics help us overcome arbitrariness, inconsistency, and flat-out bias ("I hate dog stories," "I don't like this writer's attitude," "If he can't edit better than this, I'm not interested in his ideas"). They do not, however, require teachers to abandon individuality or cease responding on a personal level—as if *anything* could do this. No teacher I know believes that rubrics make us totally objective. The good news is that subjectivity is not wrong or even harmful—unless we use it as an excuse not to make our scores or grades defensible. We *do* need to offer reasons for our reactions to writing and to

> Rubrics cannot inhibit our understanding of writing any more than a precise map can tell us where and when to travel. They record what we know *now*, but they cannot preclude exploration of new territory.

show that those reasons are based on sound criteria. One of my colleagues received, as a young student, an A on a piece because the teacher said it was "nice to see typewritten work." Another received an F because her otherwise "captivating" story was written in purple ink. Rubrics make us accountable for scores or grades that affect human lives.

Maja Wilson suggests that rubrics "encourage conformity and an overly formal style" (38). This can only happen if we use language in our rubrics that affirms the value of such things. If we describe good writing with phrases such as "[t]houghtful structure guides reader through text" or "[t]akes reader on a journey of understanding," we encourage writing as thinking, writing that is individual, compelling, and formula-free (Spandel, *Creating* 51). Wilson adds that "a fixed list enforces only the values of which we are conscious, dooming our unconscious values to repressed obscurity" (41). This is a seductive argument since the first part is true; we can hardly put things into a rubric of which we are not yet conscious. Far from "dooming our unconscious values to repressed obscurity," however, we must seek to make ourselves aware of how we respond to writing and why so that we can share our thinking with students. Shared thinking is the foundation of writing instruction. We must

> The good news is that subjectivity is not wrong or even harmful—unless we use it as an excuse not to make our scores or grades defensible. We *do* need to offer reasons for our reactions to writing and to show that those reasons are based on sound criteria.

also let students know that a writing guide does not put a ceiling on performance; many student writers, like the eighth grader with his little 4-H calf, will exceed all expectations.

Wilson also suggests that our job as teachers is "to help students realize what they cannot yet do" (30). I think our job is something much harder—to help students discover what they *can* do, and then to build on it. Many students already recognize their writing faults; too few recognize their strengths. For many teachers and students, a rubric offers a whole new perspective, like a window opening for the first time. "I always responded to this special something in my students' work," a sixth-grade teacher told me. "Now I have a name for it—voice."

The real problem with current writing assessment lies not with rubrics but with what we value. Ultimately, we do not fail to reward risk taking because a rubric tells us we should. We fail to reward risk taking because we do not value it enough—yet. It isn't rubrics pushing us around but our own lack of courage, our unwillingness to let go of tired formulas and embrace the complexity of truly fine writing. Too often, in on-demand writing, we do not honor design or thinking or voice as much as we should because these things can almost never be assessed in a rapid, assessment-at-a-glance fashion. Uncovering such qualities demands astute, perceptive reading—and time. It demands believing at the core that risk taking is just as important as spelling well. Once we believe that fully, our rubrics will echo our beliefs. Until then, we will continue to reward dimensions of writing that are easy to track even when we are pressured or tired—a ponderously obvious organizational structure, formulaic transitions, summary conclusions. Attending to such features makes our assessment task easier.

Easier should not be part of the bargain. What we demand of our students as writers we must demand of ourselves as readers. A rubric is ultimately a two-way commitment, a reader-writer contract that says, "If you write with thought and with heart, I will understand, and I will hear you. I will follow where you lead and reflect on the connections you make. I will allow you to teach me."

Let's not abandon rubrics. Let's make them better by ensuring that they honor what good readers think important in writing. Let's also create an assessment approach that allows space for thinking: opportunity for reflection, personal selection of a topic, time for true revision and editing. We have seen what students cannot do, given time restraints and topics to which they have no attachment. Do we not want to see what they

Let's not abandon rubrics.

can do under the best of circumstances? Finally, let's respond to students' writing in a way that mirrors how we would wish someone to respond to us, with consistent attention to what matters coupled with an unwavering belief that many will soar beyond all current visions of success.

Works Cited

Calkins, Lucy McCormick. *The Art of Teaching Writing*. New ed. Portsmouth: Heinemann, 1994.

Flood, Donna. Personal interview. May 2006.

Kohn, Alfie. "The Trouble with Rubrics." *English Journal, 95*.4 (2006): 12–15.

Murray, Donald M. *A Writer Teaches Writing*. 2nd ed. Boston: Houghton, 2004.

Spandel, Vicki. *Creating Writers: Through 6-Trait Writing Assessment and Instruction*. 4th ed. Boston: Pearson, 2005.

———. *The 9 Rights of Every Writer: A Guide for Teachers*. Portsmouth: Heinemann, 2005.

Wilson, Maja. *Rethinking Rubrics in Writing Assessment*. Portsmouth: Heinemann, 2006.

Excerpts From

Rubrics: Heuristics for Developing Writing Strategies

Susan De La Paz

Assessment for Effective Intervention, Vol. 34, 2009, Pages 134–146.

Transforming Rubrics into Heuristics for Developing Writing Strategies

In this section, I propose and elaborate on a four-step sequence for teachers to engage in when planning how to transform rubrics into heuristics for developing writing strategies and demonstrate how this process might unfold with the use of a comparison-contrast rubric.... [The rubric used for this study], a composite generated from several readily available rubrics, proposes that several categories are proposed relating to genre, text structure, and surface features of connected text, and it provides four gradations in quality. Other rubrics for analyzing comparison and contrast essays may be equally appropriate for classroom use; this one was selected for illustration purposes.

To work from this type of rubric and use it as a heuristic for developing a writing strategy, teachers carry out a series of actions related to four key steps (see Figure 3):

1. Examine the rubric.
2. Identify underlying skills to teach.
3. Develop a mnemonic.
4. Add supports.

Furthermore, by completing the first step, teachers will develop content to be used for the remaining steps in the planning process. In addition, although my example highlights the development of a planning strategy for writing comparison essays, it would also be possible to develop a revising strategy that is genre specific.

Step I: Examine the Rubric

In this step, teachers consider four questions: What elements are essential to the genre? What is related to text structure? What are realistic goals for the writer regarding the product? How can the writer demonstrate thinking that is of value in the discipline? Step 1 provides the most important set of actions because answers to these questions will be used for, or embedded in, each subsequent planning step. To illustrate,... to write a successful comparison paper, a writer must identify points of similarity and difference between each chosen item of a category.

FIGURE 3. Transforming rubrics into writing strategies

Step 1. Examine the rubric. In so doing, answer four questions:

What elements are essential to the genre?

What is related to text structure?

What are realistic goals for the writer regarding the product?

How can the writer demonstrate thinking that is of value to the discipline?

Step 2. Identify underlying skills to teach.

Decide how to teach. Text structure may be presented via literature or trade books, visual guides, sample essays and so on.

Task representations matter. Writing in response to literature may be less difficult than writing in response to a prompt.

Good instruction still counts. Modeling, direct instruction, and opportunities to practice all make a difference.

Step 3. Develop a mnemonic.

Remind students what is essential about genre and processes underlying effective writing.

The first letter should be a verb and the overall mnemonic should relate to the purpose.

Use known acronyms, if any.

Establish different types of goals (process, product, and domain).

Add redundancy with other elements such as supports (see below).

Limit the number of total steps to a manageable number.

Step 4. Add supports.

Lists of transition words, key phrases, or domain-specific markers.

Cue cards, especially those that provide upward or downward extensions.

Forms for recording progress (e.g., to aid in goal setting).
Plan how to systematically remove these scaffolds during instruction.

To make these terms clear for later use in this article, and given the subject of social studies, one category might be "The First Ladies of the United States of America." Within this category, three items for comparison might be as follows: (a) how they supported their husbands' presidencies, (b) the effect they had on society, and (c) how the time period in which they lived provided constraints or opportunities for them to accomplish their goals. Last, the points of similarity and difference vary, depending on which of the presidents' wives are chosen; for example, Martha Washington and Eleanor Roosevelt provide an opportunity for a broader comparison (partly because they lived in very different eras) than one between Martha Washington and Abigail Adams.

> **Step I provides the most important set of actions because answers to these questions will be used for, or embedded in, each subsequent planning step.**

Although teachers may think of ideas for each step in a recursive manner, I examine hypothetical responses to the remaining questions in this step before moving on. The second question in Step 1 asks teachers to consider text structure because it provides a critical linkage for understanding each genre. Furthermore, by determining the range of text structures (there are at least four text structures for comparison essays...), teachers also decide how to introduce each form to students. One technique is to illustrate text structure by reading stories, such as *George vs. George: The American Revolution as Seen from Both Sides* (Schanzer, 2004), and *John, Paul, George, and Ben* (Smith, 2006). Another approach is to develop visual guides...for use as procedural facilitators, meaning that students use a chart to remind themselves how text structures are formed, when generating their own essays. A third way to explain text structure is to create sample essays, composed for each text structure, for students to examine and deconstruct. Students use these to identify differences and similarities among various text structures so that they fully understand each and can then use them as sample templates in their own writing. Although all these activities help students build background knowledge of text structure, in particular, I have found visual guides to be a valuable form of support (to be discussed in Step 4).

The third question in Step 1, "What are realistic goals for the writer regarding the product?", is a reminder for some students, particularly those with disabilities, that they may not achieve competence in all areas of writing. Students with learning disabilities and other high incidence disabilities have more errors such as spelling, punctuation, capitalization, grammar, and word usage mistakes than their peers and may benefit less from instruction. Thus, although teachers may legitimately expect students to (attempt to) proof their papers for mechanical errors, it is also important to focus on ways students can improve other aspects of their writing and hope that their reader gains an overall more favorable impression. Goals such as staying on topic, using vivid or original vocabulary, choosing specific examples to illustrate each comparison, and creating complete comparisons (by stating a point of similarity and a point of difference for each item presented, for example) may be chosen and monitored for an individual or groups of students.

The last question in Step 1 is to consider how the writer can demonstrate thinking that is of value in the discipline. To some extent, this question may be ignored in early primary contexts. However, because science and social studies teachers increasingly require students to use writing as a key means for demonstrating their understanding (Bangert-Drowns, Hurley, & Wilkinson, 2004), students may benefit from their teachers' explicit instructions on how to engage in this type of thinking.

For example, in science, students may compare and contrast classification systems or taxonomies, or be asked to explain why observed effects in an experiment are similar to or different from technical descriptions of a phenomenon (Hand, Prain, & Yore, 2001).

In social studies, again in the context of writing comparison essays, students may be asked to think about similarities and difference in people's attitudes and beliefs concerning different topics (such as immigration) during specific time periods (e.g., the 1900s or the first decade of the new millennium) and what underlying issues in society influenced people's beliefs during each respective time period. Finally, to bring this discussion back to a primary context (albeit not one in which a comparison essay is needed), children in elementary school are routinely asked to explain how they arrived at their solution to mathematics problems, which requires them to be able to translate symbolic representations into pictorial or written accounts and provide some explanation or justification for their solution. In each of these cases, teachers are likely to obtain better writing samples when they first identify and then make explicit what is meant by these and other disciplinary connections.

> **Although teachers may legitimately expect students to (attempt to) proof their papers for mechanical errors, it is also important to focus on ways students can improve other aspects of their writing and hope that their reader gains an overall more favorable impression.**

Step 2: Identify Underlying Skills to Teach

Using content from the first step, teachers may now consider elements related to genre, text structure, and goals (including those that are related to the writing process, writing products, and those that are discipline specific). All are relevant and may be taught directly or embedded into mnemonics and other forms of support (see Steps 3 and 4). Using information about the comparison genre as the context, I have already claimed that writers must generate points of similarity and difference between each chosen item of a category. In some contexts, such as in writing a response to literature, students read one or more texts (e.g., one source about Martha Washington and one source about Eleanor Roosevelt) to select ideas that meet each of these criteria. However, in other situations, students retrieve ideas from long-term memory, relying on prior knowledge about one or more topics. Because the latter situation is especially challenging for students with learning disabilities, my focus here is on helping students generate content for a writing prompt.

> Using content from the first step, teachers may now consider elements related to genre, text structure, and goals (including those that are related to the writing process, writing products, and those that are discipline specific).

To elaborate, students need to first brainstorm a range of categories for a given comparison (abolitionists, wives of presidents, suffragettes—if given a broader purpose to compare and contrast famous women), and second, brainstorm specific items within these categories as the basis for their comparison (with respect to the topic of presidents' wives, additional items for comparison might be their personal upbringing, whether they overcame any personal obstacles in dealing with their husband's quest for the presidency, their political skills, whether they accomplished one or more goals in their life time, and so on). Third, students need to identify what the items have in common and how they differ, to select points of similarity and difference for use in their essay. At this stage, students should organize content (this can be done by checking off selected content to be used in the essay and ordering each point, facilitated by using a list or Venn diagram format when first generating content).

So students brainstorm and organize content based on the specific genre under study and follow corresponding forms of text structure. For comparison essays, key words and phrases signal conceptual relationships to the reader. For example, "more" and "-er" words indicate similarity, whereas "on the contrary" and "in contrast" are used to signal differences.... Providing students with lists such as these and spending time in class noting how entire sentences can be used to signal a change in focus of comparison will help ensure that students use them appropriately in their compositions. Finally, for mature writers, the comparison genre, like most genres, is really a multigenre text in that it often combines explanation as well as elements of persuasion. Writers may also include descriptive elements, such as similes, metaphors, and analogies, in their examples, and it naturally follows that showing students these devices will enrich the quality of their comparisons.

Step 3: Develop a Mnemonic

This device should remind students what is essential about the genre (and accompanying text structure), as well as the processes that they need to engage in when planning to write. In my work with secondary students with and without disabilities, the following principles have led to creating useful mnemonics: (a) start each element of the mnemonic with a verb, to prompt students to engage in an action; (b) relate the mnemonic to the purpose of the activity to make it meaningful; (c) capitalize on acronyms known for other purposes, if any exist, to ease their burden in memorizing something new; (d) establish goals that relate to different purposes, process (e.g., brainstorming), product (e.g., using different sentence structures), and domain (e.g., science), either for an entire group or for individuals; (e) add redundancy with other elements of the writing program, such as supports, again to help students internalize the strategy; and finally, (f) limit the total number of steps. If additional complexity is needed, embed a subroutine (e.g., one element of the mnemonic may trigger a series of actions that are to be executed before continuing with the remaining steps).

> [The mnemonic] device should remind students what is essential about the genre (and accompanying text structure), as well as the processes that they need to engage in when planning to write.

When thinking of a sample mnemonic for comparison essays, I used the word "COMPARE" as the guiding mnemonic. Each letter corresponds to one action or element needed to plan a comparison essay. The C stands for Consider different categories ("Can you think of three different comparisons that respond to the prompt?"). The O stands for Opt for two (or more, if required) items to be compared ("How many can you write down?). The M stands for Match up ideas (list and sequence points that are similar and points that are different). If the student has already generated ideas using a list or some graphic organizer, he or she organizes them by numbering them in the order he or she plans to use them. The P stands for Pick a text structure.... The A stands for Add supporting facts, details, and examples, to elicit elaboration. The R stands for Remember your goals, which can relate to process, product, and domain, and again be established for an entire class or individualized as needed. The final letter, E stands for Evaluate ("Reread your essay to see if it makes sense"). Thus, although the resulting mnemonic is arguably too long to use in elementary contexts, for older students in particular, it responds to the rubric for comparison essays, informs students how to engage in the skills needed to create effective papers, and provides an opportunity for teachers to embed other skills and strategies found in effective papers (e.g., elaboration and revision).

Step 4: Add Supports

The supports will be phased out over time, as students gain mastery in planning, composing, and revising their compositions. Two of these supports have been mentioned already, such as lists of transition words, phrases, or other domain-specific markers.... Students can be taught to use a range of these without memorizing the entire list to become comfortable in their use yet avoid writing formulaic essays. Second, teachers can supply (and later withdraw) text-structure guides as separate graphic organizers to provide organizational cues. With comparison essays, it is important to teach students that the underlying text structure also follows parallel construction. For instance, if using a whole-to-whole or block pattern for construction, the writer might choose to mention Martha Washington before Eleanor Roosevelt for each item (when commenting on how they supported their husbands' presidencies, the effect they had on society, and how the time period in which they lived provided constraints or opportunities for them to do these things). Two more forms of support, which can be used on an as-needed basis for individual learners are (a) cue cards that guide the sequencing of steps or add extensions for more capable learners and (b) forms for recording progress (to aid in self-monitoring and goal setting). In my previous work, each of these forms of support has been helpful to students.

> The supports will be phased out over time, as students gain mastery in planning, composing, and revising their compositions.

Summary and Conclusion

The main purpose of this article has been to show teachers how to approach rubrics with a new appreciation for their potential as instructional tools. The suggestions presented here provide a series of planning activities that transform rubrics into heuristics for developing writing strategies. This was demonstrated with a hypothetical example, in writing comparison essays, as well as an example from my prior work using strategy instruction. However, space limitations preclude other discussions, such as the delicate subject of how to use rubrics to provide meaningful feedback to writers, a process which has sometimes been called into question as too standardized and not specific enough to meet the needs of individual students (Wilson, 2007). Moreover, based on the parallels herein with the use of rubrics as heuristics for developing writing strategies, the savvy reader might ask, what is the essential difference between

> The suggestions presented here provide a series of planning activities that transform rubrics into heuristics for developing writing strategies.

this approach and the more general strategy instruction (e.g., SRSD [self-regulated strategy development] model)? I give two answers. First, the six stages of instruction in SRSD, which call for a phased transformation from teacher-led to student-independent writing performance has been omitted from this discussion. Second and perhaps more important, the role of self-regulation, found to be essential for learners with disabilities and responsible for especially powerful effects as compared to strategy instruction without its emphasis, is again neglected in this overview.

To conclude, the SRSD model provides a coherent structure, incorporating modeling, self-regulation, criterion-based mastery, and a gradual transfer of knowledge and skills from teachers to students (which teachers may wish to add to their writing program, after following suggestions presented here). Transforming rubrics into mini writing strategies can be a first step. However, because the full SRSD model has consistently led to positive, noticeable effects with students who have varying initial capabilities at multiple grade levels, my hope is that teachers and their students will use rubrics to develop mini strategies, then expand their writing programs even further by incorporating a more comprehensive model of instruction.

References

Bangert-Drowns, R. L., Hurley, M. M., & Wilkinson, B. (2004). The effects of school-based writing-to-learn interventions on academic achievement: A meta-analysis. *Review of Educational Research, 74,* 29–58.

Hand, B. M., Prain, V., & Yore, L. (2001). Sequential writing tasks' influence on science learning. In G. Rijlaarsdam (Series Ed.) & P. Tynjala, L. Mason, & K. Lonka (Vol. Eds.), *Studies in writing. Volume 7: Writing as a learning tool—Integrating theory and practice* (pp. 105–129). Dordrecht, Netherlands: Kluwer Academic.

Schanzer, R. (2004). *George vs. George: The American Revolution as seen from both sides.* Washington, DC: National Geographic Society.

Schirmer, B. R., & Bailey, J. (2000). W*riting assessment rubric. Teaching Exceptional Children, 33,* 52–58.

Smith, L. (2006). *John, Paul, George, & Ben.* New York: Hyperion Books for Children.

Wilson, M. (2007). Why I won't be using rubrics to respond to students' writing. *English Journal, 96,* 62–66.

Excerpts From

Putting Rubrics to the Test: The Effect of a Model, Criteria Generation, and Rubric-Referenced Self-Assessment on Elementary School Students' Writing

Heidi L. Andrade, Ying Du, and Xiaolei Wang

Educational Measurement: Issues and Practice, Summer 2008, Pages 3–13.

The purpose of this study was to investigate the effect of reading a model written assignment, generating a list of criteria for the assignment, and self-assessing according to a rubric, as well as gender, time spent writing, prior rubric use, and previous achievement on elementary school students' scores for a written assignment (N = 116). Participants were in grades 3 and 4. The treatment involved using a model paper to scaffold the process of generating a list of criteria for an effective story or essay, receiving a written rubric, and using the rubric to self-assess first drafts. The comparison condition involved generating a list of criteria for an effective story or essay, and reviewing first drafts. Findings include a main effect of treatment and of previous achievement on total writing scores, as well as main effects on scores for the individual criteria on the rubric. The results suggest that using a model to generate criteria for an assignment and using a rubric for self-assessment can help elementary school students produce more effective writing.

Research Questions and Hypotheses

This study was designed to test popular claims about the relationship between rubric-referenced assessment, including and especially self-assessment, and elementary school students' writing by addressing two research questions:

1. Is there a main effect of a model, generating criteria, and rubric-referenced self-assessment on scores assigned to students' writing?

2. If so, is that effect influenced by gender, previous achievement in English/Language Arts, amount of time spent on writing an assignment in class, and/or prior exposure to rubrics?

We predicted the following hypotheses would be supported by our data:

1. Reading a model paper, generating the criteria for a rubric, and using a rubric to self-assess first drafts will be associated with higher scores for students' written work.
2. On average, girls will receive higher scores for their writing than boys.
3. Amount of writing time and previous achievement in English/Language Arts will be positively associated with writing scores.
4. Prior exposure to rubrics will not be related to writing scores.

Method and Data Sources
Participants

The study employed a convenience sample of 116 volunteer participants. It took place in seven public elementary school classrooms in the northeastern United States. Three classes were grade 3 ($N = 46$) and four were grade 4 ($N = 70$). Though each class had only one teacher and a teacher's aide for all academic subjects, five of the seven classes participated in the study during English/Language Arts (ELA) class time, and two of the classes participated in the study during social studies class time. The sample consisted of intact classes, matched by grade level and subject matter: There were four classes in the treatment group (two third grade classes studying ELA, and two fourth grades, one studying ELA and one studying social studies), and three in the comparison group (one third grade studying ELA, and two fourth grades, one studying ELA and one studying social studies).

Among the participants, 52 (44.8%) were boys, and 64 (55.2%) were girls. A majority of the participants ($N = 110$; 94.8%) were Caucasian. The number of participants who were identified as having special needs was very small ($N = 3$).

Procedures

The writing process in each class resembled a Writers' Workshop: Students engaged in some form of prewriting, wrote first drafts, got feedback from the classroom teacher, and wrote final drafts.

The treatment condition differed from the comparison condition in three ways: The students in the treatment group (1) read a model story or essay, discussed its strengths and weaknesses, and generated a list of qualities of an effective story or essay; (2) received a written rubric; and (3) used the rubric to self-assess their first drafts. The students in the comparison group did not read a model story or essay but did generate a list of qualities of an effective story or essay. The comparison group did not receive a rubric. Students in the comparison group were asked to review their first drafts and note possibilities for improvement in the final draft. They did not self-assess their drafts according to a rubric.

Rubrics

The rubrics given to the treatment group classes referred to seven commonly assessed criteria for writing (e.g., the 6+1 Trait® Writing Method; see Culham, 2003; Spandel & Stiggins, 1997): ideas and content, organization, voice and tone, word choice, sentence fluency, and conventions.... We treated the essay score data as interval-level data for analysis.

Results

The average writing score for the entire sample was 26.8 (SD =5.2), with a range of 16 to 40.... Initial analysis and data screening suggested that the variables most likely to influence students' writing scores include treatment, gender, and previous achievement in English/Language Arts. Ethnicity and special needs were not included as variables because the sample sizes for each are very small.

Total Essay Scores

Controlling for previous achievement, a GLM two-way ANOVA was used to analyze the main effect of treatment and gender. The assessment is statistically significant. On average, the treatment group's writing scores (M =28.5, SD = 4.9) are higher than the comparison group's scores (M =24.3, SD =4.7), $F(1, 111) = 18.9, p = .000$, partial $\eta^2 = .15$.

Scores on Individual Criteria

The previous paragraph reported on total essay scores, which were the sum of scores received for the seven criteria on the rubrics—ideas and content, organization, paragraph formatting, voice and tone, word choice, sentence fluency, and conventions. We also examined the relationships between the treatment and particular aspects of writing, as represented by each criterion.

> On average, the treatment group's writing scores are higher than the comparison group's scores.

Table 4 contains the means and standard deviations for scores on each criterion on the rubric, by condition and gender.

TABLE 4. Means and standard deviations of scores for each criterion, by condition and gender (*N* = 116)

	Condition	Gender	Mean	SD	N
Ideas	Comparison	Male	3.02	1.32	23
		Female	2.76	1.42	23
		Total	2.89	1.36	46
	Treatment	Male	3.72	1.29	29
		Female	4.26	1.10	41
		Total	4.04	1.21	70
Organization	Comparison	Male	2.86	1.07	23
		Female	3.01	0.90	23
		Total	2.93	0.98	46
	Treatment	Male	3.61	0.94	29
		Female	3.76	1.00	41
		Total	3.70	0.97	70
Paragraphs	Comparison	Male	2.64	1.37	23
		Female	2.90	0.99	23
		Total	2.77	1.19	46
	Treatment	Male	3.46	1.42	29
		Female	3.44	1.45	41
		Total	3.45	1.42	70
Voice	Comparison	Male	3.70	1.55	23
		Female	4.03	1.20	23
		Total	3.86	1.38	46
	Treatment	Male	4.34	0.87	29
		Female	4.85	0.98	41
		Total	4.64	0.96	70
Words	Comparison	Male	3.59	0.85	23
		Female	3.97	0.81	23
		Total	3.78	0.84	46
	Treatment	Male	4.29	1.03	29
		Female	4.46	0.94	41
		Total	4.39	0.97	70
Sentences	Comparison	Male	4.17	0.70	23
		Female	4.10	0.67	23
		Total	4.14	0.68	46
	Treatment	Male	4.27	0.52	29
		Female	4.43	0.66	41
		Total	4.36	0.61	70
Conventions	Comparison	Male	3.95	0.72	23
		Female	3.96	0.89	23
		Total	3.95	0.80	46
	Treatment	Male	3.56	0.81	29
		Female	4.12	1.00	41
		Total	3.89	0.96	70

Discussion

This study provides support for the hypothesis that having students use model papers to generate criteria for a writing assignment and using a rubric to self-assess first drafts is positively related to the quality of their writing. The treatment has a statistically significant, positive association with third and fourth grade students' essay scores, even controlling for the predictably powerful effect of previous achievement in English/Language Arts. The effect size for total essay scores (partial η^2 = .15) is small but meaningful in practice: Roughly translated into typical classroom grades (an admittedly subjective process that can be undertaken in a variety of ways) by equating a score of six on each criterion with 100%, a five on each criterion with 90%, a four with 80% and so on, the average grade for the treatment group would be a low B, compared to the average comparison group grade of a high C.

> Roughly translated into typical classroom grades...the average grade for the treatment group would be a low B, compared to the average comparison group grade of a high C.

Student-reported prior rubric use was not associated with total scores on the writing assignments. We attribute this finding to minimal rubric use by most of the students prior to the study. A poll of the teachers revealed that, of the seven teachers in the study, six had already exposed their students to rubrics but only four handed their rubrics out to students before they began an assignment, and only two had asked students to use the rubrics to assess their own or each other's work. Like Andrade (2001), we conclude that simply handing out a rubric is unlikely to have a measurable effect on student work.

> In the analysis of the scores received on individual criteria (ideas and content, organization, paragraph formatting, voice and tone, word choice, sentence structure, and conventions), the treatment had a significant influence on all criteria except for sentences and conventions.

In the analysis of the scores received on individual criteria (ideas and content, organization, paragraph formatting, voice and tone, word choice, sentence structure, and conventions), the treatment had a significant influence on all criteria except for sentences and conventions. Interestingly, conventions was the only criterion not explicitly attended to during the rubric-referenced self-assessment done by the treatment group. We interpret this finding as additional evidence of the effect of formal self-assessment.

We also note that the finding regarding the effect of treatment on criteria such as voice, or ideas and content, stands as a rejoinder to recent critiques of rubrics (Kohn, 2006; Wilson, 2006). Kohn and Wilson argue that rubrics promote weak writing by focusing attention on only the most quantifiable and least important qualities of assignments. The fact that rubric-referenced self-assessment was associated with higher scores on important qualities like ideas and content testifies to the potential of such processes to help students master significant, meaningful aspects of writing—at least when the rubrics emphasize those important qualities and when students are actively involved in using them (Andrade, 2006), as in this study.

References

Andrade, H. G. (2001, April 18). The effects of instructional rubrics on learning to write. *Current Issues in Education, 4*(4). Available at http://cie.ed.asu.edu/ volume4/number4.

Andrade, H. (2006). The trouble with a narrow view of rubrics. *English Journal, 95*(6), 9.

Culham, R. (2003). *6 + 1 traits of writing: The complete guide, grades 3 and up.* Portland, OR: Northwest Regional Educational Laboratory.

Kohn, A. (2006). The trouble with rubrics. *The English Journal, 95*(4), 12–15.

Spandel, V., & Stiggins, R. J. (1997). Creating writers: *Linking writing assessment and instruction* (2nd ed.). New York: Longman.

Wilson, M. (2006). *Rethinking rubrics in writing assessment.* Portsmouth, NH: Heinemann.

Excerpts From

Reliability and Validity of Rubrics for Assessment Through Writing

Ali Reza Rezaei and Michael Lovorn

Assessing Writing, Vol. 15, 2010, Pages 18–39.

Introduction

The use of rubrics for evaluating students' writing emerged from a general dissatisfaction, among teachers and administrators, with traditional essay grading strategies. In today's educational environment of high stakes assessment, many educators regularly and confidently employ rubrics as a way to assess students' work. This is an indication that rubrics are highly regarded as tools that increase reliability and validity in assessment. It should be noted, however, that simple implementation of rubrics may not guarantee effective assessment (Breland, 1983; Ross-Fisher, 2005; Tomkins, 2003).

Several researchers have reported that teachers' assessment is more reliable if a rubric is used (Jonsson & Svingby, 2007; Silvestri & Oescher, 2006). No research has been found to show a negative effect of using rubrics (decreasing the reliability). Consequently, many teachers have used rubrics with the assumption that they increase grading objectivity, particularly, regarding students' writing submissions. As a result, another assumption exists that assessment without a rubric tends to be more subjective because it is based only on each grader's subjective judgment, and her/his overall impressions of the writer's style. With this in mind, teachers often resolve that using a rubric is better than not using one (Spandel, 2006). Researchers have asked, however, if this assumption about rubrics is based on false claims to objectivity, or if they simply make subjectivity more visible (Turley & Gallagher, 2008).

Background

Rater bias is evident in many forms (Read et al., 2005; Ross-Fisher, 2005; Tomkins, 2003). It is noteworthy that students who write neatly and display better basic writing mechanics regularly receive higher marks on their essays than students who lack these skills, even though their attention to content is otherwise identical (Briggs, 1970; Bull & Stevens, 1979; Chase, 1968; James, 1927; Markham, 1976; Marshall & Powers, 1969; Sheppard, 1929). Gage and Berliner (1992) investigated reliability and validity of essay grading by having a group of 100 teachers grade an essay without a rubric. All teachers graded the same essay, scoring it on a 100-point scale. Despite the fact that each teacher was given the same instructions, grades varied greatly. Their scores ranged from 60 to the upper 90s. As a part of this investigation, researchers also asked participating teachers to estimate the grade level of the student who wrote the paper. Again, answers varied significantly. Estimates ranged from as high as the junior year in college to as low as 5th grade elementary school level. Reasons for this variance may be found in studies in assessment bias. According to recent findings, graders' biases have related to gender, language command, and even physical attractiveness of students (Malouff, 2008), and bias effect is accentuated when raters tend to rate unusually harshly or leniently (Knoch, Read, & Randow, 2007). Additionally, essays written in good penmanship are frequently assigned higher marks than essays written in poor penmanship (Chase, 1968; Marshall & Powers, 1969). According to Scannell and Marshall (1966), essays with several composition errors, including punctuation, spelling, and grammar mistakes, often resulted in lower scores than essays free of these mistakes. This held true even when graders had been prompted to score on content alone. Related research by Marshall and Powers (1969) also found an inverse relationship between scores assigned to an essay and the number of composition errors (spelling, grammar, and punctuation) in the paper.

> **Do rubrics lead to a more reliable and less biased assessment in comparison with traditional essay grading?**

In contrast, rubrics have been lauded as tools that have effectively leveled the playing field for all (Jonsson & Svingby, 2007). However, do rubrics lead to a more reliable and less biased assessment in comparison with traditional essay grading? Today many teachers feel more confident about their assessment of student writing when rubrics are employed (Silvestri & Oescher, 2006). Rating scales used in performance assessment have been repeatedly criticized for being imprecise and therefore often resulting in holistic marking by raters. This means even if a rubric is used the grade might be mainly assigned based on teacher's overall impression. These studies have also determined that criteria that use impressionistic terminology are more open to subjective or ambiguous interpretations (Knoch, 2009; Weigle, 2002).

Teachers, schools, and school systems have adopted rubrics for more accurate assessment in every discipline. Recently, however, some educators have challenged the collective assumption that simply implementing rubrics increases inter-rater reliability and validity, and the overall accuracy and quality of assessment (Kohn, 2006; Wilson, 2006). In steadily increasing numbers, educators are coming to realize that no rubric can be completely effective in evaluation of students' individual writing idiosyncrasies or their unique understanding of the concepts. Some have even found that rubrics prematurely narrow and cement their visions of good writing (Wilson, 2007).

This paper investigates the extent to which the use of rubrics helps prevent raters from paying too much attention to writing mechanics over a focus on the reasoning, content knowledge, and logical thinking in graduate student writing.

This study intends to investigate the reliability and validity of rubrics in assessment through students' writing. The goal is to see if using a rubric leads to a more reliable assessment in comparison with the case where no rubric (holistic assessment) is used.

Method

Experiments

Experiment I

Group 1 (education students) and Group 3 (business and marketing students) participated in this experiment. Participants were asked to grade a written essay (Appendix A) on the topic of economic globalization on a 100-point scale. They were asked to grade the essay once without a rubric and then with a rubric. Participants were not privy to the writer's name, specific age, or level of education, but were instructed to assume the writer was a student of an advanced social studies class and that the essay was the student's response to the following prompt: "In an essay, discuss economic globalization in terms of its history; economic, social, and political impacts; and how information technology has influenced the speed of globalization in terms of outsourcing and off-shoring."

> The goal is to see if using a rubric leads to a more reliable assessment in comparison with the case where no rubric (holistic assessment) is used.

Although the essay response was well written in terms of skills and mechanics, it covered only a broad description of economic globalization, and it did not fully address any element of the above prompt. The goal of this experiment was to evaluate how participants were influenced by and/or impressed with the mechanics and superficial characteristics of the essay, rather than the correctness or the accuracy of the answer.

Experiment 2

Group 2 (education students) and Group 4 (business and marketing students) participated in this experiment. The research design was similar to the first experiment (the same prompt and the same rubric were used); however, the essay given to these participants was different. Unlike the first essay, this second essay accurately addressed all parts of the prompt, and according to the rubric, deserved a high score because the writer answered all questions and used a variety of proper sources (references) in a complete and concise response. The penmanship of this essay, however, was obstructed by 20 structural, mechanical, spelling and grammar errors. In fact the authors inserted these 20 spelling and grammar errors in the second essay to investigate how mechanics influenced the raters' grading.

[T]wo sample essays were designed specifically for use in this study. The first response used in the first experiment is referred to in this paper as the "Wrong Essay". Although it was eloquently and professionally written, it contained only a broad description of globalization and did not fully address or answer any of the above prompts. The second response used in the study is referred to in this paper as the "Correct Essay". The authors inserted 20 structural and mechanical errors into this essay, yet it was written to adequately answer the questions outlined in the prompt.

Summary of findings

Four hypotheses were tested in this project. First, the authors predicted that the rubric would lower the range and the variability of scores and, therefore, increase the reliability of grading. The results did not support this hypothesis. Findings indicated that using the rubric did not lessen the range of assigned scores to a given essay. In fact, on the contrary, the authors found that the assigned grade variance increased significantly after implementing the rubric. Furthermore, it showed that

> Using the rubric did not lessen the range of assigned scores to a given essay.

participants (particularly from college of education) were strongly influenced by the trivial mechanics and superficial aspects of students' writing. The authors came to this conclusion because the only problem with the second essay was the grammar and spelling errors; therefore, higher grades were expected for this essay (in comparison with the first essay). However, the authors observed that many raters assigned low scores to this essay because the writer had demonstrated poor sentence structure and mechanics. When the authors asked the participants to justify their assigned grades, several responded with explanations to this effect: "The student's poor writing style indicated she/he did not take time (or perhaps even care enough) to spell check or to revise the sentence structure, and so she/he deserves the poor grade". Statements of this nature elicited a response from the authors (among ourselves) questioning the very nature and purpose of rubrics. The authors found it interesting that although rubrics were designed to reduce or eliminate rater's bias such as this, and although this rubric placed very little assessable attention on writing mechanics (only 10 points out of 100), it was obviously still a significant factor in raters' assessments.

Second, it was predicted that in the first experiment using the rubric would lead to high scores in "mechanics" and "structural organization and clarity," and that low scores would result from "understanding and synthesis of argument" and "understanding the goals and implications of globalization". Results did not support this hypothesis. This is evident from the fact that although the first version of the essay did not address the prompt, it not only received a passing grade (overall 68.2 out of 100), but also it received a passing grade (18.1 out of 25) on the item specifically evaluating the writer's attempt to adequately address the prompt. The authors also predicted that using the rubric would lead to a very low score (ideally zero) on citations and references because the writer failed to cite any sources for the essay. It was particularly interesting to note that raters gave credit (8.6 out of 15) to some aspects (citation) of the paper that it did not contain at all. It should be noted that lack of any citation in the essay is not a subjective matter. Giving credit to something that did not exist indicated that the raters were extremely influenced by their overall impression due to the very impressive writing style of the first essay. As noted by Lumley (2002), although raters try to remain close to the rubric, they are heavily influenced by the complex intuitive impression of the text obtained when they first read it.

> **Although raters try to remain close to the rubric, they are heavily influenced by the complex intuitive impression of the text obtained when they first read it.**

Third, it was predicted that in the second experiment, the participants would be negatively influenced by essay writer's spelling errors and grammatical mistakes, and that they would assign an overall low score, particularly to the writer's mechanics. This was confirmed by the above results; however, the authors did not expect a low score on "understanding and synthesis of argument" and "understanding the goals and implications of globalization". Surprisingly, the results showed that the participants rated the second essay lower than the first essay even in these two categories.

Finally, and surprisingly, the results did not show a significant difference between education students and business/marketing students. The authors expected education students to be less influenced by the mechanics of the essay because of their familiarity with rubrics, fair assessment, and raters' bias; however, the results did not support this hypothesis. This perhaps indicates that they did not have enough training. It also could be interpreted that a general familiarity with rubrics is not enough to change the reliability of assessment and there is a need for special training for using rubrics for a specific assignment. These findings not only show low reliability for the rubric used in this study but also question its construct and criterion-based validity.

Discussion and limitations

Some educators believe that rubrics have not led to a more objective or more reliable grading. Ideally, the feedback given by employment of a rubric is better than the assignment of a simple letter grade; however, untrained users of rubrics may simply use it to justify their biased assessment. According to this group, the irrelevant variables affecting holistic assessment of a performance or an essay may still affect rubric-based assessment. Judgments ultimately turn on adjectives that are murky and end up being left to the teacher's discretion (Kohn, 2006; Lumley, 2002). The results of the present research confirmed this observation and showed that the raters graded the essay based on their overall impression rather than following the rubric. For example, we observed that some teachers gave points for citation in the essay that did not include any citations. We believe this happened because the raters were influenced by the overall quality of writing and so did not pay attention to this particular weakness.

> Ideally, the feedback given by employment of a rubric is better than the assignment of a simple letter grade; however, untrained users of rubrics may simply use it to justify their biased assessment.

However, some educators criticize rubrics due to their reductive nature (Flower & Hayes, 1981; Kohn, 2006; Mabry, 1999; Pula & Huot, 1993). This group argues that performance on an essay should be evaluated as a whole. In other words, a paper that scores high on isolated factors of good writing does not necessarily add up to good writing or vice versa. The authors think this might be a legitimate concern regarding rubrics; however, this concern applies more to composition or writing courses than written essays in other disciplines. For example, in this study (or for a social science professor) the overall quality of writing was not as important as responding to the essay prompts. Therefore, using a rubric in this study could not be considered a reductionist element. Furthermore, as Hamp-Lyons (1991) argues, sometimes, it is the holistic scoring that is reductive by reducing the writer's complex responses to a single score.

Although the results of this study were quite unexpected, the authors trusted them because the sample size was large and similar results were found across all four groups.

Conclusion

In conclusion, it appears that many teachers use rubrics without considering their reliability. Research indicates that at least some teachers believe decisions in the classroom, made on the basis of an assessment, can easily be changed if they appear to be wrong (Jonsson & Svingby, 2007). Many educators are now suggesting using portfolio assessment instead of a one-day or one-time (snapshot) writing sample (East, 2006; Elliot, 2005; Hamp-Lyons, 2002). As mentioned earlier, many teachers use rubrics simply because they believe using any rubric is better than assessing without a rubric. The authors understand the many benefits of using rubrics in assessment, and realize that rubrics should be well-designed, topic-specific (contextual), analytic, and complemented with exemplars to be effective. However, if a rubric like the one used in this project, which was designed by a group of professors in a college of education, is shown to be unreliable, then what does this say about the thousands of rubrics being used every day in schools? What does this say particularly about those rubrics downloaded from the Internet and implemented without any training? The unexpected results indicated that making a quality rubric, and using it effectively, are not as easy as one originally assumes. We learned that rubrics should be developed locally for a specific purpose and a specific group of students. Like any tool, improper use is sometimes worse than not having used the tool at all. In the same way, using a rubric may not necessarily be better than not using one. The history of writing assessment shows that achieving high reliability in writing assessment is not easy, and we should be careful not to sacrifice validity to achieve higher rates of reliability.

> **Rubrics should be developed locally for a specific purpose and a specific group of students.**

References

Breland, H. M. (1983). *The direct assessment of writing skill: A measurement review.* New York: College Entrance Examination Board.

Briggs, D. (1970). The influence of handwriting on assessment. *Educational Research, 13,* 50–55.

Bull, R., & Stevens, J. (1979). The effects of attractiveness of writer and penmanship on essay grades. *Journal of Occupational Psychology, 52,* 53–59.

Chase, C. I. (1968). The impact of some obvious variables on essay test scores. *Journal of Educational Measurement, 5,* 315–318.

East, M. (2006). The impact of bilingual dictionaries on lexical sophistication and lexical accuracy in tests of L2 writing proficiency: A quantitative analysis. *Assessing Writing, 11*(3), 179–197.

Elliot, N. (2005). *On a scale: A social history of writing assessment in America.* New York: Peter Lang.

Flower, L., & Hayes, J. R. (1981, April). *Process-based evaluation of writing: Changing the performance, not the product.* Paper presented at the annual meeting of the American Educational Research Association.

Gage, N. L., & Berliner, D. C. (1992). *Educational psychology.* Wentzville, MO: Borgasorus Books.

Hamp-Lyons, L. (1991). *Assessing second language writing in academic contexts.* Norwood, NJ: Ablex.

James, H. (1927). The effect of handwriting on grading. *English Journal, 16,* 180–205.

Jonsson, A., & Svingby, G. (2007). The use of scoring rubrics: Reliability, validity and educational consequences. *Educational Research Review, 2,* 130–144.

Knoch, U. (2009). Diagnostic assessment of writing: A comparison of two rating scales. *Language Testing, 26*(20), 275–304.

Knoch, U., Read, J., & von Randow, J. (2007). Re-training writing raters online: How does it compare with face-to-face training? *Assessing Writing, 12,* 26–43.

Kohn, A. (2006). The trouble with rubrics. *English Journal, 95*(4), 12–15.

Lumley, T. (2002). Assessment criteria in a large-scale writing test: What do they really mean to the raters? *Language Testing, 19*(3), 246–276.

Mabry, L. (1999). Writing to the rubric: Lingering effects of traditional standardized testing on direct writing assessment. *Phi Delta Kappan, 80*(9), 673–679.

Malouff, J. (2008). Bias in grading. *College Teaching, 56*(3), 191–192.

Markham, L. R. (1976). Influences of handwriting on teacher evaluation of written work. *American Educational Research Journal, 13,* 277–283.

Marshall, J. C., & Powers, J. M. (1969). Writing neatness, composition errors, and essay grades. *Journal of Educational Measurement, 6*, 97–101.

Pula, J. J., & Huot, B. A. (1993). A model of background influences on holistic raters. In M. M. Williamson & B. A. Huot (Eds.), *Validating holistic scoring for writing assessment: Theoretical and empirical foundations* (pp. 237–265). Cresskill, NJ: Hampton Press.

Ross-Fisher, R. L. (2005). Developing effective success rubrics. *Kappa Delta Pi, 41*(3), 131–135.

Scannell, D. P., & Marshall, J. C. (1966). The effect of selected composition errors on grades assigned to essay examinations. *American Educational Research Journal, 3*, 125–130.

Sheppard, E. M. (1929). The effects of quality of penmanship on grades. *Journal of Educational Research, 19*, 102–105.

Silvestri, L., & Oescher, J. (2006). Using rubrics to increase the reliability of assessment in health classes. *International Electronic Journal of Health Education, 9*, 25–30.

Spandel, V. (2006). In defense of rubrics. *English Journal, 96*(1), 19–22.

Tomkins, M. (2003). Trouble comes in threes. *Times Educational Supplement, 4547*, 23.

Weigle, S. C. (2002). *Assessing writing.* Cambridge: Cambridge University Press.

Wilson, M. (2006). *Rethinking rubrics in writing assessment.* Portsmouth: Heinemann.

Wilson, M. (2007). Why I won't be using rubrics to respond to students' writing. *English Journal, 96*(4), 62–66.

Chapter 6

New Technology, New Writing?

"After we learn the alphabet, are we going to learn how to text?"

Introduction

Although the beginnings of Internet-based writing were limited to listservs, text-only multiplayer games, and e-mail, the last two decades' technology tools have allowed a limitless venue—and audience—for writing. Important professional organizations such as the National Writing Project[1] and the National Council of Teachers of English (NCTE) have worked hard to keep writing teachers apprised of the latest iterations of technology tools—blogging, texting, social media, and collaborative resources (such as Wikipedia)—that students may wish to use for their writing work in the classroom. **Kathleen Blake Yancey,** writing for the NCTE in the first article of this chapter, welcomes the abundance of composing opportunities offered by these innovations; she highlights the participatory impulse that draws both writers and readers together in online spaces: "[O]ne of the biggest changes is the role of audience: writers are everywhere, yes, but so too are audiences...." The interweaving of computer literacy and language literacy leads Yancey to wonder how writing itself will change, how publication will encompass more products, and whether older models of composing can be retrofitted to fit the new writing spaces.

The development of Web 2.0 (and beyond) technologies has leapt ahead of researchers' ability to capture the effects of these new writing tools and spaces on children and teens, in and out of the classroom. **The Pew Internet & American Life Project** has studied the question by asking children and teens, in a series of surveys, how they use and understand technology. In the executive summary from *Writing, Technology and Teens,* authors **Amanda Lenhart, Sousan Arafeh, Aaron Smith,** and **Alexandra Rankin Macgill** discover that 85% of the students surveyed participate in some form of electronic communication, but 60% of them do not think of this activity as writing. Interestingly, the survey also finds that parents are more optimistic, in general, than are their children about the positive influence of computers on the students' writing skills. Both groups agree that electronic tools allow students to revise and edit more easily, which many teachers would recognize as assisting the development of a solid writing process.

But surveys only provide the opinions and impressions of the respondents; almost from the beginning of affordable personal computers, education researchers have attempted to investigate the real effects of computer use on writing. In the third article in this chapter,

---

[1] National Writing Project, *Because digital writing matters: Improving student writing in online and multimedia environments* (San Francisco: Jossey-Bass/Wiley, 2010).

Amie Goldberg, Michael Russell, and **Abigail Cook** perform a meta-analysis of studies of computer-based writing over the years 1992 to 2002. Compiling the research, they find that computer use has a positive effect on the quantity and quality of student writing, and some studies suggest that students made more revisions to their writing between drafts when they used computers.

The following article confirms in a later study that "the rewriting stage...benefited the most from the use of laptops." Researcher **Mark Warschauer** set up an experimental study in which students in 10 different schools used laptops for every stage of the writing process and summarizes seven benefits of this use: (1) computer-based writing became integrated into instruction, (2) students received and responded to feedback more easily, (3) student writing became both more public and more collaborative, (4) online assignments made their writing more purposeful, (5) word processing software's formatting features allowed students to produce a wide variety of genres, (6) students produced higher quality writing, and (7) students did more creative writing outside of school.

In the next article, authors **Kurt Suhr, David Hernandez, Douglas Grimes,** and **Mark Warschauer** address the effect of laptops on the "fourth grade slump." They compare the English language arts (ELA) test scores of students who had participated in two years of a one-to-one laptop program (in fourth and fifth grade) and find that "laptop students outperformed non-laptop students on changes in the ELA total score" and in subtests in writing strategies and literary response and analysis. Their analysis suggests that laptops are not a "magic bullet" because the effect on test scores is small; however, as they argue, even a small improvement in the upper elementary years' literacy development may have important long-term effects.

A long-term program that has reported its findings over a decade, the **Maine Learning Technology Initiative** studies laptop use for all subjects. In their summary of the program's effect on student writing, **David Silvernail, Caroline Pinkham, Sarah Wintle, Leanne Walker,** and **Courtney Bartlett** report that student writing performance improved on state assessments in writing. In addition, students who reported that they used their laptops for all phases of the writing process did better than students who did not use their laptops. Interestingly, the researchers also show that it did not matter whether students used computers or hand wrote their assessments—students who had used laptops to write outperformed those who did not: "writing improved regardless of the writing test medium." In essence, this study helps confirm the centrality of the writing process: technology helps more easily practice drafting, revising, and editing—and this practice improves their writing both on and off the computer.

Excerpt From

Writing in the 2lst Century: A Report from the National Council of Teachers of English

Kathleen Blake Yancey

National Council of Teachers of English, www.ncte.org, ©February 2009.

Writing in the 2lst Century

With digital technology and, especially Web 2.0, it seems, writers are *everywhere*—on bulletin boards and in chat rooms and in emails and in text messages and on blogs responding to news reports and, indeed, reporting the news themselves as I-reporters. Such writing is what Deborah Brandt has called self-sponsored writing: a writing that belongs to the writer, not to an institution, with the result that people— students, senior citizens, employees, volunteers, family members, sensible *and* non-sensible people alike—want to compose and do—on the page and on the screen and on the network—*to each other*. Opportunities for composing abound—on MySpace and Facebook and Googledocs and multiple blogs and platforms—and on national media sites, where writers upload photos and descriptions, videos and personal accounts, where they are both recipients and creators of our news.

In much of this new composing, we are writing to share, yes; to encourage dialogue, perhaps; but mostly, I think, to participate.

In fact, in looking at all this composing, we might say that *one of the biggest changes is the role of audience: writers are everywhere, yes, but so too are audiences*, especially in social networking sites like Facebook, which, according to the New York Times, provides a commons for people, not unlike the commons that used to be in small towns and large, and an interesting response to Robert Putnam's discussion of community in *Bowling Alone*. Putnam claims, based on some impressive data, that in the late twentieth century participation in community groups declined. No doubt that's so, but this is the twenty-first, and participation of many varieties is increasing almost exponentially—whether measured in the number and kinds of Facebook posts, the daily increase in activity on the NCTE Ning social site, the number of students involved in this year's elections, the numbers of blogs and the increase in little magazines, and even in the number of text messages I seem to get from persons, political campaigns, and my own institution.

Perhaps most important, seen historically this 21st century writing marks the beginning of a new era in literacy, a period we might call the Age of Composition, a period where composers become composers not through direct and formal instruction alone (if at all), but rather through what we might call an extracurricular social co-apprenticeship.

Scholars of composition (e.g., Beaufort; Ding) have discussed social apprenticeships: opportunities to learn to write authentic texts in informal, collaborative contexts like service learning sites, labs, and studios. In the case of the web, though, writers compose authentic texts in informal digitally networked contexts, but there isn't a hierarchy of expert-apprentice, but rather a peer co-apprenticeship in which communicative knowledge is freely exchanged. In other words, our impulse to write is now digitized and expanded—or put differently, newly technologized, socialized, and networked.

I want to put a face on this composing with two examples, one individual and one collective.

The first: earlier this year, on August 23, Tiffany Monk, a sixteen-year-old who lives in Melbourne, Florida, looked out her window and was alarmed. Tropical Storm Fay had passed through Melbourne, but not before leaving a flood in its wake, and Tiffany saw that something was very wrong in her trailer park.

> "There were people trapped in their homes," Monk [explained]. "Water was rising and there was no way out. (There were) people with oxygen tanks and wheelchairs and there was no way out. They needed help." ("Girl Uses Computer," par. 3)

Tiffany knows how to compose. She took pictures of Groveland Mobile Home Park showing the rising waters, she composed emails, and then she sent both on, at the same time asking for help and illustrating why it was needed. "You really have to see this," she said in emails [including] photos of tires floating by in her road. "We are trapped in. Literally, there is no way out." (par. 5)

See this they did: all Tiffany's neighbors were rescued and many of their personal possessions were salvaged as well— because a sixteen-year-old-girl saw a need; because she knew how to compose in a twenty-first-century way; and because she knew her audience.

And what did she learn in this situation? *"...[T]hat if you actually take action then someone might listen to you."* That's a real lesson in composition.

A second story of composing begins in the spring of 2008, when a high school student on Facebook decides that test-taking could be more fun for him, for other test-takers, and for the test-scorers. And the test? Advanced Placement—AP English, AP history, AP psychology, AP calculus...all AP tests. The idea was basically simple: get students to write the "iconic phrase" THIS IS SPARTA from the movie *300,* in capital letters, anywhere on the test, and then cross it out with one line. Because the rules of the test stipulate that students can cross out mistakes and cannot be penalized for doing so, none of the test-takers could be penalized. In addition, "bonus points" were available if students also wrote THIS IS MADNESS elsewhere on the test.

And write they did.

Facebook users "flocked" to join the group *Everybody Write "THIS IS SPARTA!"*—in fact over 30,000 students. And the readers of these exams enjoyed several laughs, which was the intent. According to Erica Jacobs, who teaches at Oakton High School in Virginia, AP readers participated in the joke in several ways, including exchanging notes with each other about the crossed-out lines, posting a sign proclaiming "THIS IS SPARTA" on a reader table, and beginning the last day by announcing, "This is Sparta!" (par. 9) And what were they laughing at? Two examples from AP history exams:

- As the country slid deeper into the Depression, it became clear that drastic change was needed in order to save the American banking system. Fortunately, Franklin Delano Roosevelt, after taking office, immediately declared "THIS IS MADNESS!" and established a four-day banking holiday.
- After the assassination of Abraham Lincoln, John Wilkes Booth cried, "THIS IS SPARTA" before jumping from the balcony.

Now what's interesting to me about this event is fourfold.

One is that these students understand the power of networking, which they used for a collective self-sponsoring activity, in this case a kind of smart-mob action. When you have a cause, you can organize thousands of people on very short notice—and millions when you have more time. Teenagers understand this in ways that many adults do not, and what's as important, they understand how to make it happen.

Two is that the students didn't stop with Facebook and AP. They went to Wikipedia, where they posted the line THIS IS SPARTA at one point on the entry for the College Board, and THIS IS MADNESS at another point on the same entry. Both those lines stayed on Wikipedia for at least a month, when they were later taken down: contrary to popular belief, Wikipedia is monitored. But these students understand how to contribute to Wikipedia. They understand both the reach and the impact of networking. They understand circulation of messages—from a Facebook group to high school and college teachers to a site that rivals encyclopedias in comprehensiveness and exceeds them in timeliness and that offers opportunities for all of us literally to make knowledge.

Three is that the students understood the new audiences of twenty-first century composing—colleagues across the country and faceless AP graders alike. They understood one audience—the testing system—and knew how to play it. Several of the students were concerned enough not to want their scores to be negatively affected, as they revealed on another site where college advisors answer questions (answers.yahoo.com)—and those queries were removed, too!—but these students—and there were thousands and thousands of them—were quite simply bored enough to take the chance. Put differently, they refused to write to a teacher-as-examiner exclusively; they wrote as well to live teachers who might be amused at the juxtaposition between a serious claim about John Wilkes Booth and THIS IS SPARTA. Put differently still, they wanted not a testing reader, but a human one.

Four, we can imagine the ways we might channel this energy for a cause more serious, for a purpose more worthy. In other words, these students know how to compose, and they know how to organize, and they know audience. How can we build on all that knowledge? How can we help them connect it to larger issues?

Taken together, what do these observations about new composings mean?

First, we have moved beyond a pyramid-like, sequential model of literacy development in which print literacy comes first and digital literacy comes second and networked literacy practices, if they come at all, come third and last.

And truly, this pyramid has been deconstructing for some time now. It's the same hierarchy that some want us to use with print composing. When teaching children to write in print, we don't insist that they spell every word correctly before they are allowed to write a sentence; we don't expect perfect paragraphs before they are allowed to write a story. We expect complex thinking to develop alongside and with beginning skills. Complex thinking and skills: they develop together—for the two-year-old learning to talk, for the six-year-old learning to write, and for the sixty-year-old still learning to compose—new genres and new media—because perhaps as never before, learning to write is a lifelong process. That's the way we learn to compose digitally, too, of course, in concert with print and alphabetic literacy, not in sequence.

Second, we have multiple models of composing operating simultaneously, each informed by new publication practices, new materials, and new vocabulary.

We have many questions about these new composings that we need to pursue, to document, and to share. These are questions we need to take up inside school.

For example:

- Our current model(s) of composing are located largely in print, and it's a model that culminates in publication. When composers blog as a form of invention or prewriting, rather than as a form of publication (which I did in composing this text: see kbyancey@ wordpress.org), what does that do to our print-based model(s) of composing that universally culminate in publication?

- How do we mark drafts of a text when, as Pam Takayoshi showed twelve years ago, revising takes place *inside* of discrete drafts?

- How and when do we decide to include images and visuals in our compositions, and where might we include these processes in the curriculum?

- How do we define a composing practice that is interlaced and interwoven with email, text-messaging, and web-browsing? As Mark Poster observes, composing at the screen today isn't composing alone: it's composing in the company of others. How does that change our model(s) of composing?

- How does access to the vast amount and kinds of resources on the web alter our model(s)?

- Can we retrofit our earlier model(s) of composing, or should we begin anew?

And still, *outside of school, composing is ubiquitous.* Through writing, we participate—as students, employees, citizens, human beings.

Through writing, we are.

References

Beaufort, Anne. *College Writing and Beyond.* Logan, UT: Utah State UP, 2007.

Brandt, Deborah. *Literacy in American Lives.* New York: Oxford UP, 2001.

Ding, Huiling. "The Use of Cognitive and Social Apprenticeship to Teach a Disciplinary Genre: Initiation of Graduate Students into NIH Grant Writing (National Institute of Health)." *Written Communication* 25 (2008): 3–52.

"Girl Uses Computer To Save Trapped Flood Victims." 23 Aug. 2008. *ClickOrlando.* 12 Jan. 2009, http://www.clickorlando.com/weath-er/17277174/detail.html.

Jacobs, Erica. "This Is Sparta!—Facebook Prank or Political Statement?" 16 June 2008. examiner.com. 12 Jan. 2009 http://www. examiner.com/a-1443213~This_is_Sparta_Facebook_prank_or_ political_statement_.html.

Poster, Mark. *Information Please.* Durham: Duke UP, 2006.

Putnam, Robert. *Bowling Alone.* New York: Simon, 2000.

Takayoshi, Pam. "The Shape of Electronic Writing." *Computers and Composition* 13 (1996): 235–41.

Thompson, Clive. "Brave New World of Digital Intimacy." *New York Times* 5 Sept. 2008. 16 Jan. 2009, http://nytimes.com/2008/09/07/magazine/07awareness-t.html?_ r=2&oref=slogin.

Executive Summary From
Writing, Technology and Teens

Amanda Lenhart, Sousan Arafeh, Aaron Smith,
and Alexandra Rankin Macgill

Pew Internet & American Life Project, www.pewinternet.org, ©2008.

Summary of Findings

Teenagers' lives are filled with writing. All teens write for school, and 93% of teens say they write for their own pleasure. Most notably, the vast majority of teens have eagerly embraced written communication with their peers as they share messages on their social network pages, in emails and instant messages online, and through fast-paced thumb choreography on their cell phones. Parents believe that their children write more as teens than they did at that age.

> Most teenagers spend a considerable amount of their life composing texts, but they do not think that a lot of the material they create electronically is real writing.

This raises a major question: What, if anything, connects the formal writing teens do and the informal e-communication they exchange on digital screens? A considerable number of educators and children's advocates worry that James Billington, the Librarian of Congress, was right when he recently suggested that young Americans' electronic communication might be damaging "the basic unit of human thought—the sentence."[1] They are concerned that the quality of writing by young Americans is being degraded by their electronic communication, with its carefree spelling, lax punctuation and grammar, and its acronym shortcuts. Others wonder if this return to text-driven communication is instead inspiring new appreciation for writing among teens.

While the debate about the relationship between e-communication and formal writing is on-going, few have systematically talked to teens to see what they have to say about the state of writing in their lives. Responding to this information gap, the Pew Internet & American Life Project and National Commission on Writing conducted a national telephone survey and focus groups to see what teens and their parents say about the role and impact of technological writing on both in-school and out-of-school writing. The report that follows looks at teens' basic definition of writing, explores the various kinds of writing they do, seeks their assessment about what impact e-communication has on their writing, and probes for their guidance about how writing instruction might be improved.

At the core, the digital age presents a paradox. Most teenagers spend a considerable amount of their life composing texts, but they do not think that a lot of the material they create electronically is *real* writing. The act of exchanging emails, instant messages, texts, and social network posts is communication that carries the same weight to teens as phone calls and between-class hallway greetings.

> ## At the same time that teens disassociate e-communication with "writing," they also strongly believe that good writing is a critical skill to achieving success—and their parents agree.

At the same time that teens disassociate e-communication with "writing," they also strongly believe that good writing is a critical skill to achieving success—and their parents agree. Moreover, teens are filled with insights and critiques of the current state of writing instruction as well as ideas about how to make in-school writing instruction better and more useful.

Even though teens are heavily embedded in a tech-rich world, they do not believe that communication over the internet or text messaging is writing.

The main reason teens use the internet and cell phones is to exploit their communication features.[23] Yet despite the nearly ubiquitous use of these tools by teens, they see an important distinction between the "writing" they do for school and outside of school for personal reasons, and the "communication" they enjoy via instant messaging, phone text messaging, email and social networking sites.

- 85% of teens ages 12–17 engage at least occasionally in some form of electronic personal communication, which includes text messaging, sending email or instant messages, or posting comments on social networking sites.
- 60% of teens do not think of these electronic texts as "writing."

Teens generally do not believe that technology negatively influences the quality of their writing, but they do acknowledge that the informal styles of writing that mark the use of these text-based technologies for many teens do occasionally filter into their school work. Overall, nearly two-thirds of teens (64%) say they incorporate some informal styles from their text-based communications into their writing at school.

- 50% of teens say they sometimes use informal writing styles instead of proper capitalization and punctuation in their school assignments;
- 38% say they have used text shortcuts in school work such as "LOL" (which stands for "laugh out loud");
- 25% have used emoticons (symbols like smiley faces ☺) in school work.

The impact of technology on writing is hardly a frivolous issue because most believe that good writing is important to teens' future success.

Both teens and their parents say that good writing is an essential skill for later success in life.

- 83% of parents of teens feel there is a greater need to write well today than there was 20 years ago.
- 86% of teens believe good writing is important to success in life— some 56% describe it as essential and another 30% describe it as important.

Parents also believe that their children write more now than they did when they were teens.

- 48% of teenagers' parents believe that their child is writing more than the parent did during their teen years; 31% say their child is writing less; and 20% believe it is about the same now as in the past.

Recognition of the importance of good writing is particularly high in black households and among families with lower levels of education.

- 94% of black parents say that good writing skills are more important now than in the past, compared with 82% of white parents and 79% of English-speaking Hispanic parents.
- 88% of parents with a high school degree or less say that writing is more important in today's world, compared with 80% of parents with at least some college experience.

New Technology, New Writing?

Teens are motivated to write by relevant topics, high expectations, an interested audience and opportunities to write creatively.

Teens write for a variety of reasons—as part of a school assignment, to get a good grade, to stay in touch with friends, to share their artistic creations with others or simply to put their thoughts to paper (whether virtual or otherwise). In our focus groups, teens said they are motivated to write when they can select topics that are relevant to their lives and interests, and report greater enjoyment of school writing when they have the opportunity to write creatively. Having teachers or other adults who challenge them, present them with interesting curricula and give them detailed feedback also serves as a motivator for teens. Teens also report writing for an audience motivates them to write and write well.

Writing for school is a nearly every-day activity for teens, but most assignments are short.

Most teens write something nearly every day for school, but the average writing assignment is a paragraph to one page in length.

- 50% of teens say their school work requires writing every day; 35% say they write several times a week. The remaining 15% of teens write less often for school.
- 82% of teens report that their typical school writing assignment is a paragraph to one page in length.
- White teens are significantly more likely than English-speaking Hispanic teens (but not blacks) to create presentations for school (72% of whites and 58% of Hispanics do this).

The internet is also a primary source for research done at or for school. 94% of teens use the internet at least occasionally to do research for school, and nearly half (48%) report doing so once a week or more often.

Teens believe that the writing instruction they receive in school could be improved.

Most teens feel that additional instruction and focus on writing in school would help improve their writing even further. Our survey asked teens whether their writing skills would be improved by two potential changes to their school curricula: teachers having them spend more time writing in class, and teachers using more computer-based tools (such as games, writing help programs or websites, or multimedia) to teach writing.

Overall, 82% of teens feel that additional in-class writing time would improve their writing abilities and 78% feel the same way about their teachers using computer-based writing tools.

Non-school writing, while less common than school writing, is still widespread among teens.

Outside of a dedicated few, non-school writing is done less often than school writing, and varies a bit by gender and race/ethnicity. Boys are the least likely to write for personal enjoyment outside of school. Girls and black teens are more likely to keep a journal than other teens. Black teens are also more likely to write music or lyrics on their own time.

- 47% of black teens write in a journal, compared with 31% of white teens.
- 37% of black teens write music or lyrics, while 23% of white teens do.
- 49% of girls keep a journal; 20% of boys do.
- 26% of boys say they never write for personal enjoyment outside of school.

Multi-channel teens and gadget owners do not write any more—or less—than their counterparts, but bloggers are more prolific.

Teens who communicate frequently with friends, and teens who own more technology tools such as computers or cell phones do not write more for school or for themselves than less communicative and less gadget-rich teens. Teen bloggers, however, are prolific writers online *and* offline.

- 47% of teen bloggers write outside of school for personal reasons several times a week or more compared to 33% of teens without blogs.
- 65% of teen bloggers believe that writing is essential to later success in life; 53% of non-bloggers say the same.

Teens more often write by hand for both out-of-school writing and school work.

Most teens mix and match longhand and computers based on tool availability, assignment requirements and personal preference. When teens write they report that they most often write by hand, though they also often write using computers as well. Out-of-school personal writing

New Technology, New Writing?

is more likely than school writing to be done by hand, but longhand is the more common mode for both purposes.

- 72% of teens say they usually (but not exclusively) write the material they are composing for their personal enjoyment outside of school by hand; 65% say they usually write their school assignments by hand.

As tech-savvy as they are, teens do not believe that writing with computers makes a big difference in the quality of their writing.

Teens appreciate the ability to revise and edit easily on a computer, but do not feel that use of computers makes their writing better or improves the quality of their ideas.

- 15% of teens say their internet-based writing of materials such as emails and instant messages has helped improve their overall writing while 11% say it has harmed their writing. Some 73% of teens say this kind of writing makes no difference to their school writing.
- 17% of teens say their internet-based writing has helped the personal writing they do that is not for school, while 6% say it has made their personal writing worse. Some 77% believe this kind of writing makes no difference to their personal writing.

When it comes to using technology for school or non-school writing, teens believe that when they use computers to write they are more inclined to edit and revise their texts (57% say that).

Parents are generally more positive than their teen children about the effect of computers and text-based communication tools on their child's writing.

Parents are somewhat more likely to believe that computers have a positive influence on their teen's writing, while teens are more likely to believe computers have no discernible effect.

- 27% of parents think the internet writing their teen does makes their teen child a better writer, and 27% think it makes the teen a poorer writer. Some 40% say it makes no difference.

On specific characteristics of the impact of tech-based writing, this is how parents' and teens' views match up:

The Impact of Technology on Writing

Do you think using computers makes students more likely to...?	Parents (responding about their children)	Teens (responding about students in general)
Positive Attributes	**Agree**	**Agree**
Write better because they can revise and edit easily	69%	59%
Present ideas clearly	54	44
Be creative	50	44
Communicate well	43	36
Negative Attributes	**Agree**	**Agree**
Take short cuts and not put effort into writing	45	49
Use poor spelling and grammar	40	42
Write too fast and be careless	40	41
Have a short attention span	22	28

SOURCE: Pew Internet & American Life Project Teen/Parent Survey on Writing, September–November 2007. Margin of error is ±5%.

Teens enjoy non-school writing, and to a lesser extent, the writing they do for school.

Enjoyment of personal, non-school writing does not always translate into enjoyment of school-based writing. Fully 93% of those ages 12–17 say they have done some writing outside of school in the past year and more than a third of them write consistently and regularly. Half (49%) of all teens say they enjoy the writing they do outside of school "a great deal," compared with just 17% who enjoy the writing they do for school with a similar intensity.

Teens who enjoy their school writing more are more likely to engage in creative writing at school compared to teens who report very little enjoyment of school writing (81.% vs. 69%). In our focus groups, teens report being motivated to write by relevant, interesting, self-selected topics, and attention and feedback from engaged adults who challenged them.

Writing, Technology and Teens: Summary of Findings at a Glance

Even though teens are heavily embedded in a tech-rich world, they do not believe that communication over the internet or text messaging is writing.

The impact of technology on writing is hardly a frivolous issue because most believe that good writing is important to teens' future success.

Teens are motivated to write by relevant topics, high expectations, an interested audience and opportunities to write creatively.

Writing for school is a nearly every-day activity for teens, but most assignments are short.

Teens believe that the writing instruction they receive in school could be improved.

Non-school writing, while less common than school writing, is still widespread among teens.

Multi-channel teens and gadget owners do not write any more—or less—than their counterparts, but bloggers are more prolific.

Teens more often write by hand for both out-of-school writing and school work.

As tech-savvy as they are, teens do not believe that writing with computers makes a big difference in the quality of their writing.

Parents are generally more positive than their teen children about the effect of computers and text-based communication tools on their child's writing.

Teens enjoy non-school writing, and to a lesser extent, the writing they do for school.

SOURCE: Lenhart, Amanda; Arafeh, Sousan; Smith, Aaron and Rankin Macgill, Alexandra. *Writing, Technology and Teens,* Washington, DC: Pew Internet & American Life Project, April 24, 2008.

Notes

[1] Dillon, Sam. "In Test, Few Students are Proficient Writers," *The New York Times,* April 3, 2008. http://www.nytimes.com/2008/04/03/education/03cnd-writing.html?em&ex=1207454400&en=a866a90118b1f389&ei=5087%0A

[2] Analysis of daily communications choices is based on all teens, regardless of technology ownership.

[3] Lenhart, Amanda, Madden, Mary & Hitlin, Paul. (2005) "Teens and Technology: Youth are Leading the Transition to a Fully Wired and Mobile Nation," Pew Internet & American Life Project, Washington, DC, July 27, 2005.

Excerpts From

The Effect of Computers on Student Writing: A Meta-Analysis of Studies from 1992 to 2002

Amie Goldberg, Michael Russell, and Abigail Cook

Journal of Technology, Learning, and Assessment, Vol. 2, February 2003, Pages 3–51.

Introduction

Over the past two decades, the presence of computers in schools has increased rapidly. While schools had one computer for every 125 students in 1983, they had one for every 9 students in 1995, one for every 6 students in 1998, and one for every 4.2 students in 2001 (Glennan & Melmed, 1996; Market Data Retrieval, 1999, 2001). Today, some states, such as South Dakota, report a student to computer ratio of 2:1 (Bennett, 2002).

Just as the availability of computers in schools has increased, their use has also increased. A national survey of teachers indicates that in 1998, 50 percent of K–12 teachers had students use word processors, 36 percent had them use CD ROMS, and 29 percent had them use the World Wide Web (Becker, 1999). More recent national data indicates that 75 percent of elementary school-aged students and 85 percent of middle and high school-aged students use a computer in school (U.S. Department of Commerce, 2002). Today, the most common educational use of computers by students is for word processing (Becker, 1999; inTASC, 2003). Given that, it is logical to ask: Do computers have a positive effect on students' writing process and quality of writing they produce?

> **Do computers have a positive effect on students' writing process and quality of writing they produce?**

[T]he study presented here employs meta-analytic techniques, commonly used in fields of medicine and economics, to integrate the findings of studies conducted between 1992–2002. This research synthesis allows educators, administrators, policymakers, and others to more fully capitalize on the most recent findings regarding the impact of word processing on students' writing.

Methodology

Meta-analytic procedures refer to a set of statistical techniques used to systematically review and synthesize independent studies within a specific area of research. Gene Glass first proposed such methods and coined the term "meta-analysis" in 1976. "Meta-analysis refers to the analysis of analyses ... it ... refer[s] to the statistical analysis of a large collection of results from individual studies for the purpose of integrating the findings. It connotes a rigorous alternative to the casual, narrative discussions of research studies which typify our attempts to make sense of the rapidly expanding research literature" (p. 3). The meta-analytic portion of the study was conducted using procedures set forth by Lipsey and Wilson (2001) and Hedges and Olkin (1985). The methodology followed five phases:

- identification of relevant studies,
- determination for inclusion,
- coding,
- effect size extraction and calculation, and
- data analyses.

Summary of Findings

The analyses focused on three outcome variables commonly reported by studies that examine the impact of word processors on student writing. These variables include: Quantity of Writing, Quality of Writing, and Number of Revisions. Below, findings for each of these variables are presented separately.

Quantity of Writing

Fourteen studies included sufficient information to calculate effect sizes that compare the quantity of writing, as measured by word count, between computer and paper-and-pencil groups.

Figure 3 indicates that 4 of the 14 studies had effect sizes that were approximately zero or negative, but which did not differ significantly from zero. Figure 3 also shows that 4 of the 14 studies had positive effect sizes that differed significantly from zero. In addition, the mean weighted effect size across all 14 studies is .50, which differs significantly from zero. Thus, across the fourteen studies, the meta-analysis indicates that students who write with word processors tend to produce longer passages than students who write with paper-and-pencil.

In short, the meta-analysis of studies that focused on the effect of word processing on the quantity of student writing found a positive overall effect that was about one-half standard deviation. This effect tended to be larger for middle and high school students than for elementary students.

FIGURE 3. Forest Plot of Quantity of Writing Meta-analysis

Author	Publication Year	Grand N*	Adjusted Effect Size	Lower 95% CI	Upper 95% CI
Owston, et al.	1992	136	0.00	-0.34	0.34
D'Odorico & Zammuner	1993	51	0.56	0.00	1.12
Snyder	1993	51	0.78	0.21	1.35
Peterson	1993	36	1.31	0.59	2.03
Hagler	1993	76	0.47	0.01	0.93
Olson	1994	14	0.02	-1.03	1.07
Jones	1994	20	0.48	-0.41	1.37
Brigman	1994	12	1.23	0.00	2.46
Wolfe, et al.	1996	60	-0.05	-0.41	0.3
Nichols	1996	60	0.87	0.34	1.4
Dybahl, et al.	1997	41	-0.14	-0.77	0.48
Godsey	2000	44	1.31	0.66	1.96
Padgett	2000	32	0.52	-0.18	1.23
Barrera, et al.	2001	36	0.21	-0.44	0.87
mean		669	0.541	0.380	0.702

*Grand N = n_{paper} + $n_{computer}$

Lower 95% Confidence Interval → ⊢■⊣ ← Upper 95% Confidence Interval
↑
Effect Size

Quality of Writing

Fifteen studies included sufficient information to calculate effect sizes that compare the quality of writing between computer and paper-and-pencil groups.

Figure 4 indicates that 4 of the 15 studies had effect sizes that were approximately zero or negative, but which did not differ significantly from zero. Since the power in meta-analysis is the aggregation of findings across many studies, it is not unusual to find a subset of studies that contradict the overall trend of findings. In this case, a qualitative examination did not reveal any systematic differences among these studies' features as compared with those studies reporting positive effect sizes. Figure 4 also shows that the 11 remaining studies had positive effect sizes and that seven of these effect sizes differed significantly from zero.

New Technology, New Writing?

In addition, the mean adjusted effect size across all 15 studies is .41, which differs significantly from zero. According to Cohen's criteria for effect sizes, this is considered a small to moderate effect. Thus, across the 15 studies, the meta-analysis indicates that students who write with word processors tend to produce higher quality passages than students who write with paper-and-pencil.

In short, the meta-analysis of studies that focused on the effect of word processing on the quality of student writing found a positive overall effect that was about four tenths of a standard deviation. As with the effect for quantity, this effect tended to be larger for middle and high school students than for elementary students.

> **Students who write with word processors tend to produce higher quality passages than students who write with paper-and-pencil.**

FIGURE 4. Forest Plot of Quality of Writing Meta-analysis

Author	Publication Year	Grand N*	Adjusted Effect Size	Lower 95% CI	Upper 95% CI
Owston, et al.	1992	136	0.38	0.04	0.72
Hagler	1993	38	0.96	0.49	1.44
Jones	1994	20	1.25	0.29	2.21
Jackiewicz	1995	58	0.62	0.09	1.15
Keetley	1995	23	0.20	-0.62	1.02
Lam & Pennington	1995	34	0.25	-0.42	0.93
Nichols	1996	60	0.01	-0.5	0.52
Lichetenstein	1996	32	0.77	0.05	1.49
Wolfe, et al.	1996	120	-0.06	-0.42	0.3
Breese, et al.	1996	44	0.83	0.21	1.44
Langone, et al.	1996	12	0.43	-0.71	1.58
Jones & Pellegrino	1996	20	-0.61	-1.5	0.29
Lerew	1997	150	0.88	0.55	1.22
Dybdhal, et al.	1997	41	-0.20	-0.83	0.42
Head	2000	50	0.43	-0.13	0.99
mean		838	0.410	0.340	0.481

*Grand N = n_{paper} + $n_{computer}$

Lower 95% Confidence Interval → ├──■──┤ ← Upper 95% Confidence Interval
↑
Effect Size

Revisions

Only 6 of the 30 studies that met the criteria for inclusion in this study included measures related to revisions. Of these six studies, half were published in refereed journals, half took place in elementary schools, and only one employed a sample size greater than 30.

Because of the small sample size (only 6) coupled with the reporting of multiple measures of revisions which could not be combined into a single measure for each study, it was not possible to calculate an average effect size. Nonetheless, these six studies all report that students made more changes to their writing between drafts when word processors were used as compared to paper-and-pencil. In studies that focused on both revision and quality of writing, revisions made by students using word processors resulted in higher quality writing than did students revising their work with paper and pencils. It should also be noted that one study found that students writing with paper-and-pencil produced more content-related revisions than did students who used word processors.

> **Students made more changes to their writing between drafts when word processors were used as compared to paper-and-pencil.**

In short, given the small number of studies that compared revisions made on paper with revisions made with word processors coupled with the multiple methods used to measure revisions, it is difficult to estimate the effect of computer use on student revisions.

Discussion

This study employed meta-analytic techniques to summarize findings across multiple studies in order to systematically examine the effects of computers and student learning. Although a large number of studies initially identified for inclusion in the meta-analysis had to be eliminated either because they were qualitative in nature or because they failed to report statistics required to calculate effect sizes, the analyses indicate that instructional uses of computers for writing are having a positive impact on student writing.

> **Instructional uses of computers for writing are having a positive impact on student writing.**

This positive impact was found in each independent set of meta-analyses; for quantity of writing as well as quality of writing.

Early research consistently found large effects of computer-based writing on the length of passages and less consistently reported small effects on the quality of student writing. In contrast, although our meta-analyses of research conducted since 1992 found a larger overall effect size for the quantity of writing produced on computer, the relationship between computers and quality of writing appears to have strengthened considerably. When aggregated across all studies, the mean effect size indicated that, on average, students who develop their writing skills while using a computer produce written work that is .4 standard deviations higher in quality than those students who learn to write on paper. On average, the effect of writing with computers on both the quality and quantity of writing was larger for middle and high school students than for elementary school students.

> **The relationship between computers and quality of writing appears to have strengthened.**

In addition, the findings reported in the excluded studies are consistent with both the findings of our quantitative meta-analyses and many of the findings presented in Cochran-Smith's (1991) and Bangert-Downs (1993) summaries of research conducted prior to 1992. In general, research over the past two decades consistently finds that when students write on computers, writing becomes a more social process in which students share their work with each other. When using computers, students also tend to make revisions while producing, rather than after producing, text. Between initial and final drafts, students also tend to make more revision when they write with computers. In most cases, students also tend to produce longer passages when writing on computers.

> **When students write on computers, writing becomes a more social process in which students share their work with each other.**

For educational leaders questioning whether computers should be used to help students develop writing skills, the results of our meta-analyses suggest that on average students who use computers when learning to write produce written work that is about .4 standard deviations better than students who develop writing skills on paper. While teachers undoubtedly play an important role in helping students develop their writing skills, the analyses presented here suggest that when students write with computers, they engage in the revising of their work throughout the writing process, more frequently share and receive feedback from their peers, and benefit from teacher input earlier in the writing process. Thus, while there is clearly a need for systematic and high quality research on computers and student learning, those studies that met the rigorous criteria for inclusion in our meta-analyses suggest that computers are valuable tools for helping students develop writing skills.

References

Bangert-Downs, R. L. (1993). The word processor as an instructional tool: A meta-analysis of word processing in writing instruction. *Review of Educational Research, 63*(1), 69–93.

Becker, H. J. (1999). *Internet use by teachers: conditions of professional use and teacher-directed student use.* Irvine, CA: Center for Research on Information Technology and Organizations.

Bennett, R.E. (2002). Inexorable and inevitable: The continuing story of technology and assessment. *Journal of Technology, Learning and Assessment, 1*(1). Retrieved November 1, 2002, from http://www.bc.edu/research/intasc/jtla/journal/v1n1.shtml [new address http://ejournals.bc.edu/ojs/index.php/jtla/issue/view/206]

Cochran-Smith, M. (1991). Word processing and writing in elementary classrooms: A critical review of related literature. *Review of Educational Research, 61,* 107–155.

Glass, G. V. (1976). Primary, secondary, and meta-analysis of research. *Educational Researcher, 5,* 3–8.

Glennan, T. K. & Melmed, A. (1996). Fostering the use of educational technology: Elements of a national strategy. Santa Monica, CA: Rand.

Hedges, L. & Olkin, I. (1985). *Statistical Methods for Meta-Analysis.* Orlando, FL: Academic Press.

Lipsey, M. W. W. & Wilson, D.B. (2001). *Practical Meta-Analysis* (Vol. 49). Thousand Oaks, CA: Sage Publications.

Market Data Retrieval. (1999). *Technology in education 1999.* Shelton, CT: Market Data Retrieval.

U.S. Department of Commerce. (2002). *A Nation Online: How Americans are expanding their use of the Internet.* Washington, DC: Author. Retrieved November 1, 2002, from http://www.ntia.doc.gov/ntiahome/dn/nationonline_020502.htm.

Laptops and Literacy: A Multi-Site Case Study

Mark Warschauer

Pedagogies: An International Journal, Vol. 3, 2008, Pages 52–67.

Due to the development and diffusion of information and communication technologies, we have witnessed the greatest change in our means of communication and production of knowledge since the invention of the printing press (for overviews, see Coiro, Knobel, Lankshear, & Leu, 2008; Reinking, 1998; Warschauer, 1999). The technological, economic, and social transformations of the digital era pose three important literacy and learning challenges that can be summarised as *past/future, home/school*, and *rich/poor*. Past/future refers to the gap between previously required literacy and learning skills that focus on the mastery of written texts and the broader set of digital literacy, thinking, communication, and productivity skills required for 21st-century life (see North Central Regional Educational Laboratory & the Metiri Group, 2003). Home/school refers to the gap between the media-rich and autonomous literacy experiences that many children enjoy at home and the often more restrictive literacy practices they engage in at school (see Gee, 2003, 2004). Rich/poor refers to the ever present inequity between the literacy and learning achievements of students of high and low socioeconomic status (SES)—a gap made more dangerous by the disappearance of well-paying unskilled jobs and the fact that technological fluency is required for many elite professions (see Castells, 1996; Warschauer, 2003).

Not surprisingly, educators have turned to increased infusions of technology into the classroom to try to address these challenges. However, research suggests that the potential of new educational technologies is far from being realized because logistical, administrative, and pedagogical obstacles make it difficult for teachers to effectively deploy shared computers (see studies by Cuban, 2001; Warschauer, Knobel, & Stone, 2004). In addition, unequal patterns of technological access and

> We have witnessed the greatest change in our means of communication and production of knowledge since the invention of the printing press.

use in society get reproduced in schools, as teachers make use of limited computer resources to benefit the most able or privileged students (see Schofield & Davidson, 2004).

To better integrate technology into instruction, many school districts throughout the country are working to create *one-to-one* classroom environments in which each student has access to an Internet-connected laptop computer at school and in most cases, at home. Relatively few studies have focused on one-to-one laptop programs and even fewer are considered methodologically rigorous (see review and critique in Penuel, 2005). At the same time, no prior studies have carried out extensive and systematic observations of laptop programs in more than a few schools and none have used the theoretical lens of literacy as a research focus.

> **Relatively few studies have focused on one-to-one laptop programs and even fewer are considered methodologically rigorous.**

This article presents findings from a 2-year laptop and literacy study conducted in Southern California from 2003 to 2005. The study was designed to examine the relationship of laptop use to student literacy practices. A complete report on the findings can be found in Warschauer (2006). This article is a summary of the study's major findings.

Method

The study is based on an examination of laptop use in a purposely stratified sample of 10 schools in California and Maine. The research was based on a sociocultural framework of literacy (e.g., Gee, 1996), which considers the way social and cultural environments and contexts shape and constrain the way meaning-making with diverse types of texts occurs in and out of school.

Research at the 10 schools was directed by Mark Warschauer and carried out by a team of faculty, graduate students, and undergraduates. Data collection involved a combination of observations, interviews, surveys, and document reviews. About 5 to 7 students from each school were chosen to participate in individual case studies in order to represent the student diversity at the schools. A total of 650 hours of classroom observations were conducted at the 10 schools, with detailed field notes taken during all observations. Interviews were conducted with a total of 61 teachers, 32 school staff members (administrators, librarians, counselors, and technology coordinators), 67 students, and 31 parents.

Writing

Laptops were used extensively during each stage of the writing process. Prewriting activities were assisted by the use of Internet search engines (e.g., for background information) and graphic organisers (for planning). Drafts were almost always done on computer and this caused less fatigue compared with writing by hand. It also offered additional benefits to students whose handwriting could have been affected by coordination, motor skill, or cognitive function difficulties. As a special education teacher explained,

> For many of our students with cognitive disabilities, getting the ideas from your brain onto paper is pretty much a torture. But whatever reason, and the reasons are as different as the individual students are, word processing as opposed to writing has been an incredible tool in terms of creatively being able to express themselves and then also working on just the mechanics of written language.... It levels the playing field sort of with their peers.

The rewriting stage—where students receive feedback, reread their papers, and edit their work—benefited the most from the use of laptops. Papers written on the computer were read much more easily and quickly compared with hand-written papers, thus allowing teachers to read and respond to student writing more efficiently. In 3 of the 10 schools, students also had access to an automated essay evaluation software that gave numerical scores and basic feedback. Though this software was far from perfect (see discussion in Warschauer & Ware, 2006), it did provide an additional form of feedback for earlier drafts, allowing teachers to focus on later drafts.

> **The rewriting stage—where students receive feedback, reread their papers, and edit their work—benefited the most from the use of laptops.**

Most important, once students received feedback, they could revise their papers more readily than if they had been written by hand. A middle school teacher in Maine explained how the feedback and editing stage was improved through use of laptops:

> The most exhausting part of my job was 1 to 1 writing conferences, especially when you have the red pen out, you can't read their writing, you've got to squeeze in comments in the lines—two or three of those a day were all I could handle. And it was harder for them afterward to go back and remember. So when you have the laptop, it's live, it's right there, you are editing, you are conferencing together. When I need to give them feedback on revisions they needed to make, it was

easier for them to just take what I offered and go back right there and do it.

The increased visibility and ease in revising computer-based writing also aided student collaboration, as peers frequently gathered around computer screens to work together. Natalie, a high school student in California, provided an interesting illustration of this point:

> My friend who sits with me at my table, Felicia, we'll go back and forth. If I'm not sure how to start my essay out, I'll start reading hers, and I'm like, "OK, now I see what the teacher wants," and then I'll just take it from there. I don't copy what she writes, but it gives me an idea how I should write my paper.

Natalie further explained that such collaboration would not happen in a typical classroom. "Not a lot of people have very legible writing....The intention [to share] might be there, but when you get the piece of paper, you just can't read it."

Other types of sharing and collaboration that took place (through video projectors or online discussion forums) are also not possible in a typical classroom. We witnessed a fascinating example of collaborative online writing in an English class at Plum High, Maine, where students who had read selected short stories worked in small groups, each with his or her own laptop, to collaboratively author an alternate version of the story from a particular character's perspective. They used the shareware program SubEthaEdit (CodingMonkeys, 2005) that allows multiple Macintosh users to edit the same document in real time, with each user's contribution appearing in a different colour. Although this experience may or may not help them on a standardized writing test, such forms of multivocal writing are becoming increasingly common in the real world, and learning how to accomplish such collaboration well is a valuable skill.

Students took advantage of the formatting features of computers to write in multiple and diverse genres.

Overall, we can summarise seven advantages of writing with laptops. First, computer-based writing became more naturally integrated into instruction. Second, the writing process became more iterative, with students able to receive and respond to feedback better. Third, writing became more public, visible, and collaborative. Students were able to view and improve on each other's work—whether on a classmate's laptop screen or a printout. Most of the laptop classes we observed were "print-rich" and had numerous exemplars of student work posted around the room, often with multiple versions of the same paper. Fourth, writing became more purposeful and authentic, with students able to write things with real objectives (e.g., online book reviews, authentic correspondence, materials for publication). Fifth, students took advantage of the formatting features of computers to write in multiple and diverse genres—producing, among other things, newspapers, informational brochures, pamphlets, business letters, and magazine advertisements. Sixth, by using computer-based language (e.g., spell-check, thesaurus, etc.) and formatting tools and by revising their work for authentic audiences, students produced higher quality writing in which they took more pride. Finally, by having a powerful writing tool available at school and at home, many students also became more autonomous in their writing and even engaged in creative writing during their free time. An elementary school teacher in California summarised how the multiple benefits of laptops helped his students learn to write:

> They are writing more, it's better quality, it's produced faster. I think the laptops facilitate the writing because there is less fatigue involved than with cursive or print. Again they have the Internet right there to pull up graphics, they have Apple works drawings to illustrate their stories, so I think the laptop is a great facilitator of writing. I'll give my students prompts to write a short story, and usually before the stories were 2–3 pages, but this year, their short stories are 8–10 pages long.

Conclusion

This multi-site case study of literacy practices and outcomes in 10 K–12 schools found that the processes, sources, and products of students' literacy activities changed noticeably in the one-to-one laptop classroom. Literacy processes became more public, collaborative, authentic, and iterative, with greater amounts of scaffolding and feedback provided. Literacy sources expanded to include a wealth of online materials, more student-collected data, and digital or audio archives of students' own work. Literacy products extended beyond the essays and PowerPoint presentations that dominate typical schools to include a greater variety of textual and multimedia genres. All of these changes are in line with those often touted by technology enthusiasts but have previously not been regularly achieved through shared uses of educational computers (see Cuban, 2001; Warschauer, Knobel, & Stone, 2004).

References

Castells, M. (1996). *The rise of the network society.* Maiden, MA: Blackwell.

CodingMonkeys. (2005). SubEthaEdit. Retrieved February 2, 2006, from http://www.codingmonkeys.de/subethaedit/

Coiro, J., Knobel, M., Lankshear, C, & Leu, D. J. (Eds.). (2008). *Handbook of research on new literacies*. Mahwah, NJ: Erlbaum.

Cuban, L. (2001). Oversold and underused: *Computers in classrooms, 1980–2000*. Cambridge, MA: Harvard University Press.

Gee, J. P. (1996). *Social linguistics and literacies*. London: Taylor & Francis.

Gee, J. P. (2003). *What video games have to teach us about learning and literacy*. New York: Palgrave Macmillan.

Gee, J. P. (2004). *Situated language and learning: A critique of traditional schooling*. New York: Routledge.

North Central Regional Educational Laboratory & the Metiri Group. (2003). *enGauge 21st century skills: Literacy in the digital age*. Naperville, IL, and Los Angeles: Author.

Penuel, W. R. (2005). *Research: What it says about 1 to 1 learning*. Cupertino, CA: Apple Computer.

Reinking, D. (Ed.). (1998). *Handbook of literacy and technology: Transformations in a post-typographic world*. Mahwah, NJ: Erlbaum.

Schofield, J. W., & Davidson, A. L. (2004). Achieving equality of student Internet access within schools. In A. Eagly, R. Baron, & L. Hamilton (Eds.), *The social psychology of group identity and social conflict* (pp. 97–109). Washington, DC: APA Books.

Warschauer, M. (1999). *Electronic literacies: Language, culture, and power in online education*. Mahwah, NJ: Erlbaum.

Warschauer, M. (2003). *Technology and social inclusion: Rethinking the digital divide*. Cambridge, MA: MIT Press.

Warschauer, M. (2006). *Laptops and literacy: Learning in the wireless classroom*. New York: Teachers College Press.

Warschauer, M., & Ware, P. (2006). Automated writing evaluation: Defining the classroom research agenda. *Language Teaching Research, 10,* 157–180.

Warschauer, M., Knobel, M., & Stone, L. A. (2004). Technology and equity in schooling: Deconstructing the digital divide. *Educational Policy, 18*(4), 562–588.

Excerpts From

Laptops and Fourth-Grade Literacy: Assisting the Jump over the Fourth-Grade Slump

Kurt A. Suhr, David A. Hernandez, Douglas Grimes, and Mark Warschauer

Journal of Technology, Learning, and Assessment, Vol. 9, January 2010, Pages 4–45.

Abstract

School districts throughout the country are considering how to best integrate technology into instruction. There has been a movement in many districts toward one-to-one laptop instruction, in which all students are provided a laptop computer, but there is concern that these programs may not yield sufficiently improved learning outcomes to justify their substantial cost. And while there has been a great deal of research on the use of laptops in schools, there is little quantitative research systematically investigating the impact of laptop use on test outcomes, and none among students at the fourth- to fifth-grade levels. This study investigated whether a one-to-one laptop program could help improve English language arts (ELA) test scores of upper elementary students, a group that often faces a slowdown of literacy development during the transition from learning to read to reading to learn known as the *fourth-grade slump*.

We explore these questions by comparing changes in the ELA test scores of a group of students who entered a one-to-one laptop program in the fourth-grade to a similar group of students in a traditional program in the same school district. After two years' participation in the program, laptop students outperformed non-laptop students on changes in the ELA total score and in the two subtests that correspond most closely to frequent laptop use: writing strategies and literary response and analysis.

Research Questions

The purpose of this study was to compare longitudinal changes in ELA achievement of students participating in a one-to-one laptop program (treatment group) with students who did not participate in the program (control group). We asked three closely related research questions:

1. Were there significant differences in the total ELA score changes in the California Standards Test (CST) over the two-year period from third grade to fifth grade between the one-to-one laptop group and the non-laptop group, after controlling for other factors?

2. Were there significant differences in the six subtests used to compute those total ELA scores for the same two groups?

3. Can participation in a one-to-one laptop program be used to predict changes in ELA total and subtest scores over the two-year period from third grade to fifth grade?

Methodology

We used a quasi-experimental research design to analyze the effects of the one-to-one laptop program on CST ELA achievement for students in fourth and fifth grades. We used a longitudinal measure of change in scores. Their CST scores in third grade (Spring, 2004) served as a baseline or pre-test, and their fifth-grade scores (Spring, 2006) served as a post-test. Change in academic achievement was measured by the difference between pre-test and post-test. . . . [W]e used analysis of variance (ANOVA), multivariate analysis of variance (MANOVA), and multiple regression to address the three research questions.

> After year 2, laptop students significantly outperformed non-laptop students in their change scores for literary response and analysis and writing strategies.

The CST is a criterion-referenced test designed to show students' mastery of California academic standards for their grade level. Half the questions are new each year. Since the raw scores are scaled to a normal distribution in the same range (150 to 600 points total score, with 350 as the threshold for proficient performance), the scaled scores are stable from year to year for students who maintain the same level of mastery of state standards for each advancing grade level. (From this point on, in accord with common practice, we refer only to scaled CST scores, and drop the term "scaled.") The ELA portion of the CST contains a total of 75 questions in both fourth and fifth grades.

We also surveyed teachers and students, interviewed teachers, observed classes, and collected samples of teacher and student artifacts to supplement the test score analysis with information about how laptops were used for teaching and learning.

As mentioned, participation in the laptop program was determined either by school or by class. Self-selection by students was therefore non-existent, and self-selection by teachers was effectively nil. All of the teachers in the laptop program said they were glad to join it.

Discussion

The results of the ANOVA and MANOVA analyses showed that after year 2, laptop students significantly outperformed non-laptop students in their change scores for literary response and analysis ($p < .01$) and writing strategies ($p < .05$). For both the laptop and non-laptop students, change scores for reading comprehension were negative (see Table 16), although the drop in reading comprehension scores of laptop students ($M = -0.44$) was less than for non-laptop students ($M = -1.39$). This suggests that the fourth-grade slump phenomenon may have followed

> Teacher and student surveys, observations, and interviews all confirmed that writing and revising was the most common use of the laptops in the schools in our study.

these students into fifth grade (year 2 of program implementation), and that the use of laptop computers has mitigated the full impact of the phenomenon on laptop-using students, and thus may account for the significantly higher performance of laptop students in reading comprehension than their non-laptop peers.

In the multiple regression analyses for year 2 change data, the treatment variable was found to be a significant predictor for changes in ELA total score, literary response and analysis, and writing strategies. The square of the semi-partial correlation (sr^2) yields the coefficient of determination for the unique contribution of each predictor. *By itself,* the treatment variable (i.e., being enrolled in the laptop program) explained approximately 3% of the variation in the change in ELA total scores, 4% of the variation in the change in literary response and analysis scores, and 7% of the variation in the change in writing strategies scores.

According to Cohen (1992), an *ES* of .02 is small and an *ES* of .15 is moderate. The treatment effect of being in the laptop program had small to moderate effects on the change scores for which significant predictors were found—ELA total score *ES* = .04, literary response and analysis *ES* = .04, and writing strategies *ES* = .08.

TABLE 16. Means and Standard Deviations of Changes in Laptop and Non-Laptop Students' CST ELA Total Score and Subtest Scores

ELA test or subtest/ Group	Year 1 M	Year 1 SD	Year 2 M	Year 2 SD	Combined M	Combined SD
Total scale score						
Non-laptop	26.67	29.64	−16.83	28.35	9.83	40.41
Laptop	19.56	29.35	2.19	34.33	21.74	32.43
Word analysis and vocabulary development						
Non-laptop	−1.11	2.23	−3.70	2.59	−4.81	2.84
Laptop	−1.83	1.89	−3.30	1.55	−5.13	1.92
Reading comprehension						
Non-laptop	1.19	2.49	−1.39	2.51	−0.20	2.74
Laptop	0.87	1.66	−0.44	2.38	0.43	2.54
Literary response and analysis						
Non-laptop	−0.04	1.48	2.76	2.29	2.72	2.30
Laptop	−0.06	1.65	3.76	1.62	3.70	1.95
Written and oral language conventions						
Non-laptop	3.85	2.74	0.20	2.18	4.06	2.58
Laptop	4.17	2.08	−0.35	2.28	3.81	1.96
Writing strategies						
Non-laptop	4.57	2.20	0.19	2.47	4.76	2.90
Laptop	4.37	2.32	1.89	2.57	6.26	2.44

Teacher and student surveys, observations, and interviews all confirmed that writing and revising was the most common use of the laptops in the schools in our study. These benefits are consistent with what has been noted in other case studies of laptop programs which also report increased opportunities to practice diverse writing strategies and critically analyze literature (e.g., Warschauer, 2008; Warschauer et al., 2004).

> The positive effects for laptop use appeared only after the second year and not after the first year.

Further large scale research correlating students' use of laptops with test score outcomes would be necessary to better understand the more specific benefits of laptop use for English language arts instruction.

It is also not surprising to us that the positive effects for laptop use appeared only after the second year and not after the first year. During the first year of the study, there was a steep learning curve as both teachers and students first experienced a one-to-one classroom. But, as the teachers explained in interviews, in the second year they could focus their teaching more on content and learning and less on basic computer skills. This is consistent with what has been found in other research on laptop programs as well (e.g., Silvernail & Gritter, 2007; Grimes & Warschauer, 2008).

> **Laptop use over multiple years may have a small positive effect on literacy test score outcomes.**

Conclusion

Laptop programs have a strong allure to educational administrators seeking to promote the kinds of thinking, learning, and creativity required in the 21st century. However, a major question of many administrators when considering this or any other educational intervention is the effect it may have on standardized test scores.

The modest sample size and small effect sizes of this study make it difficult to draw definitive conclusions. Nevertheless, the study adds to an emerging body of literature suggesting that laptop use over multiple years may have a small positive effect on literacy test score outcomes. Given that the tests themselves are taken on paper, thus potentially disadvantaging students who have done much of their learning via computer (for example, see Russell & Plati, 2002), the actual benefits vis-à-vis knowledge of the material covered on the tests may be understated for laptop students. It also may be the case, as advocates suggest, that much of what is best taught and learned with laptops is not covered on standardized tests at all. Finally, since the upper elementary grades have proven to be a critical turning point at which many students begin a downward trajectory in literacy and learning, even a small upward bump at this grade level could have an important long-term effect.

> **Since the upper elementary grades have proven to be a critical turning point at which many students begin a downward trajectory in literacy and learning, even a small upward bump at this grade level could have an important long-term effect.**

Laptops are not the magic bullet that will single-handedly overcome unsatisfactory ELA test scores. However, this study suggests that laptops may have a small effect on increasing such scores, with particular benefits in the areas of literary response and analysis and writing strategies. Further research, with larger sample sizes, more diverse student demographics, longitudinal evaluation, a wider array of outcome measures (including those taken on both paper and computer and those involving both standardized tests and alternative forms of assessment), and, where possible, random assignment, will help us continue to shed light on the effects of laptop use on literacy and learning.

References

Cohen, J. (1992). A power primer. *Psychological Bulletin, 112*(1), 155–159.

Grimes, D., & Warschauer, M. (2008). Learning with laptops: A multi-method case study. *Journal of Educational Computing Research 38*(3), 305–332.

Russell, M., & Plati, T. (2002). Does it matter with what I write? Comparing performance on paper, computer, and portable writing devices [Electronic version]. *Current Issues in Education, 5*(4), 1–25.

Silvernail, D.L., & Gritter, A.K. (2007). *Maine's middle school laptop program: Creating better writers.* Retrieved August 6, 2008, from http://www.usm. maine.edu/cepare/Impact_on_Student_Writing_ Brief.pdf.

Warschauer, M. (2008). Laptops and literacy: A multi-site case study. *Pedagogies, 3*(1), 52–67.

Warschauer, M., Grant, D., Del Real, G., & Rousseau, M. (2004). Promoting academic literacy with technology: Successful laptop programs in K–12 schools. *System, 32*(4), 525–537.

Excerpts From

A Middle School One-to-One Laptop Program: The Maine Experience

David L. Silvernail, Caroline A. Pinkham, Sarah E. Wintle,
Leanne C. Walker, Courtney L. Bartlett

Center for Education Policy, Applied Research, & Evaluation, University of Southern Maine,
©August 2011, www.usm.maine.edu/cepare/publications.htm

Background

Over a decade ago Maine embarked on a bold new initiative, an initiative designed to:

> ...transform Maine into the premier state for utilizing technology in kindergarten to grade 12 education in order to prepare students for a future economy that will rely heavily on technology and innovation. (Task Force on Maine's Learning Technology Endowment, 2001, p. vi)

The Maine Learning Technology Initiative (MLTI) has provided all 7th and 8th grade students and their teachers with laptop computers, created a wireless internet infrastructure in all of Maine's middle schools, and provided teachers and staff technical assistance and professional development for integrating laptop technology into their curriculum and instruction.

Does the availability and use of laptops by teachers and students translate into higher achievement?

The concept of the Maine Learning Technology Initiative (MLTI) began with a vision of former Governor Angus King. He believed that if Maine wanted to prepare Maine's students for a rapidly changing world, and wanted to gain a competitive edge over other states, it would require a sharp departure in action from what Maine had done in the past.

In late 1999 a one-time State surplus of general funds provided Governor King the opportunity to act upon his beliefs. He proposed that all middle school students and teachers in Maine be provided laptop computers. In the summer of 2000 the Legislature and Governor King convened a Joint Task Force on the Maine Learning Technology Endowment and charged the task force with conducting an in-depth examination of the issues surrounding Governor King's proposal, and to recommend the best course for Maine to follow.

The task force concluded:

We live in a world that is increasingly complex and where change is increasingly rampant. Driving much of this complexity and change are new concepts and a new economy based on powerful, ubiquitous computer technology linked to the Internet.

Our schools are challenged to prepare young people to navigate and prosper in this world, with technology as an ally rather than an obstacle. The challenge is familiar, but the imperative is new: we must prepare young people to thrive in a world that doesn't exist yet, to grapple with problems and construct new knowledge which is barely visible to us today. It is no longer adequate to prepare some of our young people to high levels of learning and technological literacy; we must prepare all for the demands of a world in which workers and citizens will be required to use and create knowledge, and embrace technology as a powerful tool to do so.

If technology is a challenge for our educational system, it is also part of the solution. To move all students to high levels of learning and technological literacy, all students will need access to technology when and where it can be most effectively incorporated into learning. (Task Force on Maine's Learning Technology Endowment, 2001, p. i)

In the Fall of the 2002–2003 academic year, the first full implementation phase of the MLTI began. In this first phase, over 17,000 seventh graders and their teachers in over 240 middle schools across the state of Maine received laptop computers. The following year all eighth graders and their teachers also received laptops, and each subsequent year thereafter, all seventh and eighth graders and their teachers have received laptop computers, paid for by the State of Maine.

> **Teacher training through professional development was believed to be paramount for the successful implementation of the laptop program.**

Concurrently, with the first deployment of the laptops, the Maine Department of Education initiated a professional development program to assist teachers in integrating the laptops into their curriculum and instruction. Teacher training through professional development was believed to be paramount for the successful implementation of the laptop program. In each of the State's middle schools, both a Teacher Leader and a Technology Coordinator were selected and trained to serve as leaders within their schools for the MLTI. These teacher leaders and technology coordinators now serve as contact and support personnel for

New Technology, New Writing?

the classroom teachers in the buildings where they teach. Subsequently new roles were created and added to the MLTI professional development network. These positions were created to facilitate greater integration of curriculum and technology and as support for the transformation of teaching and learning in Maine's classrooms.

This report describes some of the major impacts of the Maine middle school laptop program. It presents evidence on both the use and impacts of the laptop technology with teachers and students, evidence of the impacts of the program on student achievement, and a cost analysis of the program.

Impacts on Student Learning: A Summary of Findings

Does the availability and use of laptops by teachers and students translate into higher achievement? The answer is that it depends. The evidence indicates that if teachers specifically target content and/or skills and integrate the use of laptops in teaching these, the evidence indicates greater achievement. If the integration is less targeted, the results are less clear.

> The results from this study suggest that improvements in writing performance may be attributed, at least in part, to the laptop program.

An underlying premise of the laptop program has been that the State of Maine will make the laptops available to all middle school students and their teachers, but that individual schools and teachers will decide how they are used. Consequently, use levels vary...and types of use also vary across classrooms and schools. A further consequence of this underlying premise is that there is little consistent statewide evidence of the impacts of the laptops on student achievement, (except in the area of writing). But there is some evidence of the positive impacts of the laptops on achievement in cases where use of the laptops is specifically targeted to improve achievement.

The research team has conducted several small and large scale research studies designed to assess the impacts of the laptop program on student achievement. To date research has been completed in the areas of mathematics, writing, and science. Additionally, two research projects have been completed to determine what impact the introduction of ubiquitous computing may have on students' ability to evaluate sources, specifically sources found on the Internet. Full reports of each of the studies...are available at www.usm.maine.edu/cepare/publications.htm.

Report 2: Maine's Middle School Laptop Program: Creating Better Writers

The purpose of a second research study was to determine the impact that Maine's laptop program was having on students' writing ability. Student test scores on the Maine Educational Assessment (MEA), the annual statewide test, were examined by researchers for two separate years. The primary examination looked at student test scores for the years 2000 and 2005 in order to determine if there was a difference in scores at two points in time: *before* the laptop program was implemented in any schools (2000) and *after* the program had been implemented for several years (2005).

TABLE 21. MEA Writing Scale Scores 2000 and 2005

Year	Number of Students	Average Scale Score	Standard Deviation	Effect Size
2000	16,557	534.11	10.61	0.32
2005	16,251	537.55	9.17	

Table 21 reports the MEA Writing Scale Scores for 2000 and 2005. The writing portion of the MEA at that time consisted of a writing prompt that was double scored. Scale scores could range from 500–580. As may be seen in the table, in 2005 the average writing scale score was 3.44 points higher than in 2000. Analysis of these average scale scores indicated that, in fact, there was a statistically significant difference in writing scores between the two time periods ($t = 31.51$; $df = 32806$; $p < .001$). The results indicated writing performance had improved. Undoubtedly other factors beyond implementation of the laptop program may have contributed to improved writing performance over the course of five years (implementation of new writing programs in schools, more teacher professional development, etc.), but since these other interventions did not occur in all Maine middle schools, and the results are based on the total population of all 8th graders and all Maine middle schools, the results from this study suggest that

> Students who reported not using their laptop in writing (No Use Group) had the lowest scale score, whereas students who reported using their laptops in all phases of the writing process (Best Use Group) had the highest scale score.

improvements in writing performance may be attributed, at least in part, to the laptop program.

A secondary analysis of the 2005 scale scores revealed an additional key finding. How the laptops were being used in the writing process influenced writing performance. As shown in Table 22, writing scale scores are related to how, and to what extent students used their laptop to produce writing. Students who reported not using their laptop in writing (No Use Group) had the lowest scale score, whereas students who reported using their laptops in all phases of the writing process (Best Use Group) had the highest scale score. Analysis of variance revealed a significant difference between the groups ($F=123.67$; $df=3$, 15,877; $p <.001$), and post hoc analysis indicated significant differences between all four groups shown in the table. In essence the findings revealed greater levels of use of the laptop in the writing process as a writing development tool (e.g., drafts, edits, final copy) was related statistically to writing scores.

TABLE 22. Type of Laptop Use in Writing

Survey Question		Number of Students	Scale Score	
Stem	Responses		Average	Standard Deviation
How do you use your laptop for writing?	Drafts and Final copy	11593	538.8	8.97
	Final copy only	3413	537.7	8.89
	Drafts only	233	533.0	9.74
	Not at all	642	532.0	9.63

However, one may ask if the laptops helped students to become better writers in general or just better writers when using the laptops? To answer this third key research question, the way in which students produced their MEA writing sample was examined. In 2005, some Maine students completed the MEA writing assessment online, while many others produced their writing sample in longhand. Table 23 reports the average writing scale scores for students who produced their writing sample online and those who were developing their writing sample in the traditional paper and pencil fashion. As shown in the table, the scale scores are almost identical. In fact, an analysis of these scores using an independent sample t-test statistic indicated no statistically significant difference between the scale scores of the two groups ($t = .810$; $df = 16249$; $p >.05$). In other words, writing improved regardless of the writing test medium.

TABLE 23. MEA 2005 Writing Scale Scores by Mode of Writing (Assessment)

Writing Sample	Number of Students	Average Scale Score	Standard Deviation
Online	3,251	537.68	10.52
Longhand	13,000	537.52	8.80

Thus, the evidence indicated that implementation of Maine's one-to-one ubiquitous laptop program was related positively to middle school students' writing. Five years after the initial implementation of the laptop program, students' writing scores on Maine's statewide test had significantly improved. Furthermore, students scored better the more extensively they used their laptops in developing and producing their writing. And finally, the evidence indicated that using their laptops in this fashion helped them to become better writers in general, not just better writers using laptops.

> **Writing improved regardless of the writing test medium.**

References

Maine Department of Education, Task Force on the Maine Learning Technology Endowment, Augusta, Maine (2001). *Teaching and Learning for Tomorrow: A Learning Technology Plan for Maine's Future.* http://maine.gov/mlti/resources/history/mlterpt.pdf